CW00548895

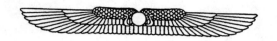

A Hymn To Osiris

"Glory be to Osiris Un-nefer, the great god within Abydos, king of eternity, lord of the everlasting, who passeth through of years in his existence. Eldest son of the womb of Nut, by Seb, lord of the crowns of the North and South, lord of the lofty white crown. As Prince of gods and of men he hath received the crook and the flail and the dignity of his divine fathers. Let thy heart which is in the mountain of Amenta be content, for thy son Horus is established upon thy throne. Thou art crowned lord of Tattu and ruler in Abtu. Through thee the world waxeth green in triumph before the might of Neb-er-tcher. He leadeth in his train that which is and that which is not yet, in his name Ta-her-seta-nef; he toweth along the earth in triumph in his name Seker. He is exceeding mighty and most terrible in his name Osiris. He endureth forever and forever in his name Un-nefer. Homage to thee, King of kings, Lord of lords, Prince of princes, who from the womb of Nut hast possessed the world and hast ruled all lands and Akert. Thy body is of gold, thy head is of azure, and emerald light encircleth thee. O An of millions of years, all-pervading with thy body and beautiful in countenance in Ta-sert."

From the Book of Coming Forth By Day Of Ani

The
Ausarian Resurrection

was edited by

Dr. Karen Vijaya Asha Clarke-Ashby

Cruzian Mystic Books
P.O.Box 570459
Miami, Florida, 33257
(305) 378-6253 Fax: (305) 378-6253

Ashby, Muata.
    The Ausarian resurrection : the ancient Egyptian bible
/ Reginald Muata Abhaya Ashby. -- 1st ed.
    p. cm.
    Preassigned LCCN:
    ISBN: 1-884564-27-5

    1. Osiris (Egyptian deity) 2. Resurrection (Egyptian
religion)--Popular works. 3. Mythology, Egyptian. 4.
Egypt--Religion. 5. Gods, Egyptian.   I. Title.

BL2450.O7A84 1998   299.31
                            QBI98-66756

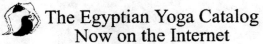

The Egyptian Yoga Catalog
Now on the Internet

Check out the latest books, audio and video presentations on Egyptian Yoga and seminars, classes and courses now on the World Wide Web!
INTERNET ADDRESS:
http://members.aol.com/Semayoga/index.htm

E-MAIL ADDRESS: Semayoga@aol.com

ALSO BY MUATA ASHBY

EGYPTIAN YOGA VOLUME I: THE PHILOSOPHY OF ENLIGHTENMENT

EGYPTIAN YOGA VOLUME II: THE SUPREME WISDOM OF ENLIGHTENMENT

INITIATION INTO EGYPTIAN YOGA

MYSTICISM OF USHET REKHAT

EGYPTIAN PROVERBS

THEF NETERU: THE MOVEMENT OF THE GODS AND GODDESSES

THE CYCLES OF TIME

THE HIDDEN PROPERTIES OF MATTER

THE WISDOM OF ISIS: GOD IN THE UNIVERSE

THE MYSTICAL TEACHINGS OF THE AUSARIAN RESURRECTION

THE WISDOM OF MAATI

THE SERPENT POWER

EGYPTIAN TANTRA YOGA

THE BLOOMING LOTUS OF DIVINE LOVE

MEDITATION: THE ANCIENT EGYPTIAN PATH TO ENLIGHTENMENT

Sema
Institute of Yoga

Sema (ψ) is an Ancient Egyptian word and symbol meaning *union*. The Sema Institute is dedicated to the propagation of the universal teachings of spiritual evolution which relate to the union of humanity and the union of all things within the universe. It is a non-denominational organization which recognizes the unifying principles in all spiritual and religious systems of evolution throughout the world. Our primary goals are to provide the wisdom of ancient spiritual teachings in books, courses and other forms of communication. Secondly, to provide expert instruction and training in the various yogic disciplines including Ancient Egyptian Philosophy, Christian Gnosticism, Indian Philosophy and modern science. Thirdly, to promote world peace and Universal Love.

A primary focus of our tradition is to identify and acknowledge the yogic principles within all religions and to relate them to each other in order to promote their deeper understanding as well as to show the essential unity of purpose and the unity of all living beings and nature within the whole of existence.

The Institute is open to all who believe in the principles of peace, non-violence and spiritual emancipation regardless of sex, race, or creed.

About the author and editor:
Dr. Muata Abhaya Ashby

About The Author

Reginald Muata Ashby holds a Doctor of Philosophy Degree in Religion, and a Doctor of Divinity Degree in Holistic Healing. He is also a Pastoral Counselor and Teacher of Yoga Philosophy and Discipline. Dr. Ashby is an adjunct faculty member of the American Institute of Holistic Theology and an ordained Minister. Dr. Ashby has studied advanced Jnana, Bhakti and Kundalini Yogas under the guidance of Swami Jyotirmayananda, a world renowned Yoga Master. He has studied the mystical teachings of Ancient Egypt for many years and is the creator of the Egyptian Yoga concept. He is also the founder of the Sema Institute, an organization dedicated to the propagation of the teachings of Yoga and mystical spirituality.

About the Editor

Karen Clarke-Ashby, "Vijaya-Asha", is the spouse and spiritual partner of Muata. She is an independent researcher, practitioner and teacher of Yoga, a Doctor in the Sciences, a Pastoral Counselor, and the editor of *Egyptian Proverbs, Egyptian Yoga: The philosophy of Enlightenment* and *The Ausarian Resurrection* by Muata.

Sema Institute
P.O. Box 570459, Miami, Fla. 33257 (305) 378-6253, Fax (305) 378-6253
©1996 Sema Institute

DEDICATIONS

First and foremost I would like to dedicate this volume to the Neters whose story
has brought drama, delight, passion and spiritual enlightenment to the world,
Osiris, Isis and Horus.

Asar (Osiris)
Who is the Innermost Reality of All Existence

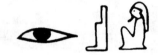

Ast (Isis)
Who is the Revelation of the Innermost Reality of All Existence

Hor (Horus)
Who is the Fulfillment of the Innermost Reality of All Existence

Table of Contents

Foreword   13

INTRODUCTION: THE ANCIENT   **18**
ORIGINS OF THE OSIRIAN MYTH

Religion   18

Myth, Ritual and Mysticism   19

Religion and Yoga   19

Myth and Ritual   21

The Keys to Reading and   25
Understanding a Myth

The Importance of Scriptures and Symbols   29

The Scriptures and Symbols of Shetaut Neter   30

A Compendium of The Ausarian Myth   31

The Unabridged Myth of Shetaut Asar-Aset-   35
Heru

THE   **39**
AUSARIAN RESURRECTION

A Hymn to Ra   41

The Creation   41

The Destruction of Evil Men and Women   43

The Story of Hathor and Tehuti   49

The Birth of Osiris and Isis   51

Osiris: The First King of Egypt and Teacher of   53
the World

The Ancient History of Osiris and Isis   55

Osiris Travels to India and Europe   55

The Murder of Osiris   57

Isis Finds the Body of Osiris   61

A Hymn to Isis   63

The Dismemberment of the Body of Osiris   65

The Search for the pieces of the Body of Osiris   65

A Hymn to Anubis   67

A Hymn to Horus   67

The Death and Resurrection of Horus   71

The Initiation of Horus   85

The Mystical Secrets of Creation   91

The Battle of Horus and Set   105

The Evil of Set   115

A Hymn to Osiris   121

GLOSS ON   **127**
THE AUSARIAN RESURRECTION

The Substratum of Creation   127

Mystical Symbolism of the Characters   131

Osiris   132

Set   132

Isis   133

Nephthys   134

Horus   136

Anubis   138

Horus and Set   139

Tehuti and the Eye   139

Osiris and the Duat   145

The Characters of the Osirian Myth as   149
Psycho-spiritual Stages of Human Evolution

Osiris and Nephthys   150

Set: Slave to the Lower Self   151

Anubis: Sheti-Saa-Maat   154

Horus-Hathor: Righteous Action, Virtue and   157
Spiritual Power - Min: Self Control

What is the Pert-em-Hru?   161

Christianity and the Osirian Religion   163

The Christian Eucharist and The Osirian Mystery   165

Opening the Mouth of The Osiris (Initiate)   172

Isis and the Wakening of the Soul   174

Incorporating the Osirian Rituals Into Your Life   175

Conclusion   179

Meditation on the Ausarian Myth: A Jour-   185
ney to the Duat

"If you are a man who leads,

Who controls the affairs of the many,

Seek out every beneficent deed,

That your conduct may be blameless.

Great is justice, lasting in effect,

Unchallenged since the time of Osiris.

One punishes the transgressor of laws,

Though the greedy overlooks this;

Baseness may seize riches,

Yet crime never lands its wares;

In the end it is justice that lasts,

Man says: "It is my father's ground.""

—Sage Ptahotep (circa 3,000 B.C.E. Ancient Egypt)

Asar (Osiris), *Aset* (Isis) and *Nebthet* (Nephthys)

FOREWORD

What do you want most in life? For what are you truly looking? What is there in life to fulfill your deepest longings, needs and desires?

In every walk of life, there are people who seek for the ultimate fulfillment of their existence. If you have picked up this book, you must have begun to realize by now that what you are seeking is not to be found in the world of ordinary human experiences. If it were, you would have already found it and experienced complete fulfillment by now, or you would have witnessed someone who had discovered such happiness and peace. If you believe in the law of reincarnation, you must at least understand intellectually that you have been in all parts of the world and have experienced vast amounts of prosperity as well as the depths of degradation through countless embodiments, and still you have not discovered that for which you are looking. This points to the simple fact that if you have not discovered what you have been looking for after all of this time, then there is no guarantee that you will find it in the future either.

When you become tired of following the trite rhetoric given by society as to the importance of material values and weary of religious dogmas and un-fulfilling popular rituals such as the fanaticism over sports, sex or thrill seeking activities, you might begin to hunger for something more abiding, substantial and real.

The earliest seekers of mystical truth decided to forsake the world of human experience and in so doing, discovered that the world of human experience, that is, the experiences within society and nature which appear to be so real and abiding, are not the only realities nor the absolute truths of existence. In this realization they discovered that they were more than just mortal individuals who seemed to come out of the union of a man and woman, only to grow up experiencing the frailties and fleeting pleasures of human existence, and then to ultimately die. They realized that beyond the physical nature there is a vast and eternal consciousness which is the source of the spirit that enlivens the physical body. In this experience they discovered that they were not separate from the universe, but that the universe is indeed an expression of the Divine wherein cosmic forces originate, sustain, interact with and interpenetrate all that exists. They realized that it was their ignorance of this truth which led them to the erroneous search in the wilderness of human experience for the ultimate fulfillment of their desires, supreme peace and happiness.

In their discovery of that which sustains the universe and human consciousness, they discovered the source of supreme peace and abiding happiness. Out of universal love and compassion, derived from that peace and bliss which they discovered, they set about to develop systems of mythology and philosophy along with mental and physical disciplines which would allow others to come into the same experience.

Religion, in its original form, is meant to lead people from ignorance of the true Self to the light of knowledge. Religion is a composite of myth and certain mental and physical exercises, known under the general term "Yoga", which are designed to enhance the spiritual development of the person who practices them. While yoga is technically not to be considered a religion or a philosophy, yogic disciplines have been used by philosophers and religions throughout history in order to promote the spiritual process as prescribed by the particular religious or philosophical system. Yoga is more akin to a science or technology for controlling and purifying the mind and body which will allow the spirit within to emerge.

The goal of yoga is to promote integration of the mind-body-spirit complex in order to produce optimal health of the human being. This is accomplished through mental and physical exercises which promote the free flow of spiritual energy by reducing mental complexes caused by ignorance. There are two roads which human beings can follow; one of wisdom and the other of ignorance. The path of the masses is generally the path of ignorance which leads them into negative situations, thoughts and deeds. These in turn lead to ill health and sorrow in life. The other road is based on wisdom and it leads to health, true happiness and enlightenment.

The ancient religion of Osiris, Isis and Horus, if properly understood, contains all of the elements necessary to lead the sincere aspirant to attain immortality through inner self-discovery. The Osirian myth is so powerful that it is still having an effect on the world religions. Therefore, it is my great honor to present the complete Osirian myth and to expound on the mystical and mythological implications and teachings of the myth. It is my hope that all who read of this wonderful epic and then practice the yogic disciplines prescribed by it will discover supreme peace and eternal bliss in this very lifetime!

Muata Abhaya Ashby 1996

14

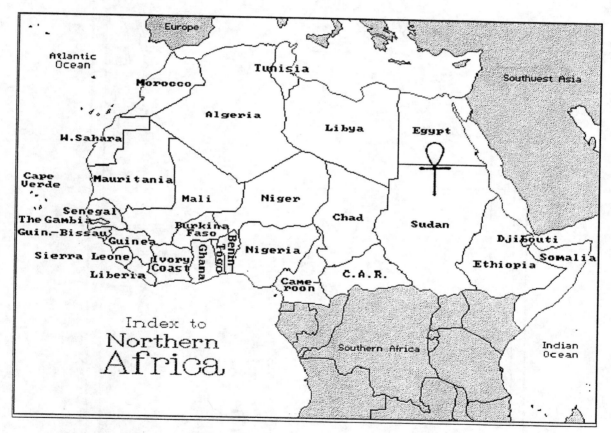

Above: A map of North East Africa showing the location of the land of *Ta-Meri* or *Kamut,* also known as ancient Egypt.

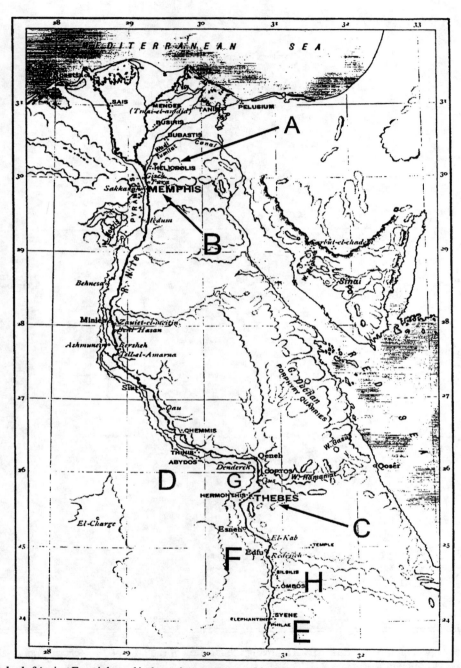

The land of Ancient Egypt is located in the north-eastern corner of the African Continent. The cities wherein the theology of the Trinity of Amun-Ra-Ptah was developed were: A- Anu (Heliopolis), B-Hetkaptah (Memphis), and C-Waset (Thebes). The cities wherein the theology of the Trinity of Osiris-Isis-Horus was developed were A- Anu, D-Abydos, E-Philae, F- Edfu, G-Denderah, and H- Ombos.

Introduction To The Ausarian Resurrection

The Complete Myth
of
Shetaut Asar-Aset-Heru

The Ancient Origins of The Osirian Myth

The Osirian Mystery is the most important myth of Ancient Egypt. It influenced all other centers of spirituality in Ancient Egypt and continues to have far reaching implications for modern civilization as to the origin and deeper meaning of present day religious beliefs. From pre-dynastic times (before-5,500 B.C.E.) up to 500 A.C.E., well after the dawn of Christianity, the story of Osiris, Isis and the struggle of Horus was well known. It was the most popular among myths all over the ancient world, including Asia Minor, Africa, Greece and later throughout the Roman Empire.

The story of Osiris is so meaningful because the principle ideas about human existence and destiny are embodied in this timeless story. These ideas were carried on in other religious systems of ancient times and their influences can be detected in present day religions as well. The myth took many forms in other religions and mystery systems which had contact with the Ancient Egyptian system. The most notable similarities are within the Christian and Hindu religions. In order to better understand the purpose and function of religion, we will need to define "religion" and its levels of practice.

Religion

The term religion comes from the Latin "*Relegare*" which uses the word roots "*RE*", which means "*BACK*", and "*LIGON*", which means "*to hold, to link, to bind.*" Therefore, the essence of true religion is that of linking back, specifically, linking its followers back to their original source and innermost essence. In this sense the terms "religion" and "yoga" are synonymous. This source which is the underlying reality behind every object in Creation is described as unborn, undying, eternal and immortal, and is known by an endless number of names, some of which are: Consciousness, Self, Higher Self, God, Goddess, Supreme Being, Divine Self, Eternal Self, Soul, Pure Consciousness, Brahman, All, Allah, Jehovah, Neter Neteru, Creator, Absolute, Heavenly Father, Divine Mother, Great Spirit. These various names, while arising from various traditions and separate cultures, in reality represent the same divine and transcendental principle.

Although religion in its purest form is a Yoga system, the original intent and meaning of the scriptures are often misunderstood, if not distorted. This occurs because the various religions have developed in different geographic areas, and therefore, the lower levels (historical accounts, stories and traditions) have developed independently, and sometimes without proper guidance. Under these conditions, the inner meanings of the myths and symbols become lost and the exoteric meanings are emphasized. This leads to deism and a phenomenal (an occurrence or fact which is perceptible by the senses) approach to religion rather than a mystical, symbolic and transcendental understanding.

Most religions tend to be *deistic* at the elementary levels. Deism, as a religious belief or form of theism (belief in the existence of a God or gods), holds that God's action was restricted to an initial act of creation, after which He retired (separated) to contemplate the majesty of His work. Deists hold that the natural creation is regulated by laws put in place by God at the time of creation which are inscribed with perfect moral principles. Therefore, deism is closely related to the exoteric or personal understanding of the Divinity.

Myth → Ritual → Mysticism

In its complete form, religion is composed of three aspects, *mythology*, *ritual* and *metaphysical* or the *mystical experience* (mysticism - mystical philosophy). While many religions contain rituals, traditions, metaphors and myths, there are few professionals trained in understanding their deeper aspects and psychological implications (metaphysics and mystical). Thus, there is disappointment, frustration and disillusionment among many followers as well as leaders within many religions, particularly in the Western Hemisphere, because it is difficult to evolve spiritually without the proper spiritual guidance. Through introspection and spiritual research, it is possible to discover mythological vistas within religion which can rekindle the light of spirituality and at the same time increase the possibility of gaining a fuller experience of life. The exoteric (outer, ritualistic) forms of religion with which most people are familiar is only the tip of an iceberg so to speak; it is only a beginning, an invitation or prompting to seek a deeper (esoteric) discovery of the transcendental truths of existence.

Religion and Yoga

Yoga is the practice of mental, physical and spiritual disciplines which lead to self-control and self-discovery by purifying the mind, body and spirit, so as to discover the deeper spiritual essence which lies within every human being and object in the universe. In essence, the goal of yoga practice is to unite or *yoke* one's individual consciousness with universal or cosmic consciousness. Therefore, Ancient Egyptian religious practice, especially in terms of the rituals and other practices of the Ancient Egyptian temple system known as *Shetaut Neter* (the way of the hidden Supreme Being), may be termed as a yoga system: *Egyptian Yoga*. In this sense, religion, in its purest form, is a yoga system, as it seeks to reunite people with their true and original source.

The disciplines of Yoga fall under five major categories. These are: *Yoga of Wisdom*, *Yoga of Devotional Love*, *Yoga of Meditation*, *Tantric Yoga* and *Yoga of Selfless Action*. Within these categories there are subsidiary forms which are part of the main disciplines. The emphasis in the Osirian Myth is on the Yoga of Wisdom, Yoga of Devotional Love and Yoga of Selfless Action. The important point to remember is that all aspects of yoga can and should be used in an integral fashion to effect an efficient and harmonized spiritual movement in the practitioner. Therefore, while there may be an area of special emphasis, other elements are bound to become part of the yoga program as needed. For example, while a yogin may place emphasis on the Yoga of Wisdom, they may also practice Devotional Yoga and Meditation Yoga along with the wisdom studies.

So the practice of any discipline that leads to oneness with Supreme Consciousness can be called yoga. If you study, rationalize and reflect upon the teachings, you are practicing *Yoga of Wisdom*. If you meditate upon the teachings and your Higher Self, you are practicing *Yoga of Meditation*. If you

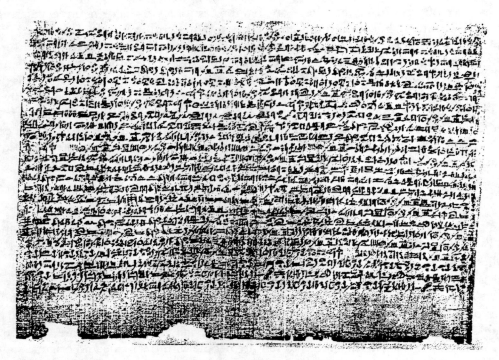

Above: The papyrus containing the ancient Egyptian myth of the History of Creation.

practice rituals which identify you with your spiritual nature, you are practicing *Yoga of Ritual Identification* (which is part of the Yoga of Wisdom and the Yoga of Devotional Love of the Divine). If you develop your physical nature and psychic energy centers, you are practicing *Serpent Power (Kundalini or Uraeus) Yoga* (which is part of Tantric Yoga). If you practice living according to the teachings of ethical behavior and selflessness, you are practicing *Yoga of Action* (Maat) in daily life. If you practice turning your attention towards the Divine by developing love for the Divine, then it is called *Devotional Yoga* or *Yoga of Divine Love*. The practitioner of yoga is called a yogin (male practitioner) or yogini (female practitioner), and one who has attained the culmination of yoga (union with the Divine) is called a yogi. In this manner, yoga has been developed into many disciplines which may be used in an integral fashion to achieve the same goal: Enlightenment. Therefore, the aspirant should learn about all of the paths of yoga and choose those elements which best suit his/her personality or practice them all in an integral, balanced way.

Enlightenment is the term used to describe the highest level of spiritual awakening. It means attaining such a level of spiritual awareness that one discovers the underlying unity of the entire universe as well as the fact that the source of all creation is the same source from which the innermost Self within every human heart arises.

> *As one can ascend to the top of a house by means of a ladder or a tree or a staircase or a rope, so diverse are the ways and means to approach God, and every religion in the world shows one of these ways.*

> Ramakrishna (1836-1886)

All forms of spiritual practice are directed toward the goal of assisting every individual to discover the true essence of the universe both externally, in physical creation, and internally, within the human heart, as the very root of human consciousness. Thus, many terms are used to describe the attainment of the goal of spiritual knowledge and the eradication of spiritual ignorance. Some of these terms are: *Enlightenment, Resurrection, Salvation, The Kingdom of Heaven, Moksha or Liberation, Buddha Consciousness, One With The Tao, Self-realization, to Know Thyself,* etc.

Myth and Ritual

First, we must begin by gaining a deeper understanding of what mythology is and then to understand its purpose. With this understanding, we may then undertake the study of the Osirian myth or any other mystical story and be able to understand the psycho-spiritual implications which are being imparted through it.

The American Heritage Dictionary defines *Myth* as follows:

> 1. A traditional story presenting supernatural beings, ancestors, or heroes that serve as primordial types in a primitive view of the world.
> 2. A fictitious or imaginary story, person, or thing.
> 3. A false belief.

The American Heritage Dictionary defines *Mythology* as follows:

    1. A body of myths about the origin and history of a people.
    2. The study of myths.

The Random House Encyclopedia defines *Mythology* as follows:

> Mythology, a body of myths or traditional stories dealing with gods and legendary heroes. The mythology of a people serves to present their world view, their explanations of natural phenomena, their religious and other beliefs. Mythological literature includes the Greek *Iliad* and *Odyssey*, the Scandinavian *Edda*, the Indian *Ramayana*, and the Babylonian *Gilgamesh*, among others. Various interpretations of mythology have been made by anthropologists such as Sir James Frazer and Claude Lévi-Strauss. In literature, myth has been used as the basis for poetry, stories, plays, and other writings.

In relation to mythology, the term epic is also used. The American Heritage Dictionary defines an *Epic* as:

    1. A long narrative poem that celebrates episodes of a people's heroic tradition.

The Encarta/Funk & Wagnall's Encyclopedia defines an Epic as:

> A long narrative poem, majestic both in theme and style. Epics deal with legendary or historical events of national or universal significance, involving action of broad sweep and grandeur. Most epics deal with the exploits of a single individual, thereby giving unity to the composition. Typically, an epic involves the introduction of supernatural forces that shape the action, conflict in the form of battles or other physical combat, and certain stylistic conventions: an invocation to the Muse, a formal statement of the theme, long lists of the protagonists involved, and set speeches couched in elevated language. Commonplace details of everyday life may appear, but they serve as background for the story, and are described in the same lofty style as the rest of the poem.

These definitions have been included here to give you a reference as to what society at large, especially in the West, has accepted as the definition and purpose of mythological and epic literature. Now we will explore the initiatic-yogic-mystical meaning of *Mythology*. First however, one more definition is required. We need to understand what is a *Metaphor*. The American Heritage Dictionary defines *Metaphor* as follows:

A figure of speech in which a term that ordinarily designates an object or idea is used to designate a dissimilar object or idea in order to suggest comparison or analogy, as in the phrase *evening of life.*

Mystical mythology is much like a metaphor in that its stories and characters are designed to provide a reference toward something other than the story itself. This means that there is an exoteric meaning which refers to the events and circumstances in the story, which may or may not have a basis in fact, and also an esoteric or mystical meaning which refers to a deeper teaching or message which transcends the boundaries of the events in the story. Through the myth many ideas which are not easily explained in rational, logical terms can be freely explored and elucidated in imaginative and colorful ways. Mystical myths are particularly important because their purpose is to point to where the answers to the most important questions of every individual may be found. Everyone is searching for answers to questions like, "Who am I really?", "Is this all that I am?", "Where do I come from?" and "What is my purpose in life?" Through myths, the teachings of Sages and Saints can take full flight, free of the constraints of normal literary writing. Therefore, myths are an ideal ways to impart spiritual truths which transcend ordinary human experiences.

The essence of Creation and therefore, of each individual human being, is transcendental; it transcends the ordinary bounds of mental perception and understanding. However, all human experiences occur in and through the mind. Therefore, the heart of all human experiences, be they pain or pleasure, is rooted in the mind, the *psyche*. The purpose of mythology is to bridge the gap between the limited human mind and that which transcends all. Thus, mythology must be understood in the light of its psychological and mystical implications. So here we will introduce a new term: "Psycho-Mythology".

The study of mythical stories is important in order to gain insight into the "Psycho-Mythology" or psychological implications of mythology for the psycho-spiritual transformation of the individual which leads to the attainment of Enlightenment. Enlightenment implies the attainment of an expanded state of consciousness, termed as *dilation* (expansion) *of the heart* in Ancient Egyptian Yoga Philosophy, in which there is a full and perfect awareness of one's existence beyond the mind and body. So the term *psycho*, as it is used here, must be understood as far more than simply that which refers to the mind. "Psycho" must be understood to mean everything that constitutes human consciousness in all of its stages and states. Therefore, psycho implies the conscious, subconscious and unconscious workings of the mind. "Mythology" refers to the codes, messages, ideas, directives, beliefs, etc., that affect the psyche through the conscious, subconscious and unconscious aspects of the mind of an individual, specifically those effects which result in psycho-spiritual transformation, that is, a transpersonal or transcendental change in the personality of an individual which leads to the discovery of the transcendental reality of existence.

A myth should never be understood literally. This would be like going to a theater to see a fictional movie or reading a fantasy novel, and believing it to be real. Yet, as a movie or novel may be based on real events and carry an important message which is being imparted through the medium of actors, a plot and so on, mystical myths are not to be understood as being completely baseless nor as having been put together purely for entertainment. Myths are symbols which speak to people in a psycho-symbolic way. This psychological language of myths can lead people to understand and experience the transcendental truths which cannot be easily expressed in words.

The Ausarian Resurrection myth holds deep implications for psycho-mythological study and must be approached with reverence and patience by an aspirant. The actual story of Osiris is a simple collection of facts with which several rituals have been associated. The story itself represents a set of events which together compose a plot like any other story or life situation. This level of understanding is the first level of religious practice: Mythology. At this level we must understand the principles which the Osirian Mystery is conveying to us. These principles are universal truths, and thus, they are common to the life experiences of every human being. However, a mystical myth goes much further than just telling a story about human pain and pleasure, and beyond mere entertainment. A mystical myth also provides the answers to the most fundamental questions of the human experience as to the origins of existence, the universe and humanity. It elucidates the fate of human existence, providing a guiding light for traversing the many winding roads of life in such a way as to avoid pain and sorrow and reach the abode of supreme peace and happiness. Behind each principle there are many implications which must be understood and practiced in daily life in order for the teachings to become an integral part of life.

The rituals, hymns and prayers associated with the Osirian myth may be found in such texts as the *Ancient Egyptian Pyramid Texts*, *Coffin Texts* and the various versions of the *Egyptian Book of Coming Forth By Day* (Book of the Dead). Their correspondent rituals in the Christian religion would be akin to the mass service, the passion plays and the Eucharist. These constitute the second level religion: Ritual. Myths constitute the heart and soul of rituals. Mythology is a mystical language for transmitting and teaching the principles of life and creation. Rituals are the medium through which the myths are practiced, lived and realized. As previously discussed, rituals represent the second stage in the process of religion.

Thus, when you delve into a myth, you must expect more than just entertainment. You should be equipped with the knowledge which will allow you to decipher the hidden meanings in the story so that you may also begin to experience and benefit from them on a personal level. Only then will you be able to engender a real transformation in your life which will lead you to Enlightenment. This is the third level of religious practice, the mystical or metaphysical level.

The Keys to Reading and Understanding a Myth

Religion without myth not only fails to work, it also fails to offer man the promise of unity with the transpersonal and eternal.

—C. G. Jung (1875-1961)

The first and most important key to understanding a mystical myth is comprehending that the myth is not talking about some ancient personality or story which occurred a long time ago and which has no relevance to the present. In fact, the myth is speaking about you. It is a story about human life, its origins, its destiny, its plight and the correct action for leading a truly successful life which paves the way to Enlightenment and true happiness.

The second key to understanding a mystical myth is comprehending that it is usually written in the form of a journey in which the subject must learn about himself/herself and transcend the ordinary human consciousness. In this movement there are experiences of happiness, sorrow, struggle and learning. It is a movement from ignorance and darkness towards light, wisdom and ultimately, to spiritual Enlightenment.

The third key to understanding a mystical myth comes from living the myth. Living a myth does not mean simply reading a myth, being able to recount the events with perfect memory or simply practicing the rituals of a myth without a deeper understanding of their implications and purpose. It means making the essence of the teaching being conveyed through the myth an integral part of your life. If this practice is not implemented, the teachings remain at the intellectual level and the deeper truths of the myth are not revealed. Therefore, you must resolve to discover the myth in every facet of your life, and in so doing, you will be triumphant as the hero(ine) of the myth.

The philosophy of spiritual transcendence and Enlightenment did not begin with the dawn of the dynastic period in Ancient Egyptian history. The evidence from ancient texts and the history of Manetho* show that the Ancient Egyptian history which is known and written about in modern times is only the descendent of a much more ancient era of Egyptian civilization which began many thousands of years before the dynastic era. *(See *Egyptian Yoga: The Philosophy of Enlightenment* and *Egyptian Yoga Guide Book Two: The Ancient Origins of Yoga*)

Ancient Egyptian civilization originated in the unfathomable reaches of antiquity. Records indicate that Ancient Egypt existed as early as 36,000 B.C.E. The Osirian Myth centers around the life of the first king of Egypt, Asar, (Osiris), his wife and sister, Aset, (Isis), and their son Hor or Heru, (Horus). Osiris was an incarnation of the Divine Supreme Being who came into mortal form in order to establish civilization, agriculture, philosophy and religion. Upon his death he was accorded immortality and divinity as the High God.

There were several "High God" systems in Ancient Egyptian Mythology. High God means that the highest God or Goddess within that particular system of theology is considered to be the original deity from which all others emanated as cosmic forces. Thus, Osiris is known as *Pa Neter* or *The God* (High God) and Creation is composed of the cosmic forces which originated from Osiris. The cosmic forces are known as *neters* or gods and goddesses. It is important to understand that the High Gods and Goddesses as well as the Egyptian Trinities* originated from the same transcendental Supreme Being which was without name or form, but was referred to as *Neter Neteru* (Neter of Neters - Supreme Being above all gods and goddesses) and *Neb-er-tcher*.

In this manner, the initiate is to understand that all of the gods and goddesses are in reality symbols, with names and forms, which represent the Divine in the varied manifest forms of nature. This produces a two aspected format of religion in which there is a *personal* aspect and a *transpersonal* aspect of God. The personal aspect is fixed in time and space with a name and form. This form is readily understood by the masses of human beings with ordinary spiritual awareness and is used in myths and stories. The second aspect, the *transpersonal* side, points our interest towards that which lies beyond the symbolic form. This is the *unmanifest* form of the Divine as it is expressed in the mystical teachings of religious mythology. Thus, the High God is a personal symbol or representation, with a name and form, of the nameless, formless, unmanifest and transcendental Supreme Being. (*There were several forms of the Trinity in Ancient Egyptian religion depending on the geographic locality where the teaching was espoused. These included: Amun-Mut-Khons, Ptah-Sekhmet-Nefertem, Horus-Hathor-Harsomtus (Horus the Younger), Khnum-Anukis-Satis, Ptah-Seker-Ausar (Osiris). However, the most popular Trinity throughout all of Ancient Egypt was that of Osiris-Isis-Horus).

Single Supreme, Transcendental Being - *Pa Neter - Neter Neteru - Nebertcher*
(unmanifest realm beyond time and space - names and forms)

High Gods and Goddesses manifesting as a Trinity: *Amun-Ra-Ptah; Osiris-Isis-Horus*

The activity or awareness within the manifest or symbolic area of religious practice is within the purview of the mythological and ritual stages of religious practice while the activity within the unmanifest area is covered by the third and final level of religious practice, the mystical or metaphysical level.

The first sophisticated system of religion and yoga mystical philosophy in historical times occurred in Ancient Egypt. This system included all of the gods and goddesses which in later times became individually popular in various cities throughout Ancient Egypt. At the heart of this system of gods and goddesses was *Shetai*, the hidden and unmanifest essence of the universe, also known as *Nebertcher* and *Amun*. The system of religion of Ancient Egypt was called *Shetaut Neter* or the *Hidden Way of The Unmanifest Supreme Being*.

The term "unmanifest" relates to the fact that the Ancient Egyptians realized the illusory nature of physical reality. The phenomenal world, as it is perceived by the ordinary senses in a human being, is not the absolute reality of existence. In modern times, Quantum Physics experiments have uncovered the fact that "physical matter" is not "physical" at all, that it is "energy" in various states of manifestation or vibration. Thus, the Ancient Egyptians discovered that the phenomenal universe is only a "manifest" form which arises from a deeper, unmanifest source. This notion was extensively explained in *Memphite Theology**. The theory of relativity relating to time and space was also expressed in the Ancient Egyptian creation stories long before Albert Einstein proposed his theory of relativity. *(See *Egyptian Yoga: The Philosophy of Enlightenment*)

The entire system of mystical philosophy of the hidden Supreme Being, as well as the method through which that Being manifests in the form of the phenomenal physical universe and individual human consciousness, was explained in progressive stages in the theology of the Trinity known as *Amun-Ra-Ptah*, which was said to have arisen out of the Supreme Being: *Nebertcher*. As Ancient Egyptian history moved on through thousands of years, each segment of this Trinity was adopted by a particular priesthood and locality which then set about to explain and expound the philosophy of that particular segment of the Trinity. The priests of the Ancient Egyptian city of *Anu* adopted Ra, the priesthood of the Ancient Egyptian city of *Hetkaptah* adopted Ptah, and the Ancient Egyptian city of *Weset or Newt* (Thebes) adopted Amun.

In a similar manner, the theology of the city of Abydos centered around the myth of Osiris while the theology of Philae and other localities centered around the teachings if Isis. One of the reasons why the Osirian Trinity of Osiris, Isis and Horus was so powerful is that it incorporated the teachings given in the entire primordial Trinity system of *Nebertcher: Amun Ra Ptah*, and brought them to the level of the *common folk**. It personalized the Divinity in such a way that every man and woman could partake of the myth and practice the rituals in everyday life, thereby attaining greater and greater closeness to the Divine. In this sense, every Ancient Egyptian citizen and the followers of the Osirian religion outside Egypt understood that the myth was in reality about every individual. This is why everyone, especially the Pharaoh, was mystically referred to as "The Osiris". Therefore, the mystical name of an Ancient Egyptian initiate in the mysteries of Osiris would not be Ani, but Osiris-Ani. Other examples, using modern names, would be Osiris-Alice instead of Alice, or Osiris-Benjamin instead of Benjamin, etc. *(See *Egyptian Yoga: The Philosophy of Enlightenment*)

The mystical philosophy concerning the Trinity myth is so powerful, especially the Trinity of Osiris-Isis-Horus, that when correctly understood, it holds the key to understanding the nature of Creation and of the nature of human consciousness. This is why the system of a Trinity was used in the religious system of India and later in Christianity, the former being modeled after the Ancient Egyptian system indirectly and the latter being directly modeled after the Ancient Egyptian system of the Osirian Resurrection.

The portrayal of God as a Father who begets a son who becomes his *paraclete* and revealer occurs first, and with most primacy, in Ancient Egypt, in the mythology of Nebertcher and Osiris. Horus, in Egypt, was the reincarnation of Osiris, his father, who was himself an incarnation of the High God Ra, the Absolute abode of all things. At the same time, Horus is the symbol of the human soul, the essential nature and the innate hero/heroine within every human being. In much the same way, Jesus is the revealer and paraclete of God, The Father. In Eastern mystical philosophy, Buddha and Krishna are considered to be *Avatars* or incarnations of God. The original idea of Avatarism was that from time to time when unrighteousness reaches a certain level and threatens to overwhelm righteousness, God would manifest on earth in human form to restore virtue in the world. In the Hindu tradition, the God Vishnu had ten important Avatars, one of whom was Krishna. The purpose of Avatarism from the divine point of view is to sustain creation by maintaining the balance between the pairs of opposites in creation. The disparity in the pairs of opposites is most evident in the rise of unrighteousness in society. In Ancient Egyptian mythology, the concept of Avatarism goes back to the incarnations of Hathor, as the destructive Eye of Ra, Osiris and Isis.

In Ancient Egyptian Mythology, the children of God (the Company of gods and goddesses) are not only Avatars, but they are also symbols or aspects of the human soul, and of creation itself. They, through their symbolic forms, are to be treated as models for the kind of behavior which leads to happiness and spiritual freedom. In this respect, the incarnation of God as an Avatar is really a metaphor which relates to the potential within every human being to discover and manifest their divine nature, and in so doing, become an Avatar. Thus, the passions, teachings and fates of the gods and goddesses reveal the story of the human soul and the path it must follow in order to attain knowledge of its true divine nature and achieve liberation from ignorance, pain and suffering due to bondage to the world of time and space.

In Ancient Egypt, the concept of God, the ultimate and absolute reality behind all physical manifestations, was called *Amn* or *Amun*** or *Nebertcher* or *Pa Neter* (The God, The Supreme Being). In Hindu mythology, it is *Brahman*; to the Taoists, it is *The Tao*; in Judaism it is referred to as *Yahweh*; in Islam it is *Allah*; in Christianity it is *God* and *The Kingdom of Heaven*; and to modern physics it is *Energy*. *(Other spellings include *Amun, Amen, Amon, Amonu, Amunu*.)

> *"God is a metaphor for a mystery that transcends all human categories of thought...It depends on how much you want to think about it, whether or not it's doing you any good, whether it's putting you in touch with the mystery which is the ground of your own being."*
>
> **—Joseph Campbell**

In this manner, the ancient Sages who originally established the teachings of mystical philosophy used metaphors and symbols to describe the ultimate and transcendental reality which is beyond the grasp of the human senses and mind. To describe this transcendental reality, the terms

"God", "Supreme Being", "The Absolute", Pa Neter", "Nebertcher", etc., were created in an attempt to provide a concept which the human mind could understand.

The Importance of Scriptures and Symbols

The importance of scriptures and symbols of mystical spirituality cannot be overstated. It is a powerful experience to hear a mystical story being given by word of mouth through an oral tradition, but there is an even more intense effect when one can actually view the very pictographs, hieroglyphs, steles, and reliefs, and see how every aspect of the myth can be incorporated into all areas of ordinary life. This is why spiritual art can be a powerful force to engender spiritual feeling. When the deeper, mystical implications are understood, spiritual art in the form of symbols, deities, etc., can produce a meditative effect in the mind which leads to an expansion in consciousness. This is the deeper teaching behind the creation of Temples, Cathedrals and other monuments as places of worship and ritual exercises. These symbols and myths are not necessary nor essential for spiritual enlightenment, since nature herself shows human beings the ways of the Divine. However, the path of nature is long and arduous. It involves many reincarnations and countless experiences of pain and sorrow before a human being learns the nature of creation, and the proper way to live so that one becomes closer to the Divine and experiences greater peace and happiness in life.

The scriptures and teachings serve the purpose of enlightening those who have discovered that there is a deeper basis to life other than what is promoted by the general society. The Sages of ancient times created the scriptures to assist those who would like to discover this inner reality and would be otherwise lost in the wilderness of ignorance and suffering which constitutes ordinary human life. It is for spiritual aspirants that the inner chambers of the temple are designed. The Ancient Egyptian temple basically consisted of three main sections to which several rooms that were used for various purposes were attached. These sections were (A) the Court, (B) the Hypostyle Hall and (C) the Chapel (Holy of Holies). This format follows the system of the three levels of religion, *Mythological, Ritualistic,* and *Mystical,* the manner of spiritual study prescribed by the ancient Temple of Isis, *Listening, Reflection, Meditation,* and the Ancient Egyptian initiatic education levels of aspirants, *The Mortals, The Intelligences,* and *The Creators or Beings of Light.*

The Ancient Egyptian system of education of the Temple of Isis prescribe a three tiered format for transmitting the teachings of mystical spirituality. These were: 1- Listening to the teachings. 2- Constant study and reflection on the teachings. 3- Meditation on the meaning of the teachings. It is important to note here that the same teaching which was practiced in Ancient Egypt of **Listening** to, **Reflecting** upon, and **Meditating** upon the teachings is the same process used in Vedanta-Jnana Yoga of India today. According to the teachings of *Jnana Yoga* or the Yoga of Wisdom, the process of yoga consists of three steps: 1- **Shravana** (Listening), 2- **Manana** (Reflection) and 3- **Niddidhyasana** (Meditation). In the *Shetaut NETER* system of yoga, there were three levels of aspirants.

1- **The Mortals:** Students who were being instructed on a probationary status, but had not experienced inner vision.

2- **The Intelligences:** Students who had attained inner vision and had received a glimpse of cosmic consciousness.

3- **The Creators or Beings of Light:** Students who had become IDENTIFIED with or UNITED with the light (GOD).

It is clear to see from the outline above that the Trinity system is a profound teaching which extended from the philosophy centering around the deities themselves down to the format of the educational process and the very foundation of the temple structure.

The Scriptures and Symbols of Shetaut Neter

The most important elements of the myths, wisdom teachings and rituals associated with the Shetaut Neter can be found in the Pyramid Texts, Coffin-Texts, Papyrus Texts, Temple Reliefs, Steles, Obelisks and other monuments of Ancient Egypt. All of these put together constitute what is referred to as the sacred texts of Ancient Egypt or the teachings of Egyptian mystical spirituality. The writings are referred to as "Khu" or "Hekau," meaning *utterances* or *words of power*, and collectively they are known as "Metu Neter" (Words of The God) or "Neter Metu" (Divine Speech). Modern Egyptology, the scholarly study of Ancient Egyptian civilization from the early nineteenth century to the present has labeled these utterances as *spells* or *incantations*. In a way this assessment is correct because these utterances are to be understood as incantations or words which, when understood, can have the effect of transforming the mind, allowing an expansion of consciousness and spiritual enlightenment. However, they are not to be understood in the context of Western magic, witch's spells or voodoo, etc. To do so would be a grievous error of either ignorance, in the case of the uneducated masses, or intellectualism and conceit, in the case of highly educated but uninitiated scholars. These faulty interpretations would yield the conclusion that Ancient Egyptian spirituality as well as other myths from around the world are a conglomerate of a myriad of conflicting stories and baseless ritualism devoted to idol worshipping, imagination and primitive occult nonsense. In reality, the Shetaut Neter is an extremely sophisticated philosophy and educational process for understanding and realizing the transcendental reality of life which is the basis of all existence.

A COMPENDIUM OF THE AUSARIAN RESURRECTION MYTH

THE CREATION

The process of creation is explained in the form of a cosmological system for better understanding. Cosmology is a branch of philosophy dealing with the origin, processes, and structure of the universe. Cosmogony is the astrophysical study of the creation and evolution of the universe. Both of these disciplines are inherent facets of Ancient Egyptian philosophy through the main religious systems or Companies of the gods and goddesses. A Company of gods and goddesses is a group of deities which symbolize a particular cosmic force or principle which emanates from the all-encompassing Supreme Being, from which they have emerged. The Self or Supreme Being manifests creation through the properties and principles represented by the *Pautti* Company of gods and goddesses - cosmic laws of nature. The system or Company of gods and goddesses of Anu is regarded as the oldest, and forms the basis of the Osirian Trinity. It is expressed in the diagram below.

Shetai - Neter Neteru - Nebertcher
(unseen, hidden, omnipresent, Supreme Being, beyond duality and description)

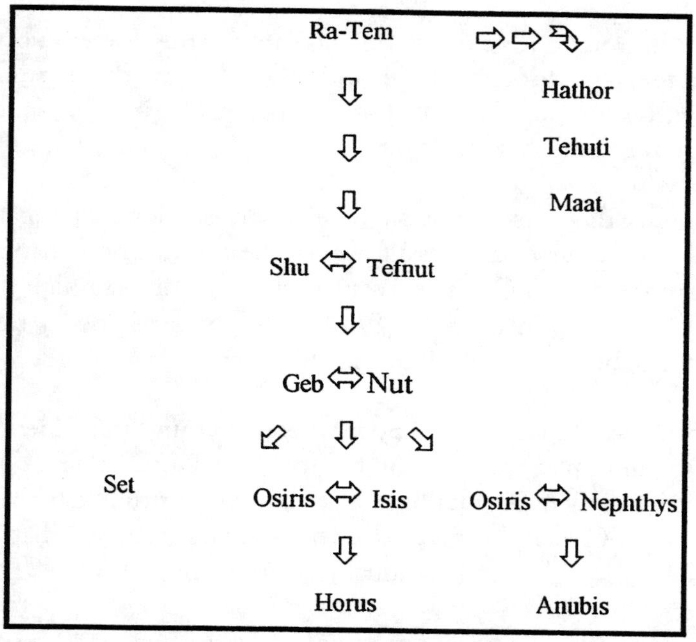

```
Ra-Tem            ⇨ ⇨ ⇛
   ⇩              Hathor
   ⇩              Tehuti
   ⇩              Maat
Shu ⇔ Tefnut
   ⇩
Geb ⇔ Nut
 ⇖   ⇩   ⇘
Set   Osiris ⇔ Isis   Osiris ⇔ Nephthys
        ⇩                ⇩
       Horus            Anubis
```

The diagram above shows that the *Psedjet* (Ennead), or the creative principles which are embodied in the primordial gods and goddesses of creation, emanated from the Supreme Being. Ra or Ra-Tem arose out of the "*Nu*", the Primeval waters, the hidden essence, and began sailing the "*Boat of Millions of Years*" which included the Company of gods and goddesses. On his boat emerged the "neters" or cosmic principles of creation. The neters of the Ennead are Ra-Atum,

Shu, Tefnut, Geb, Nut, Osiris, Isis, Set, and Nephthys. Hathor, Tehuti and Maat represent attributes of the Supreme Being as the very *stuff* or *substratum* which makes up creation. Shu, Tefnut, Geb, Nut, Osiris, Isis, Set, and Nephthys represent the principles upon which creation manifests. Anubis is not part of the Ennead. He represents the feature of intellectual discrimination in the Osirian myth. "Sailing" signifies the beginning of motion in creation. Motion implies that events occur in the realm of time and space, thus, the phenomenal universe comes into existence as a mass of moving essence we call the elements. Prior to this motion, there was the primeval state of being without any form and without existence in time or space.

Osiris, Isis and Horus

Osiris and Isis dedicated themselves to the welfare of humanity and sought to spread civilization throughout the earth, even as far as India and China.

During the absence of Osiris from his kingdom, his brother Set had no opportunity to make innovations in the state because Isis was extremely vigilant in governing the country, and always upon her guard and watchful for any irregularity or unrighteousness.

Upon Osiris' return from touring the world and carrying the teachings of wisdom abroad there was merriment and rejoicing throughout the land. However, one day after Osiris' return, through his lack of vigilance, he became intoxicated and slept with Set's wife, Nephthys. Nephthys, as a result of the union with Osiris, begot Anubis.

Set, who represents the personification of evil forces, plotted in jealousy and anger (the blinding passion that prevents forgiveness) to usurp the throne and conspired to kill Osiris. Set secretly got the measurements of Osiris and constructed a coffin. Through trickery Set was able to get Osiris to "try on" the coffin for size. While Osiris was resting in the coffin, Set and his assistants locked it and then dumped it into the Nile river.

The coffin made its way to the coast of Syria where it became embedded in the earth and from it grew a tree with the most pleasant aroma in the form of a DJED or TET. The TET is the symbol of Osiris' BACK. It has four horizontal lines in relation to a firmly established, straight column. The DJED column is symbolic of the upper energy centers (chakras) that relate to the levels of consciousness of the spirit within an individual human being.

The King of Syria was out walking and as he passed by the tree, he immediately fell in love with the pleasant aroma, so he had the tree cut down and brought to his palace. Isis (Auset, Ast), Osiris' wife, the personification of the life giving, mother force in creation and in all humans, went to Syria in search of Osiris. Her search led her to the palace of the Syrian King where she took a job as the nurse of the King's son. Every evening Isis would put the boy into the "fire" to consume his mortal parts, thereby transforming him to immortality. Fire is symbolic of both physical and mental purification. Most importantly, fire implies wisdom, the light of truth, illumination and energy. Isis, by virtue of her qualities, has the power to bestow immortality through the transformative power of her symbolic essence. Isis then told the king that Osiris, her husband, is inside the pillar he made from the tree. He graciously gave her the pillar (DJED) and she returned with it to Kamit (Kmt, Egypt).

Upon her return to Kmt Isis went to the papyrus swamps where she lay over Osiris' dead body and fanned him with her wings, infusing him with new life. In this manner Isis revived Osiris through her power of love and wisdom, and then they united once more. From their union was conceived a son, Heru (Horus), with the assistance of the gods Thoth (Tehuti) and Amon.

One evening, as Set was hunting in the papyrus swamps, he came upon Isis and Osiris. In a rage of passion, he dismembered the body of Osiris into several pieces and scattered them throughout the land. In this way it is Set, the brute force of our bodily impulses and desires, that "dismembers" our higher intellect. Instead of oneness and unity, we see multiplicity and separateness which give rise to egoistic (selfish) and violent behavior. The Great Mother, Isis, once again sets out to search, now for the pieces of Osiris, with the help of Anubis and Nephthys.

After searching all over the world they found all the pieces of Osiris' body, except for his phallus which was eaten by a fish. In Eastern Hindu-Tantra mythology, the God Shiva, who is the equivalent of Osiris, also lost his phallus in one story. In Ancient Egyptian and Hindu-Tantra mythology, this loss represents seminal retention in order to channel the sexual energy to the higher spiritual centers, thereby transforming it into spiritual energy. Isis, Anubis and Nephthys re-membered the pieces, all except the phallus which was eaten by the fish. Osiris thus regained life in the realm of the dead, the Tuat.

Horus, therefore, was born from the union of the spirit of Osiris and the life giving power of Isis (Creation). Thus, Horus represents the union of spirit and matter and the renewed life of Osiris, his rebirth. When Horus became a young man, Osiris returned from the realm of the dead and encouraged him to take up arms (vitality, wisdom, courage, strength of will) and establish truth, justice and righteousness in the world by challenging Set, its current ruler.

The Battle of Horus (Heru) and Set

The battle between Horus and Set took many twists, sometimes one seeming to get the upper hand and sometimes the other, yet neither one gaining a clear advantage in order to decisively win. At one point Isis tried to help Horus by catching Set, but due to the pity and compassion she felt towards him she set him free. In a passionate rage Horus cut off her head and went off by himself in a frustrated state. Even Horus is susceptible to passion which leads to performing deeds that one later regrets. Set found Horus and gouged out Horus' eyes. During this time Horus was overpowered by the evil of Set. He became blinded to truth (as signified by the loss of his eyes) and thus, was unable to do battle (act with MAAT) with Set . His power of sight was later restored by Hathor (goddess of passionate love, desire and fierce power), who also represents the left Eye of

Ra. She is the fire spitting, destructive power of light which dispels the darkness (blindness) of ignorance.

When the conflict resumed, the two contendants went before the court of the Ennead gods (Company of the nine gods who ruled over creation, headed by Ra). Set, promising to end the fight and restore Horus to the throne, invited Horus to spend the night at his house, but Horus soon found out that Set had evil intentions when he tried to have intercourse with him. The uncontrolled Set also symbolizes unrestricted sexual activity. Juxtaposed against this aspect of Set (uncontrolled sexual potency and desire) is Horus in the form of ithyphallic (erect phallus) MIN, who represents not only the control of sexual desire, but its sublimation as well. Min symbolizes the power which comes from the sublimation of the sexual energy.

Through more treachery and deceit Set attempted to destroy Horus with the help of the Ennead, by tricking them into believing that Horus was not worthy of the throne. Osiris sent a letter pleading with the Ennead to do what was correct. Horus, as the son of Osiris, should be the rightful heir to the throne. All but two of them (the Ennead) agreed because Horus, they said, was too young to rule. Osiris then sent them a second letter (scroll of papyrus with a message) reminding them that even they cannot escape judgment for their deeds; they too will be judged in the end when they have to finally go to the West (abode of the dead).

This signifies that even the gods cannot escape judgment for their deeds. Since all that exists is only a manifestation of the absolute reality which goes beyond time and space, that which is in the realm of time and space (humans, spirits, gods, angels, neters) are all bound by its laws. Following the receipt of Osiris' scroll (letter), Horus was crowned King of Egypt. Set accepted the decision and made peace with Horus. All the gods rejoiced. Thus ends the legend of Osiris, Isis, and Horus.

The Resurrection of Osiris and his reincarnation in the form of Horus is a symbol for the spiritual resurrection which must occur in the life of every human being. In this manner, the story of the Osirian Trinity of Osiris-Isis-Horus and the Egyptian Ennead holds hidden teachings, which when understood and properly practiced, will lead to spiritual enlightenment.

THE UNABRIDGED MYTH OF SHETAUT ASAR-ASET-HERU

What follows is the synthesis of the entire myth of the Osirian Trinity story. It has been carefully and lovingly sutured together from various ancient sources, including the inscriptions of the Temples of Isis, Osiris, Horus and Hathor, the Pyramid Texts, *The Book of Coming Forth By Day of Ani*, the writings of Plutarch, and the Hermetic writings. It constitutes one of the most complete renditions of the entire story as it was known to the Ancient Egyptians, and later to their Greek disciples, who codified large sections of the story upon their initiation into the teachings of the Egyptian temple system.

Every line in the story is based on the original ancient Hieroglyphic, Hieratic, Demotic and Greek texts, and each section has been given a title. Line numbers have been added for easy reference. A brief gloss or limited commentary has been included at the end of the story.

Each line in the myth constitutes the litany of the mystical story of Osiris, Isis and Horus which was told to the Ancient Egyptian and Greek initiates who sought to discover a spiritual awakening or enlightenment. Therefore, they are to be considered as Hekau or Words of Power (known as mantras in India). They are special utterances, which when correctly understood and recited or chanted, impart wisdom, and have a transformative effect on the human mind because they contain information about the ultimate truth of the universe, and therefore, of each individual human being. This process of psycho-spiritual transformation leads the reciter towards inner peace, contentment, divine awareness and communion with the Higher Self.

No one knows exactly when the myths of any particular country originated. Like all legends, the Osirian Mystery cannot be said to be a completely historical fact nor can it be said to be a story without any reality. Osiris, Isis, Horus and the other neters did exist, and they continue to exist even today as the energy which sustains life on earth. This is the same energy which courses through every human being, causing birth, growth, death and reincarnation. The symbolic meaning of the story has been true from the beginning of time, and is occurring in the life of every human being at this very moment. Therefore, while certain historical information is needed to set a context for our study in relation to world history, the most important aspect of the myth is the mystical meaning contained in it. In this sense, the Osirian Myth is absolutely true and factual in every detail.

The ancient Sages created stories based on human and superhuman beings whose struggles, aspirations, needs and desires ultimately led them to discover their true Self (God). The myth of Osiris, Isis and Horus is no exception in this area. While there is no single place where the entire story may be found, pieces of it are inscribed in various ancient temples walls, tombs, steles and papyri. In a way it would not have been necessary for Ancient Egyptian civilization to record the story in its entirety because its knowledge was so pervasive throughout every area of society, including the government, businesses and educational institutions.

This being the case, it might even have been considered detrimental to codify the myth because this would tend to curtail the freedom of its use as a method of teaching spiritual truths. Sages sometimes introduce seemingly new concepts and twists into old myths in order to revive and

35

update them for the present time, according to the level of intellectual and spiritual development of the people at large (the masses). In this manner they are able to cultivate a positive development for society as a whole with an exoteric or outer teaching which imparts the basic teachings of spirituality and engenders Maat (ethical behavior), while at the same time looking out for those individuals who display a certain special interest in the spiritual disciplines, and imparting onto them an esoteric teaching which leads them to the heights of inner self-discovery. The inner teachings were imparted to the spiritual aspirant who was ready to understand the psycho-mystical meanings behind the story through the initiation process.

In its form as a myth which was carried on for thousands of years through the power of folklore and oral tradition, the Osirian Mystery remained in the special domain of a legend which the Ancient Egyptian people accepted as real and true. As an object to be recorded, it might have lost its power of expression because the act of codification itself tends to lock things down to a particular time, place, idea or expression, and tends to invalidate any other variations or expressions. This is the normal attitude in the "civilized" nations. Often times there is a desire among those who are intellectually advanced to reduce things to their elementary components and hold onto them as possessions, and then to exclude whatever seems to be outside or different from the accepted models. Along with this attitude, there is a reverence for scriptures which are considered old and a disdain for younger or updated teachings given by modern day Sages.

As a spiritual aspirant, you must realize that the scriptures themselves are not alive with the wisdom which leads to realization of the Higher Self until their mystical meaning is fully understood. This is why an authentic teacher is needed to direct you towards the correct understanding and practice of the teachings. In the myth of Osiris the teacher takes many forms. Isis becomes the teacher of Horus and later, Horus seeks conference with Hathor and Tehuti. Also, the Ennead seeks council from the goddess Neith. Therefore, spiritual wisdom is a living essence which cannot be fully captured in scriptures alone. It requires initiation into (being taught) the esoteric meanings of the symbols and metaphors. However, as you become spiritually sensitive, having gained some higher knowledge through contact with others of higher development, you will begin to discover the wisdom that is latent in all of the world's great scriptures.

Myths cannot be held as a possession nor can their wisdom be understood by having them in a written form and keeping them on a bookshelf. They must be studied and understood thoroughly, and ultimately, they must be lived in order for their truths and significance to be fully realized.

Nearly every culture has a sacred book or books which extol(s) the beliefs in reference to the Divine and Its relationship to humanity. The *Bhagavad Gita, Tao Te Ching, Dhammapada, Zend Avesta, Popol Vu, Koran, Christian Bible, Torah* and other sacred texts from around the world have been sources of inspiration and means by which people have learned about spiritual matters. Many have suggested that the Egyptian *Book of Coming Forth By Day* is to be considered as the Ancient Egyptian Bible, and deservedly so, because it includes rituals for divine worship, elucidates the nature of the Divine, and emphasizes the importance of virtue and devotion to the Divine as a means to achieve contact with the Divine. There is one important element missing from the *Book of Coming Forth By Day* however. This factor is the mythological basis. While the *Book of Coming Forth By Day* alludes to the Osirian myth upon which it is based and a working knowledge of it may be gained by studying the texts, the texts were really prepared for those who were already well acquainted with (initiated into) the teachings of the myth of Osiris, Isis and Horus. Thus, it was necessary to provide only a brief or indirect reference to the myth.

The myth, being the heart of rituals, is the origin and basis of all religious practices. Therefore, myths are to be considered as the archetype and primary underlying essence of the rituals and mystical philosophy of a religious system. The following texts are offered as the "Bible" or sacred text of Ancient Egypt. They constitute the foundation and quintessence of Ancient Egyptian civilization, mystical wisdom and religious philosophy.

(Nehas-t)

"resurrection" or "spiritual awakening".

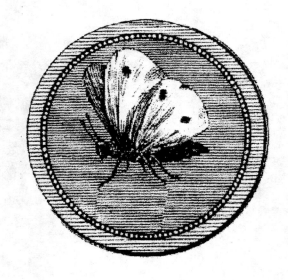

38

The Ausarian Resurrection

Om Asar Aset Heru,
Om Asar Aset Heru,
Om Asar Aset Heru,
Om Asar Aset Heru,

The Creation
The High God arising out of the primeval waters in the form of Khepera.

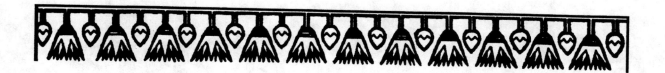

Shetaut Asar-Aset-Heru
The Myth Of Osiris, Isis and Horus

1

A Hymn to Ra
(From the Egyptian Book of Coming Forth By Day of Oenna)

"A HYMN OF PRAISE TO RA WHEN HE RISETH IN THE EASTERN PART OF HEAVEN. Behold Osiris, Oenna the merchant, who saith: "Homage to thee, in thy rising thou Tmu in thy crowns of beauty. You risest, you risest, you, Ra, shinest, you shinest, at dawn of day. You are crowned like unto the king of the gods, and the goddess Shuti doeth homage unto thee. The Company of the gods and goddesses praise thee from the double-dwelling. You goest forth over the upper air and thy heart is filled with gladness. The Sektet boat draweth onward as Ra cometh to the haven in the Atet boat with fair winds. Ra rejoiceth, Ra rejoiceth. Thy father is Nu, thy mother is Nut and you are crowned as Ra-Harmachis. Thy sacred boat advanceth in peace. Thy foe has been cast down and his head has been cut off; the heart of the Lady of Life rejoiceth in that the enemy of her lord has been overthrown. The mariners of Ra have content of heart and Annu rejoiceth"

The Creation
(From the hieroglyphic text entitled: The History of Creation.)

2   Here is the story of Ra, the God who was self-begotten and self-created. He created men and women from his own being. He assumed the sovereignty over men and women, and gods, and all things, the ONE God. Upon rising for the first time out of Nu, the Primeval Ocean, Ra emitted from himself Shu (air and space or ether) and Tefnut (moisture). These two gave rise to Geb (earth, physical matter) and Nut (sky, heaven). Maat is a daughter of Ra. It is said that Maat is the foundation of creation and that Maat is what everything is based on since Ra stands in his boat of creation on the pedestal of Maat.

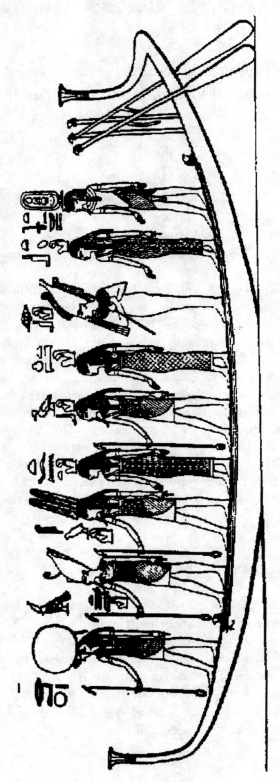

Ra and the Company of Gods and Goddesses in the Barque of Millions of Years

The Destruction of Evil Men and Women
(From the hieroglyphic text entitled: The Destruction of Evil Men and Women.)

3   Now men and women were speaking words of complaint, saying: "Behold, his Majesty (Life, Strength, and Health to him! has grown old, and his bones have become like silver, and his members have turned into gold and his hair is like unto real lapis-lazuli." His Majesty heard the words of complaint which men and women were uttering, and his Majesty (Life, Strength, and Health to him!) said unto those who were in his train: "Cry out, and bring to me my Eye, and Shu, and Tefnut, and Seb (Geb), and Nut, and the father-gods, and the mother-gods who were with me, even when I was in Nu side by side with my god Nu. Let there be brought along with my Eye, its ministers, and let them be led to me here secretly, so that men and women may not perceive them coming, and may not therefore take to flight with their hearts. Come thou with them to the Great House, and let them declare their plans fully, for I will go from Nu into the place wherein I brought about my own existence, and let those gods be brought unto me there. Now the gods were drawn up on each side of Ra, and they bowed down before his Majesty until their heads touched the ground, and the maker of men and women, the King of those who have knowledge, spake his words in the presence of the Father of the first-born gods.

4   And the gods spoke in the presence of his Majesty, saying: "Speak unto us, for we are listening to your words." Then Ra spoke unto Nu, saying: "0 you first born god from whom I came into being, 0 ye gods of ancient time, my ancestors, take ye heed to what men and women are doing; for behold, those who were created by my Eye are uttering words of complaint against me. Tell me what ye would do in the matter, and consider this thing for me, and seek out a plan for me, for I will not slay them until I have heard what ye shall say to me concerning it." Then the Majesty of Nu, to son Ra, spoke, saying: "You are the god who are greater than he who made thee. You are the sovereign of those who were created with thee. Thy throne is set, and the fear of thee is great; let thine Eye go against those who have uttered blasphemies against thee." And the Majesty of Ra said: "Behold, they have betaken themselves to flight into the mountain lands, for their hearts are afraid because of the words which they have uttered." The gods spoke in the presence of his Majesty, saying: "Let thine Eye go forth and let it destroy for thee those who revile thee with words of evil, for there is no eye whatsoever that can go before it and resist thee and it when it journeyeth in the form of Hathor."

Above: Shu separates Nut and Geb while Ra traverses over Nut (the heavens) in the barque of day (at left) and the barque of night (at right).

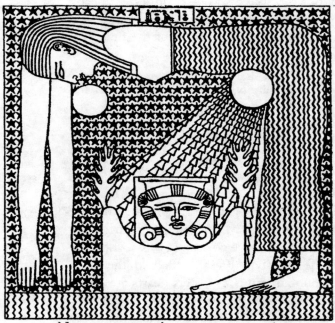

Nut consuming the evening sun and giving birth to the morning sun.

Above: The goddess Nut, from a mummy case at Turin.

At right: Nut in the form of a cow goddess.

4a   Thereupon this goddess went forth and slew the men and the women who were on the mountains and desert lands. And the Majesty of this god said, "Come, come in peace, O Hathor, for the work is accomplished." Then this goddess said, "You have made me to live, for when I gained the mastery over men and women it was sweet to my heart. I should like to continue feeding upon men and women." Then the Majesty of Ra said, "I myself will be master over them as their King, and I will destroy them." And it came to pass that *She of the offerings*, Hathor, waded about in the night season in their blood, beginning at Suten-henen. Then the Majesty of Ra spake saying:, "Cry out, and let there come to me swift and speedy messengers who shall be able to run like the wind . . . ." and straightway, these messengers were brought unto him. And the Majesty of this god spake saying: "Let these messengers go to Abu, and bring unto me mandrakes in great numbers"; and when these mandrakes were brought unto him the Majesty of this god gave them to Sekhet, the goddess who dwelleth in Annu (Heliopolis) to crush. And behold, when the maidservants were bruising the grain for making beer, these mandrakes were placed in the vessels which were to hold the beer, and some of the blood of the men and women who had been slain. Now they made seven thousand vessels of beer. Now when the Majesty of Ra, the King of the South and North, had come with the gods to look at the vessels of beer, and behold, the daylight had appeared after the slaughter of men and women by the goddess in their season as she sailed up the river, the Majesty of Ra, said: "It is good, it is good that she has displayed the power of righteousness and punished the evil ones, nevertheless I must protect men and women against her." And Ra, said, "Let them take up the vases and carry them to the place where the men and women were slaughtered by her."

4b   Then the Majesty of the King of the South and North, in the three-fold beauty of the night, caused to be poured out these vases of beer which make men to lie down (sleep), and the meadows of the Four Heavens (the South, North, West, and East of the sky) were filled with beer (divine nectar) by reason of the Souls of the Majesty of this God. And it came to pass that when this goddess arrived at the dawn of day, she found these Heavens flooded with the nectar, and she was pleased thereat; and she drank of the beer and blood, and her heart rejoiced, and she became drunk, and she gave no further attention to men and women. Then said the Majesty of Ra, to this goddess, "Come in peace, come in peace, O Amit (most beautiful one)" and thereupon beautiful women came into being in the city of Amit (or, Amem). And the Majesty of Ra spake in homage to this goddess, saying: "Let there be made for her vessels of the beer which produceth sleep at every holy time and season of the year, and they shall be in number

MAAT

MAATI

Maat is a daughter of Ra. It is said that Maat is the foundation of creation and that Maat is what everything is based on since Ra stands in his boat of creation on the pedestal of Maat.

Maat with eyes closed.

Top left: The ancient Egyptian Goddess MAAT, holding a papyrus reed scepter. Maat is a philosophy, a spiritual symbol as well as a cosmic energy or force which pervades the entire universe. She is the symbolic embodiment of world order, justice, righteousness, correctness, harmony and peace. She is also known by her headdress composed of a feather of truth. She is a form of the goddess Isis, who represents wisdom and spiritual awakening.

In ancient Egypt, the judges and all those connected with the judicial system were initiated into the teachings of MAAT. Thus, those who would discharge the laws and regulations of society were well trained in ethical and spiritual values of life, fairness, justice and the responsibility to serve society in order to promote harmony in society and the possibility for spiritual development in an atmosphere of freedom and peace, for only when there is justice and fairness in society can there be an abiding harmony and peace. Harmony and peace are necessary for the pursuit of true happiness and inner fulfillment in life.

Along with her associates, the god *Tehuti* and the goddesses *Shai*, *Rennenet* and *Meskhenet*, Maat encompasses the teachings of Karma and the destiny of every individual. Thus, they have an important role to play in the Judgment scene of the Book of Coming Forth By Day.

according to the number of my hand-maidens." And from that early time until now men have been wont to make on the occasions of the festival of Hathor vessels of the beer which make them to sleep in number according to the number of the hand-maidens of Ra.

4c   And the Majesty of Ra spake unto this goddess, saying: "I am smitten with the pain of the fire of sickness; whence cometh to me this pain?" And the Majesty of Ra said, "I live, but my heart has become exceedingly weary with existence with these men and women who have forgotten me and become boastful, prideful and full of themselves. I have slain some of them, but there is a remnant of worthless ones, for the destruction which I wrought among them was not as great as my power." Then the gods who were in his following said unto him, "Be not overcome by thy inactivity, for thy might is in proportion to thy will." And the Majesty of this God (Ra) said unto the Majesty of Nu, "My members are weak and have suffered pain since primeval time, and I shall not recover until another period comes".

4d   And the Majesty of the god Nu said, "Son Shu, be thou the Eye for thy father . . . . . and assist him, and you goddess Nut, place him on your back." And the goddess Nut said, "How can this be then, O my father Nu ?" " Hail," said Nut . . . . . to the god Nu, and the goddess straightway became a cow, and she set the Majesty of Ra upon (her) back . . . . . And when these things had been done, men and women saw the god Ra upon the back of the cow. Then these men and women said, "Remain with us, and we will overthrow thine enemies who speak words of blasphemy against thee, and destroy them."

4e   Then his Majesty, Ra, set out for the Great House, and the gods who were in the train of Ra remained with the men and women; during that time the earth was in darkness. And when the earth became light again, and the morning had dawned, the men came forth with their bows and their other weapons, and they set their arms in motion to shoot the enemies of Ra.

4f   Then said the Majesty of this god, "Your transgressions of violence are placed behind you, for the slaughtering of the enemies is above the slaughter of sacrifice." Thus came into being the slaughter of enemies. And the Majesty of this god said unto Nut, "I have placed myself upon my back in order to stretch myself out."

4g   And the Majesty of this God said, "Call to me the god Tehuti," and one brought the god to him forthwith. And the Majesty of this god said unto Tehuti, "Let us depart to a distance from heaven, from my place, because I would make

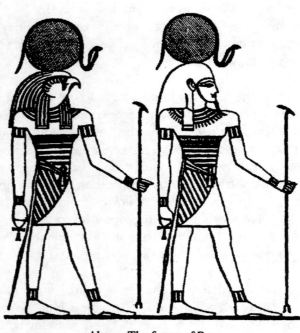

Above: The forms of Ra

Above: The forms of Shu

Above: The forms of Geb

48

light and the god of light in the Ṭuat and the Land of Gaves. You shall write down the things which are in it, and you shall punish those who are sinful, that is to say, the workers who have worked iniquity (rebellion-unrighteousness). Through thee I will keep away from the servants whom this heart of mine loathes. You shall be in my place ASTI (ast-throne or support), and you shall therefore be called, O Tehuti, the "ASTI of Ra." Moreover, I give thee power to send forth light. . . . . ; thereupon shall come into being the Ibis (jcabi) bird of Tehuti. I moreover give thee "power" to lift up thine hand before the two Companies of the gods who are better than you, and what you do shall be fairer than (the work of the god KHEN; therefore shall the divine bird of Tehuti come into being. Moreover, I give thee power to embrace the two heavens with thy beauties and with thy rays of light; therefore shall come into being the Moon-god of Tehuti. Moreover, I give thee power to drive back the Ha-nebu (unrighteous northerners); therefore shall come into being the dog-headed Ape (anan) of Tehuti, and he shall act as governor for me. Moreover, you are now in my place in the sight of all those who see thee and who present offerings to thee, and every being shall ascribe praise unto thee, O you who are God."

The Story of Hathor and Tehuti†

4h   Some say that Hathor, the goddess of beauty, the eye of Ra, transformed herself into the form of a lioness or lynx and killed the evil people who plotted against the Lord of All. Having killed all those who were evil, she forgot her true identity and became addicted to the taste of human blood. She continued to kill everyone she could find as she roamed the earth. Then, seeing that humankind would soon come to an end, Ra sent the messenger of wisdom, Tehuti, to bring his daughter back. Straightway Tehuti transformed himself into a baboon and found Hathor. At first she threatened to devour him but he cleverly enticed her into listening to the divine stories of gods and goddesses. He told her about Ra, her father and reminded her of her beautiful human form. He spoke of her glory as the Eye of Ra, and the honor which the people of Egypt bestowed upon her. Gradually her desire for blood and killing dwindled and she began to desire to regain her former place as the mighty goddess of beauty and passion. Thus, Tehuti led her back to Egypt and back to her rightful place among the pantheon of gods and goddesses.

† For the unabridged version of The Story of Hathor and Tehuti see the book *Mysticism of Ushet Rekhat* by Dr. Muata Ashby.

Below: The forms of Hathor

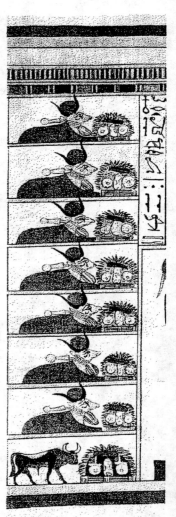

Above: Hathor as the scorching (right) eye of Ra.

Above: The Seven Hathors (seven celestial cows) and the Bull of Heaven (Osiris) who provide sustenance to the initiate.

Mystically, Osiris is the spirit which manifests as creation through the seven levels of energy-consciousness.

From the Papyrus of Ani

ᒋᒋᒋᒋᒋᒋᒋᒋᒋ
The Ennead: Nine Principles of Creation

5   In the beginning, there was the primeval ocean, Nu, and from it arose Ra. Upon his emergence this magnificent God created all that came into being from his own self and he existed within his creation as one exists within one's own body. He emanated Shu and Tefnut and they in turn gave rise to Nut and Geb. The goddess Nut and the god Geb were united in amorous embrace since they had loved each other so deeply from the beginning of time. Their embrace was so close that no other living being could exist in the world.

6   From their union Nut became pregnant, but Ra had decreed that they should be separated and that Nut could not give birth in any month of the year. At this time he also decided to retreat as an active participant in his creation and to abide in heaven wherein all who would seek him must go. From this position he supports creation as he traverses in the form of the sun making it possible for life to exist and flourish. In the morning he is known as Kheper, at noon he is known as Ra and at sunset he is known as Tem.

7   Also from here he witnesses all of the activities and events of creation. In his absence he created Tehuti, his minister and messenger through whom he, Ra, would manage and sustain his creation.

8   Ra instituted himself as the sustainer of creation during the day and illumines creation as the sun, ☉, while setting Tehuti up in the form of the baboon to watch over creation at night as the the moon, ☽.

The Birth of Osiris and Isis

9   Having become pregnant as a result of her sexual union with Geb, Nut gave birth to Osiris, Set, Isis, Nephthys, Hathor, Maat, and Tehuti.

10   Tehuti, who being wise and caring for Nut, was able to win the seventieth part of each day of the year and to have these added up and added to the year. These Epagomenal Days or "the five days over the year" he added to the three hundred and sixty days of which the year formerly consisted. These five days are to this day

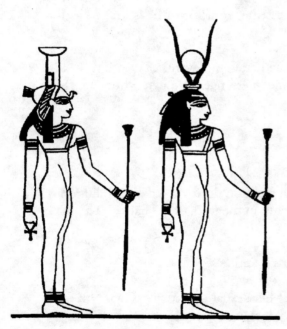

Top: Forms of Tehuti, also known as Thoth

Middle: Forms of Nephthys

Right: Forms of Set

called the "Epagomenae," that is, the "superadded", and they are observed as the birthdays of the gods. On the first of these days, Osiris was born, and as he came into the world a voice was heard saying, *"The Lord of All, Nebertcher, is born."*

10a   Upon the second of these days was born Horus the Elder. Upon the third day Set was born, who came into the world neither at the proper time nor by the right way, but he forced a passage through a wound which he made in his mother's side. Upon the fourth day Isis was born in the marshes of Egypt, and upon the fifth day Nephthys was born. As regards the fathers of these children, the first two are said to have been begotten by Ra, Isis by Tehuti, and Set and Nephthys by Geb. Therefore, since the third of the superadded days was the birthday of Set, the kings considered it to be unlucky and in consequence, they neither transacted any business in it, nor even suffered themselves to take any refreshment until the evening.

11   They further added that Set married Nephthys and that Isis and Osiris, having a mutual affection, enjoyed each other in their mother's womb even before they were born, and that from this union sprang Horus the Elder. Osiris and Isis gave birth to Horus, and Osiris and Nephthys gave birth to Anubis.

Osiris: The first King of Egypt and Teacher of the World

12   Osiris, having become king of Egypt, applied himself to civilizing his countrymen by turning them from their former indigent and barbarous course of life. Isis discovered the use of barley and wheat and Osiris developed the cultivation process for these and established the custom of offering the first fruits to the neters. He taught them how to cultivate and improve the fruits of the earth and he gave them a body of laws whereby to regulate their conduct, and instructed them in the reverence and worship which they were to pay to the gods. With the same good disposition he afterwards traveled over the rest of the world, inducing the people everywhere to submit to his discipline, not indeed compelling them by force of arms, but persuading them to yield to the strength of his reasons which were conveyed to them in the most agreeable manner, in hymns and songs, accompanied with instruments of music.

The Travels of Osiris in Ancient Times

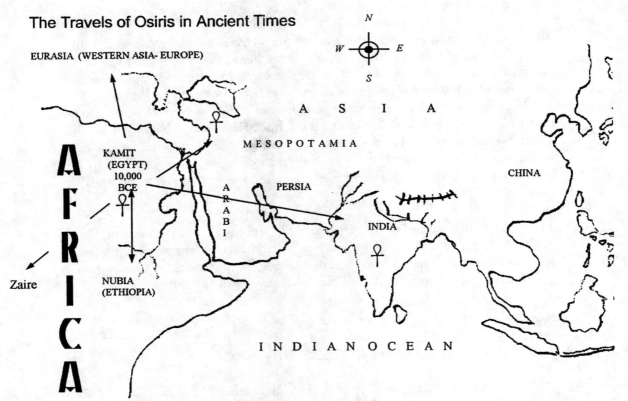

Above: A map of North-east Africa, Asia Minor and India, showing the three main locations of the use of the ancient Egyptian Ankh symbol and also the geographic area where Osiris traveled and spread the teachings of mystical spirituality (Yoga) which later became associated with Christianity in the Middle East, Rome and Greece, and Vedanta - Yoga in India.

THE ANCIENT HISTORY OF OSIRIS AND ISIS
(From the history of Diodorus Siculus - 100 BCE)

13   The wise ones say that the Egyptians are colonists sent out by the Ethiopians, Osiris having been the leader of the colony. For, speaking generally, what is now Egypt, they maintain, was not land, but sea, when in the beginning the universe was being formed; afterwards, however, as the Nile during the times of its inundation carried down the mud from Ethiopia, land was gradually built up from the deposit...And the larger parts of the customs of the Egyptians are, they hold, Ethiopian, the colonists still preserving their ancient manners. For instance, the belief that their kings are gods, the very special attention which they pay to their burials, and many other matters of a similar nature, are Ethiopian practices, while the shapes of their statues and the forms of their letters are Ethiopian; for of the two kinds of writing which the Egyptians have, that which is known as popular (demotic) is learned by everyone, while that which is called sacred (hieratic) is understood only by the priests of the Egyptians, who learnt it from their fathers as one of the things which are not divulged, but among the Ethiopians, everyone uses these forms of letters. Furthermore, the orders of the priests, they maintain, have much the same position among both peoples; for all are clean who are engaged in the service of the gods, keeping themselves shaven, like the Ethiopian priests, and having the same dress and form of staff which is shaped like a plough and is carried by their kings who wear high felt hats which end in a knob in the top and are circled by the serpents which they call asps; and this symbol appears to carry the thought that it will be the lot who shall dare to attack the king to encounter death-carrying stings. Many other things are told by them concerning their own antiquity and the colony which they sent out that became the Egyptians...

Osiris Travels to India and Europe

14   Osiris visited Ethiopia and established more cities there. From Ethiopia, he (Osiris) passed through Arabia, bordering upon the Red Sea to as far as India and the remotest inhabited coasts; he built likewise many cities in India, one of which he called Nysa, willing to have remembrance of that (Nysa) in Egypt where he was brought up. At this Nysa in India he planted ivy which continues to grow there, but nowhere else in India or around it. He left likewise many other marks of his being in those parts, by which the latter inhabitants are induced and do affirm that this God was born in India. He likewise addicted himself to the hunting of elephants, and took care to have statues of himself in every place as lasting monuments of his expedition. From India Osiris traveled through the Hellespont

Horus The Child, sitting on the primeval Lotus which symbolizes creation rising from the primeval ocean.

"For the one 'sitting above the lotus-blossom' expresses enigmatically an exaltation above the slime, and likewise denotes spiritual and empyrial supremacy. For everything pertaining to the lotus, both the forms in the leaves and the appearance of the seed, is observed to be circular. This very energy is akin to the unique circle-like motion of the mind, manifesting it in like manner according to the same forms, in a single arrangement, and according to one principle.

The god himself, however, is seated alone, above any such dominion or energy, august and holy, filled abundantly, and remaining in himself without change, as the figure of one sitting is intended to signify."

—Iamblichus, Egyptian Initiate (circa 250-330 A.C.E.)

56

into Europe and established cities there as well. He was a benefactor to the entire world and discovered the right types of foods for people to eat. Along with his minister, Tehuti, he established standards of justice and righteousness for the whole world to follow.

The Columns of Osiris in Arabia

15   There are Egyptian columns as far off as NYASA, Arabia...Isis and Osiris led an army into India, to the source of the Ganges, and as far as the Indus Ocean.

Isis (Aset): Queen of Egypt

16   During one of Osiris' absences from his kingdom, Set had no opportunity to make innovations in the state because Isis was extremely vigilant in the government of the country and always upon her guard and watchful for any irregularity or unrighteousness. Isis took to the mystic arts of the study of wisdom and the practice of meditation. She meditated on Ra and obtained the wisdom of life from him and thus became as great as Ra in power and glory, having discovered his most secret and sacred name. This is known as the story of Ra and Aset.‡

16a   Upon Osiris' return from touring the world and carrying the teachings of wisdom abroad there was merriment and rejoicing throughout the land. However, one day after Osiris' return, through his lack of vigilance, became intoxicated and slept with Set's wife, Nephthys. Nephthys, as a result of this union with Osiris, begot Anubis.

The Incarnation and Passion of the Spirit: The Death, Dismemberment and Resurrection of Osiris
(From the Greek text entitled: The History of Isis and Osiris)

The Murder of Osiris

16b   Set, who was already full of jealousy and greed, wanting to be revered and loved as Osiris was, and desiring to be the king of all Egypt, became even more angry and hateful towards Osiris. Having first persuaded seventy-two other people to join with him in a conspiracy against Osiris, Set formed a crafty plot to kill Osiris. For having privately taken the measure of the body of Osiris, he caused a chest to be made of exactly the same size, and it was very beautiful and highly decorated. This chest he brought into a certain banqueting room where it was

‡ For the unabridged version of the Story of Ra and Aset see the book *Mysticism of Ushet Rekhat* by Dr. Muata Ashby.

Isis

Osiris.
From the Papyrus of
Iuâu, Plate XXII.

Horus

Below: Horus as the Hawk from the Temple at Ombos, Nubia, Africa.

greatly admired by all who were present, and Set, as if in jest, promised to give it to that man whose body, when tried, would be found to fit it. Thereupon the whole company, one after the other, went into it, but it did not fit any of them; last of all Osiris himself lay down in it. Thereupon all the conspirators ran to the chest and clapped the cover upon it, and then they fastened it down with nails on the outside and poured melted lead over it. They next took the chest to the river which carried it to the sea through the Tanaitic mouth of the Nile; and for this reason this mouth of the Nile is still held in the utmost abomination.

17   As soon as the report reached Isis, she immediately cut off one of the locks of her hair and put on mourning apparel in that very place where she happened to be; for this reason the place has ever since been called "Koptos," or the "city of mourning, and deprivation." After this she wandered round about through the country, being full of disquietude and perplexity, searching for the chest, and she inquired of every person she met, including some children whom she saw, whether they knew what has become of it.

18   Now, it so happened that these children had seen what Set's accomplices had done with the body, and they accordingly told her by what part of the mouth of the Nile it had been conveyed to the sea. Isis meanwhile, having been informed that Osiris, deceived by her sister Nephthys who was in love with him, had unwittingly enjoyed her instead of herself, as she concluded from the melilot-garland which he had left with her, made it her business likewise to search out the child, the fruit of this unlawful union, for her sister, dreading the anger of her husband Set, had hidden it as soon it was born.

19   Accordingly, after much pains and difficulty, by means of some dogs that conducted her to the place where it was, she found it and bred it up, and in the process of time it became her constant guard and attendant, and obtained the name of Anubis, and it has come about that it watches and guards the gods as dogs do men.

20   At length Isis received more particular news that the chest had been carried by the waves of the sea to the coast of Byblos, and there gently lodged in the branches of a bush of tamarisk, which in a short time had grown up into a large and beautiful tree and had grown around the chest and enclosed it on every side so completely that it was not to be seen. Moreover, the king of the country, amazed at its unusual size and the fragrant aroma of the tree, had it cut down and made that part of the trunk wherein the chest was concealed, into a pillar to support the roof of his house.

Above: The body of Osiris grows into a tree. (From a bas relief at the temple of Denderah)

The king handing the Ṭeṭ to Isis.
From a bas-relief at Abydos.

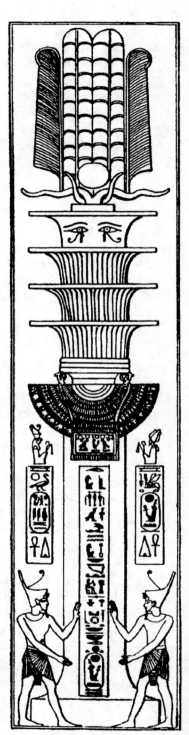

The Ṭeṭ of Osiris, with the plumes, horns, disk, breast-plate and pectoral of the god. From a bas-relief at Abydos.

60

Isis Finds The Body of Osiris

21   These things, they say, having been made known to Isis in an extraordinary manner by the report of divine spirits, she immediately went to Byblos, where, setting herself down by the side of a fountain, she refused to speak to anybody except the queen's women who chanced to be there. These, however, she saluted and caressed in the kindest manner possible, plaiting their hair for them, and transmitting into them part of that wonderful odor which issued from her own body. This raised a great desire in the queen, their mistress, to see the stranger who had this admirable faculty of transfusing so fragrant a smell from herself into the hair and skin of other people. She therefore sent for Isis to come to the royal court, and after a further acquaintance with her, made her nurse to one of her sons.

22   Isis nursed the child by giving it her finger to suck instead of the breast. She likewise put him each night into the fire in order to consume his mortal part, whilst, having transformed herself into a swallow, she circled round the pillar and bemoaned her sad fate. This she continued to do for some time, till the queen, who stood watching her, observing the child to be all of a flame, cried out and broke the spell which was transforming him from a mortal being into immortal, and thereby deprived him of some of that immortality which would otherwise have been conferred upon him. The goddess then made herself known. She revealed her true identity to the queen and related to her the story of her husband Osiris. She then asked that the pillar which supported the roof of their house might be given to her. Realizing the nature of her being and the truth of her story, the king and queen immediately agreed to give Isis the pillar.

Isis Retrieves The Body of Osiris and Returns to Egypt

23   Having taken the pillar down, she cut it open easily, and taking out what she wanted, she wrapped up the remainder of the trunk in fine linen and poured perfumed oil over it. Then she delivered it again into the hands of the king and queen. Now, this piece of wood is to this day preserved in the temple and worshipped by the people of Byblos. When this was done, Isis threw herself upon the chest, and made at the same time such loud and terrible cries of lamentation over it that the younger of the king's sons who heard her was frightened out of his life. But the elder of them she took with her, and set sail with the chest for Egypt. Now, it being morning, the river Phaedrus sent forth a keen and chilly air, and becoming angry she dried up its current.

Anubis, under the direction of Thoth, reconstituting the body of Osiris with the help of the Frog-goddess Ḥeqet. Nephthys sits at the head of the bier and Isis at the foot.

Osiris in the character of Menu, the "god of the uplifted arm," and Harpokrates as they sat in the disk of the moon, from the third day of the new moon until the fifteenth day. Below is the Crocodile-god Sebek bearing the mummy of the god on his back. To the left stands Isis.

From a bas-relief at Philae.

Below: A temple relief of Sebek
Relief from Kom Ombo, Nubia, Africa

62

24a   Isis retreated to the papyrus swamps where, with the assistance of the goddess Arat or Uatchet, the Uraeus, she was able to find safety. The crocodile God, Sebek, assisted in protecting Osiris by carrying him on his back.

24b   At the first place where she stopped, and when she believed that she was alone, she opened the chest, and laying her face upon that of her dead husband, she embraced him and wept bitterly. Then, seeing that the little boy had silently stolen up behind her, and had found out the reason of her grief, she turned upon him suddenly, and in her anger gave him so fierce and terrible a look that he fell into the sea. Afterwards he received the greatest honor on account of the goddess. Isis laid over Osiris' dead body and conceived a son, Heru (Horus), and gave birth to him with the assistance of the Gods Tehuti and Amon (Amun). Upon his birth, the gods Saa and Hu and the goddesses Uatchit and Nekhebet presented life and sovereignty to the son of Isis.

25   **A HYMN TO ISIS**
(From an Ancient Egyptian Relief
(2,400-1,400 B.C.E.), now in the Louvre.)

Oh benevolent Isis, who protected her brother Osiris, who searched for him without wearying, who traversed the land in mourning and never rested until she had found him. She who afforded him shadow with her wings and gave him air with her feathers, who rejoiced and carried her brother home.

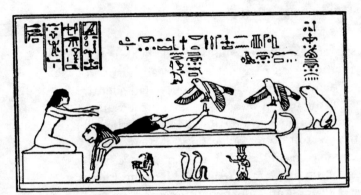

Isis addressing the mummy of Osiris as it lay in her boat ready for removal to the tomb.

"His sister [Isis] protected him [Osiris], driving off his enemies, turning aside evil happenings with the spells of her mouth, the weighty utterances of her tongue, the infallibility of her speech, and the effectiveness of her command and word. Isis the enchantress, the avenger of her brother [Osiris], sought him untiringly, and traveled about over this earth sorrowing, and rested not until she had found him. She produced warmth from her hair, she caused air to come by [the beating of] her wings, and she uttered doleful cries for her brother. She caused movement to take place in what was inert in the still heart (i.e. the dead Osiris), she drew essence from him, she made flesh and blood, she suckled [her] babe in loneliness, no man knowing where he was. The child grew up, his hand became mighty in the House of Geb (i.e. the earth), and the Company of the gods and goddesses rejoiced greatly at the coming of Horus, the son of Osiris, established of mind, true of voice, son of Isis, heir of Osiris." (From a stele in Paris.)

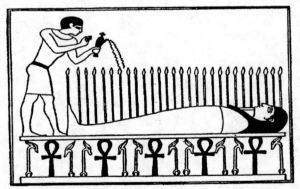

Above: Isis, in the form of a hawk over the body of Osiris, is begetting Horus by Osiris. The second hawk is Nephthys. At the head of the bier sits Hathor, and at the foot, the frog goddess Heqet.

Above: Isis (representing the creation) and the dead body of Osiris (representing the spirit, that essence which vivifies matter) are shown in symbolic union begetting Horus. Horus represents the birth of the spiritual life in every human: the birth of the soul (Ba) in a human is the birth of Horus, who is an incarnation of the Supreme Being (Osiris).

From a Stele at the British Museum 1372. 13th Dyn.

Above: After being resurrected by Isis and begetting Horus, Osiris becomes the Life Force energy which causes all things in nature to grow. (From a Bas Relief at the Temple of Philea)

She who revived what was faint for the weary one, who received his seed and conceived an heir, and who nourished him in solitude while no one knew where he was. . . .

I am your sister Isis. There is no other god or goddess who has done what I have done. I played the part of a man, although I am a woman, to let your name live on earth, for your divine seed was in my body.

The Dismemberment of The Body of Osiris

26   When Isis had come to her son Horus who was being reared at Buto, she deposited the chest in a remote and unfrequented place. One night however, when Set was hunting by the light of the moon, he came upon it by chance, and recognizing the body which was enclosed in it, he tore it into several pieces, fourteen in all, and scattered them in different places all over the world.

27   The fourteen members were: head, feet, bones, arms, heart, interior, tongue, eyes, fists, fingers, back, ears, loins, and body.

The Search For The Pieces of The body Of Osiris

28   When Isis knew what had been done, she set out, along with Anubis and Nephthys, in search of the scattered portions of her husband's body, and in order to pass more easily through the lower, marshy parts of the country, she made use of a boat made of the papyrus plant. For this reason, they say, either fearing the anger of the goddess, or else venerating the papyrus, the crocodile never injures anyone who travels in this sort of vessel. Notwithstanding all her efforts, Isis was never able to discover the phallus of Osiris which was eaten by a fish..

29   Thus, Isis, Anubis, and Nephthys, with the help of the Serpent god Nehebka, re-membered the pieces, all except the phallus which was eaten by the fish. In this way, assisted by the words of power of Isis, Osiris was reconstituted. Following this, he became the ruler in the realm of the dead, the beautiful West, the Amenta or Ṭuat.

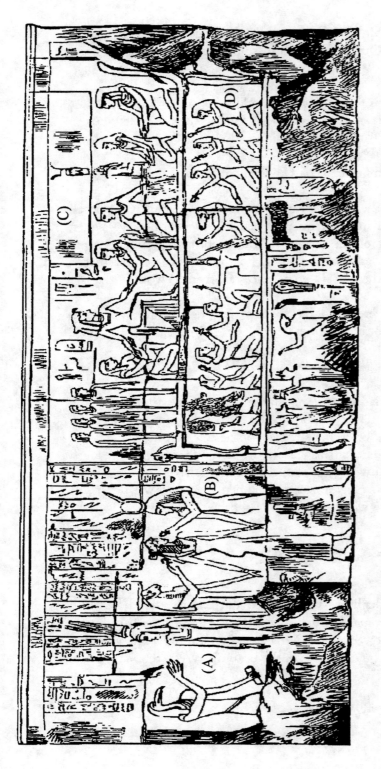

The Annunciation of The Birth of Horus

The origins of the transcendental themes of Christianity reach far into ancient Egyptian antiquity. In the New Testament Book of Matthew 1:20-23, the story of the Annunciation, Conception, Birth and Adoration of the child, Jesus, is presented. It tells how the "angel of the Lord" appears to Joseph, informing him that his wife Mary is pregnant by the Holy Spirit of God. The figure above is a drawing of the image engraved in the Holy of Holies or *Mesken*, in the temple of Luxor (5,500-1,700 BCE). In the first scene (A) at left, the god Tehuti, the transmitter of the *word* (logos), is depicted in the act of announcing to queen Mut-em-Ua (who has assumed the role of Isis) that she will give birth to the child who will be the righteous, divine heir (Horus). In the next scene (B) Knum (Kneph), the ram headed god (also associated with Amun), along with Hathor, provide her with the Life Force (spirit) through two Ankhs. In this same scene (B), the virgin is pictured as becoming pregnant (conceiving) through that spirit. In the following scene (C), the mother is being attended to while the child is being supported by nurses. The next scene (D) is the Adoration wherein the child is enthroned and adored by Amun, the hidden Holy Spirit behind all creation, and three men behind him (Amun) who offer boons or gifts with the right hand (open facing up) and eternal life with the left (holding the Ankh).

This set of scenes attests to the deeper significance of the virgin birth mystery. Every mother is a goddess and every child is a product or mixture of Creation or physical nature and the spirit of God. Through this metaphor, we are to understand that each human being has a divine origin, heritage and birthright. Therefore, it is clear to see the meaning of the Christian statements: *"I and [my] Father are one."* , *"Jesus answered them, 'Is it not written in your law that ye are gods?' "* ; from John 10:30 and 34, respectively.

A HYMN TO ANUBIS:
(From The Book of Coming Forth By Day, The Pyramid Texts and
The Shabaka Inscription)

"O Apuat, opener of the ways, the roads of the North, O Anpu, opener of the ways, the roads of the South. The messenger between heaven and hell, displaying alternately a face black as night, and golden as the day. He is equally watchful by day as by night."

"May Anubis make my thighs firm so that I may stand upon them".

30

A HYMN TO HORUS
(From the hieroglyphic text The Death of Horus)

"HORUS is the savior who was brought to birth, as light in heaven and sustenance on earth. Horus in spirit, verily divine, who came to turn the water into wine. Horus who gave his life, and sowed the seed for men to make the bread of life indeed. Horus, the comforter, who did descend in human fashion as the heavenly friend. Horus, the word, the founder in youth, Horus, the fulfiller of the word made truth. Horus, the Lord and leader in the fight against the dark powers of the night. Horus, the sufferer with cross bowed down, who rose at Easter with his double crown. Horus the pioneer, who paved the way of resurrection to the eternal day. Horus triumphant with the battle done, Lord of two worlds, united and made one."

31   Horus says:

"I am the hawk in the tabernacle, and I pierce through the veil."

Scenes of the resurrection of Osiris from the Temple of Denderah

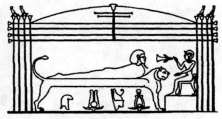

Horus presenting a Lotus Flower To Osiris

Osiris lying on a funeral bier as Isis and Nephthys look on.

Osiris, ithyphallic, wearing the Atef crown, with Isis and Horus.

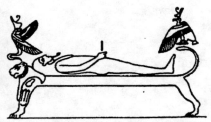

Osiris, ithyphallic, with the vulture goddess Nekhebet at the foot and the Uraeus goddess Uatchet at the head.

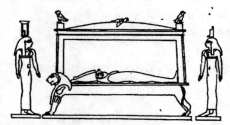

Osiris lying on a funeral bier as Isis, at the foot, and Nephthys, at the head, look on.

Osiris, ithyphallic, being watched over by three hawks, a frog headed Horus, Isis, two apes and two snake goddesses.

Osiris lying on a funeral bier as Anubis embalms him.

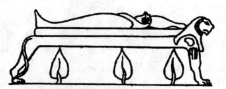

Osiris as a hawk headed mummy with three trees below his bier.

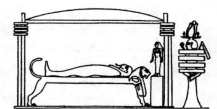

Osiris lying in his chest with Isis at his head, and Osiris in the form of the Djed Pillar looks on holding crook and flail.

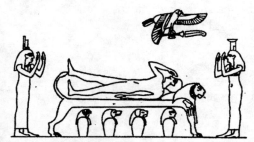

Osiris lying on a funeral bier as Isis, at the foot, and Nephthys, at the head, look on. Below are the canopic jars in the form of the four sons of Horus.

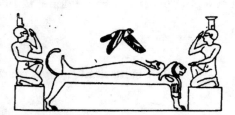

Osiris lying on a funeral bier as Isis, at the foot, and Nephthys, at the head, look on. Above is a hawk.

Scenes of the resurrection of Osiris from the Temple of Denderah

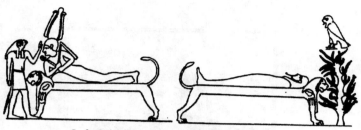

Left: Osiris rising up at the command of Horus.
Right: Osiris lying in his bier, at the head of which is a *persea* tree. Above the tree is his soul.

Horus, Isis and Nephthys raise up the pillar of Osiris, and raise Osiris himself.

Hathor kneels before Osiris, who is conceiving Horus with Isis (swallow-hawk), as the frog-god at the foot looks on. Below are Tehuti who is holding the Utchat (Eye of Horus), the two serpent goddesses and Bes.

Anubis addressing Osiris lying on a funeral bier as Isis and Horus, at the foot, and Nephthys, at the head, look on. The swallow-hawk hovers above.

Osiris rising as Isis looks on at the head of the bier. Below are his crowns.

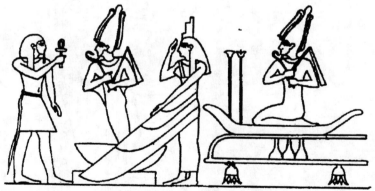

At left, Osiris is rising as Isis looks on.
At right, Osiris kneels on a boat at the head of which are a Lotus plant and a Papyrus plant (Upper and Lower Egypt). The boat sits on a sledge which is supported by two inverted Lotuses - symbols of the morning, the dawn, which brings new life.

Uatchit and Saa presenting life and sovereignty to
the son of Isis.

Nekhebit and Ḥu presenting life and
sovereignty to the son of Isis.

Above: The birth of Horus. Isis is assisted by Tehuti and Amun.

The Death and Resurrection of Horus

32   For a brief time after he found them, Set imprisoned Isis. Isis said: "I am Isis, and I have come forth from the prison wherein my brother Set placed me. Behold the god Tehuti, the great god, the Chief of Maat, both in heaven and on the earth, said unto me, 'Come now, O Isis, thou goddess, moreover it is a good thing to hearken, for there is life to one who shall be guided by the advice of another. Hide yourself with your son the child, and there shall come unto him these things. His members shall grow, and two-fold strength of every kind shall spring up in him. And he shall be made to take his seat upon the throne of his father, whom he shall one day redeem, and he shall take possession of the exalted position of ruler of the Two Lands.' "

33   Isis said: "I came forth from the prison at the time of evening, and there came forth the Seven Scorpions which were to accompany me and protect me. Two scorpions, Tefen and Befen, were behind me, two scorpions, Mestet and Mestetef, were by my side, and three scorpions, Petet, Thetet, and Maatet, were for preparing the road for me. I charged them very strictly, and my words penetrated into their ears, 'Have no knowledge of the Tesheru beings, and pay no attention to anyone who belongeth to a man of *no account*; let your faces be turned to make to live again him that was free from fault.' "

34   Fleeing from danger with no certain place to go, Isis came upon the house of a woman and asked for shelter. This woman slammed the door in the face of Isis. As a punishment for her disrespect, one of the scorpions who was protecting Isis and Horus forced its way into the lady's house and stung her child to death. Isis took pity on this poor woman whose cries of lamentation were so full of pain. Then Isis used certain words of power which she had learnt from her father and restored the child back to life.

35   Thereupon I cried out to the noble lady, "Come to me. Come to me. Verily my mouth possesses life. I am a daughter well-known in her town, and I can destroy the demon of death by the utterances which my father taught me to know. I am his daughter, the beloved offspring of his body." Then Isis placed her two hands on the child in order to make to live him whose throat was stopped.

36   Isis said: "O poison of the scorpion Tefent, come forth and appear on the ground! You shall neither enter nor penetrate further into the body of the child. O poison of the scorpion Befent, come forth and appear on the ground! I am Isis, the goddess, the lady of words of power, and I am the maker of words of power and I know how to utter words with magical effect. Hearken ye unto me, O every reptile which possesses the power to bite, and fall headlong to the ground! O poison of the scorpion Mestet, make no advance into his body. O poison of the scorpion Mestetef, rise not up in his body. O poison of the scorpions Petet and Thetet, penetrate not into his body. O poison of the scorpion Martet, fall down on the ground."

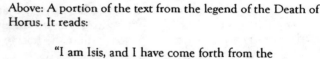

Above: A portion of the text from the legend of the Death of Horus. It reads:

"I am Isis, and I have come forth from the prison wherein my brother Set placed me. Behold, the god Tehuti, the great god, the Chief of Maat both in heaven and on the earth, said unto me, "Come now, O Isis, thou goddess, moreover it is a good thing to hearken, for there is life to one who shall be guided by the advice of another. Hide yourself with your son, the child, and there shall come unto him these things. His members shall grow, and two-fold strength of every kind shall spring up in him. And he shall be made to take his seat upon the throne of his father, whom he shall one day redeem, and he shall take possession of the exalted position of ruler of the Two Lands."

"Isis says: "I came forth from the prison at the time of evening, and there came forth the Seven Scorpions which were to accompany me and protect me."

ISIS

37   And Isis, the goddess, the great mistress of words of power, she who is at the head of the gods, unto whom the god Geb gave his own magical spells for the driving away of poison at noon-day, and for making poison to go back, and retreat, and withdraw, and go backward, spake, saying, "Ascend not into heaven, through the command of the beloved one of Ra, the egg of the Smen goose which cometh forth from the sycamore. Verily my words are made to command the uttermost limit of the night. I speak unto you, O scorpions, I am alone and in sorrow because our names will suffer disgrace through out the nomes. Do not make love, do not cry out to the Tesheru fiends, and cast no glances upon the noble ladies in their houses. Turn your faces towards the earth and find so that we may arrive at the hidden places in the town of Khebt. Oh the child shall live and the poison die! Ra, liveth and the poison dieth! Verily Horus shall be in good health for his mother Isis. Verily he who is stricken shall be in good case likewise." And the fire was extinguished, and heaven was satisfied with the utterance of Isis, the goddess.

38   "Lo, a bread-cake made of barley meal shall drive out the poison, and natron shall make it to withdraw, and the fire made of hetchet-plant shall drive out fever-heat from the limbs."

39   The woman was filled with such gratitude that she gave to Isis all kinds of things which she had in the house and offered her shelter.

40   A short time passed and it happened that Horus was stung by a scorpion, not one of those which were in the service of Isis, but one which had been sent by Set to kill Horus. Horus died then, while Isis had gone to perform a religious ceremony in honor of Osiris when the gods brought her the terrible news. "O Isis, O Isis, come to thy Horus, O you, woman of the wise mouth! Come to thy son", thus cried the gods who dwelt in her quarter of the town, "for he is as one whom a scorpion has stung, and like one whom the scorpion Uhat, which the animal Antesh drove away, has wounded."

41   She returned immediately and found Horus with a sting fresh with poison, his skin discolored and froth coming from his mouth. Isis began to utter lamentations from deep within herself. Then Isis ran out like one who had a knife stuck in her body, and she opened her arms saying: "Behold me, behold me, my son Horus, have no fear, have no fear, O son my glory! No evil thing of any kind whatsoever shall happen unto thee, for there is in thee the fluid-essence which made the things which exist. You are the son from the country of Mesqet (other world), you have come forth from the celestial waters Nu, and you shall not die by the heat of the poison. You are the Great Bennu, born on the top of the balsam-trees which are in

Above: The Goddess Selket, a form of Isis.

the House of the Aged One in Anu. You are the brother of the Abut Fish, who orders what is to be, and are the nursling of the Cat who dwelleth in the House of Neith. The goddess Reret, the goddess Hat, and the god Bes protect thy members. Thy head shall not fall to the Tchat fiend that attacketh thee. Thy members shall not receive the fire of that which is thy poison. You shall not go backwards on the land, and you shall not be brought low on the water. No reptile which bites shall gain the mastery over thee, and no lion shall subdue thee or have dominion over thee. You are the son of the sublime god (Osiris) who proceeded from Geb. You are Horus, and the poison shall not gain the mastery over thy members. You are the son of the sublime god who proceeded from Geb, and thus likewise shall it be with those who are under the knife. And the four august goddesses shall protect thy members."

42   "I am he who rolleth up into the sky, and who setteth in the Ṭuat, whose form is in the House of Height, through whom when he openeth his Eye, the light cometh into being, and when he closeth his Eye, it becometh night. I am the Water-god, Het, when he giveth commands, whose name is unknown to the gods. I illumine the Two Lands, night betaketh itself to flight, and I shine by day and by night. I am the Bull of Bakha, the land of the East and the Lion of Manu, the land of the West. I am he who traverseth the heavens by day and by night without being repulsed. I have come by reason of the voice of the son of Isis. Verily the blind serpent Na has bitten the Bull. O you, poison which floweth through every member of him that is under the knife, come forth, I charge thee, upon the ground. Behold, he that is under the knife shall not be bitten. You are Menu, the Lord of Coptos, the child of the White Shat which is in Anu, which was bitten by a reptile. O Menu, Lord of Coptos, give thou air unto him that is under the knife, and air shall be given to thee."

43   "I am Isis, who conceived a child by her husband, and became heavy with Horus, the Divine. I gave birth to Horus, the son of Osiris, in a nest of papyrus plants. I rejoiced exceedingly over this, because I saw in him one who would make answer for his father. I hid him, and I concealed him through fear of that evil one, Set. I went away to the city of Am, wherein the people gave thanks for me even through their fear of my bringing trouble for them. I passed the day in seeking to provide food for the child, and on returning to take Horus into my arms, I found him, Horus, the beautiful one of gold, the boy, the child, without life. He had bedewed the ground with the water of his eye, and with foam from his lips. His body was motionless, his heart was powerless to move, and the muscles of his members were helpless. I sent forth a cry: 'I, even I lack a son to stand up for me.

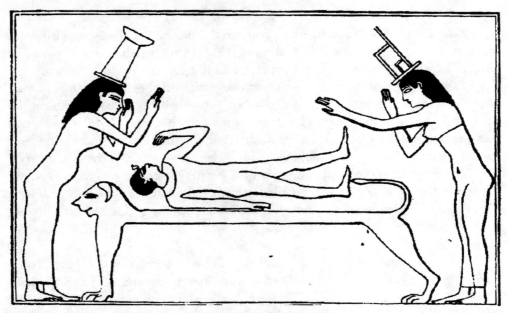

Isis and Nephthys bewailing over the dead body of Osiris as they would later do over the dead body of Horus. From a bas relief at the temple of Isis in Philae.

At left: The serpent god Nehebka, who assisted Anubis in reconstituting the body of Osiris.

Above: Anubis in the aspect of warrior who fights against the enemies of Osiris.

My two breasts are full to overflowing, but my body is empty.' My mouth wished for that which concerned him. A cistern of water and a stream of the inundation was I. The child was the desire of my heart, and I longed to protect him. I carried him in my womb, I gave birth to him, I endured the agony of the birth pangs, I was all alone, and the great ones were afraid of disaster and to come out at the sound of my voice. My father is in the Tuat (Other World), my mother is in Aqert (Other World), and my elder brother is in the sarcophagus. Think of the enemy and of how prolonged was the wrath of his heart against me, when I, the great lady was in his house. I cried then, saying, 'Who among the people will indeed let their hearts come round to me?' I cried then to those who dwelt in the papyrus swamps, and they inclined to me straightway. And the people came forth to me from their houses, and they thronged about me at the sound of my voice, and they loudly bewailed with me the greatness of my affliction. There was no man there who set restraint on his mouth, every person among them lamented with great lamentation. There was none there who knew how to make my child to live."

44   Isis said: "Horus is bitten, the heir of heaven, the son of Unefer is bitten, the child of the gods, he who was wholly uncorrupt, is bitten! He for whose wants I provided, he who was to avenge his father, is bitten! He for who I cared and suffered when he was being fashioned in my womb is bitten! He whom I tended so that I might gaze upon him, is bitten! He for whose life I prayed for is bitten! Calamity has overtaken the child and he has perished."

45   As Isis was uttering these words, the goddess Nephthys who was also mourning over her nephew Horus came upon the Scorpion Goddess Serqet (Selket). Serqet advised Isis to pray to those in the Boat of Ra, the Ennead who traverse in the Boat of Millions of Years, so that they may halt and cause time and all progress on earth to stop because they cannot continue while Horus lies dead.

46   Then Isis cried out to heaven, and her voice reached the Boat of Millions of Years, and the *Disk* ceased to move onward, and came to a standstill. As per the command of Ra, Tehuti descended from the Boat, being equipped with words of power and spells of all kinds, and bearing with him the great command of *maak-heru* or the righteous "WORD", whose commands were performed, instantly and completely, by every god, spirit, fiend, human being, and by every thing, animate and inanimate, in heaven, earth, and the Other World.

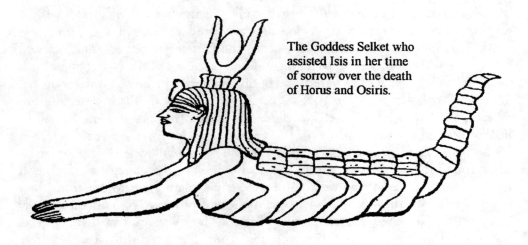

The Goddess Selket who assisted Isis in her time of sorrow over the death of Horus and Osiris.

Ra and the Company of gods and goddesses in the Barque of Millions of Years which traverses the heavens, and thereby sustains creation, is stopped by the words of power of Isis.

47   A HYMN OF PRAISE TO HORUS TO GLORIFY HIM, WHICH IS TO BE SAID OVER THE WATERS AND OVER THE LAND. Tehuti speaketh and this god reciteth the following:

"Homage to thee, god, son of a god. Homage to thee, heir, son of an heir. Homage to thee, bull, son of bull, who was brought forth by him whose throat is closed up. Then shall mankind give thee praise, and the righteous shall give thanks unto thy forms. And all the gods likewise shall invoke thee, and in truth thy name shall be invoked this day, 'I am Horus of Shetenu, the hidden place.' "

48   "O you who are in the cavern, you who are in the cavern. O you who are at the mouth of the cavern. O you who are on the way, O you who are on the way. O you who are at the mouth of the way. He is Urmer (Mnevis) who approacheth every man and every beast. He is like the god Sep who is in Anu. He is the Scorpion-god who is in the Great House (Het-ur). Bite him not, for he is Ra. Sting him not, for he is Tehuti. Shoot ye not your poison over him, for he is Nefer-Tem. O every male serpent, O every female serpent, O every creature which bite with your mouths, and sting with your tails, bite ye him not with your mouths, and sting ye him not with your tails. Get ye afar off from him. Make ye not your fire to be against him, for he is the son of Osiris. Vomit ye. (Say four times:) I am Tehuti, I have come from heaven to make protection of Horus, and to drive away the poison of the scorpion which is in every member of Horus. Thy head is to thee, Horus; it shall be stable under the Urert Crown."

49   "Thine eye is to thee, Horus, for you are Horus, the son of Geb, the Lord of the Two Eyes, in the midst of the Company of the gods. Thy nose is to thee, Horus, for you are Horus the Elder, the son of Ra, and you shall not inhale the fiery wind. Thine arm is to thee, Horus, great is thy strength to slaughter the enemies of thy father. Thy two thighs are to thee, Horus receive thou the rank and dignity of thy father Osiris. Ptah has balanced for thee thy mouth on the day of thy birth. The heart is to thee, Horus, and the Disk maketh thy protection. Thine eye is to thee, Horus, thy right eye is like Shu, and thy left eye like Tefnut, who are the children of Ra. Thy belly is to thee, Horus, and the children are the gods who are therein, and they shall not receive the fluid-essence of the scorpion. Thy strength is to thee, Horus, and the strength of Set shall not exist against thee. Thy phallus is to thee, Horus, and you are Kamutef, the protector of his father, who maketh an answer for his children in the course of every day. Thy thighs are to thee, Horus, and thy strength shall slaughter the enemies of thy father. Thy calves are to thee, Horus, the god Khnemu has built them, and the goddess Isis has covered them with flesh (changed them). The soles of thy feet are to thee, Horus, and the nations who fight

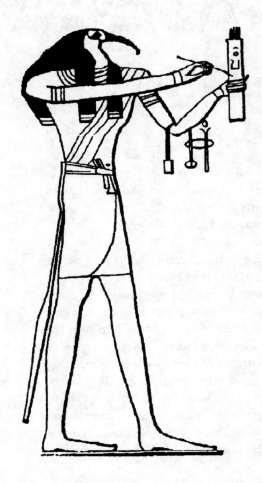 

Above: Tehuti is the transporter of the WORD of God (Ra). He brings the magic (spiritual power) of the Supreme Being (Ra) which will heal Horus.

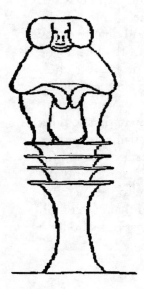

Left: Tehuti in the form of a baboon sitting atop the pillar of Osiris.

with the bow (Peti) fall under thy feet. You rulest the South, North, West, and East, and you seest like Ra. (Say four times.) And likewise him that is under the knife."

50   "Beautiful god, Senetchem-ab-Ra,-setep-[en] Amen, son of Ra, Nekht-Heru-Hebit, you are protected, and the gods and goddesses are protected, and conversely. Beautiful god, Senetchem-ab Ra-setep-[en]-Ra, son of Ra; Nekht-Heru-Hebit, you are protected, and Heru-Shet [enu], the great god, is protected, and conversely."

51   Then Tehuti came to Isis and told her that no harm could possibly have happened to Horus, for he was under the protection of the Boat of Ra, but his words failed to comfort Isis, and though she acknowledged the greatness of his designs, she complained that they savored of delay. "What is the good," she asked, "of all thy spells, and incantations, and magical formulas, and the great command of Maak-heru, if Horus is to perish by the poison of a scorpion, and to lie here in the arms of Death?" "Evil, evil is his destiny, for it has entailed the deepest misery for him and death."

52   In answer to these words, Tehuti, turning to Isis and Nephthys, bade them to fear not, and to have no anxiety about Horus, for, said he, "I have come from heaven to heal the child for his mother." And Tehuti said: "Fear not, fear not, O goddess Isis, fear not, fear not, O Nephthys, and let not anxiety be with you. I have come from heaven having the power of life to heal the child for his mother, let thy heart be firm; he shall not sink under the flame." He then pointed out that Horus was under protection as the Dweller in his Disk (Aten), the Great Dwarf, the Mighty Ram, the Great Hawk, the Holy Beetle, the Hidden Body, the Divine Bennu, etc., and proceeded to utter the words of power to restore life back to Horus."

53   And Tehuti said: "Wake up, Horus! Thy protection is established. Make happy the heart of thy mother Isis. The words of Horus shall bind up hearts. He shall cause to be at peace him who is in affliction. Let your hearts be happy, O ye who dwell in the heavens. Horus, he who has redeemed his father shall cause the poison to retreat. Verily that which is in the mouth of Ra shall circulate, and the tongue of the Great God shall repulse opposition. The Boat of Ra standeth still, and travelleth not onwards. The Disk is in the same place where it was yesterday to heal Horus for his mother Isis. Come to the earth, draw near, O Boat of Ra. Make the Boat to travel, O mariners of heaven. Transport provisions of Sekhem to heal Horus for his mother Isis. Hasten away, O pain which is in the region round about,

Above: Horus, the child, being victorious over the lower nature in the forms of animals. (From the Meterniche Stele)

At left: Horus as the Supreme Divinity, Lord of Creation, sitting atop the primeval lotus (creation) which rises out of the primeval ocean.

Horus as the Hawk. From the tomb of King Tutankhamun.

82

and let the Boat descend upon the place where it was yesterday to heal Horus for his mother Isis."

54   "I am Tehuti, the firstborn son, the son of Ra, and Tem and the Company of the gods have commanded me to heal Horus for his mother Isis, and to heal him that is under the knife likewise. O Horus, O Horus, thy Ka protecteth thee, and thy image worketh protection for thee. The poison is as the daughter of its own flame; it is destroyed because it smote the "strong son". Your temples are in good condition, for Horus liveth for his mother, and he who is under the knife likewise."

55   And the goddess Isis said: "Set your face towards those who dwell in the North Land (Ateh), the nurses who dwell in the city Pe-Tept (Buto), for they have offered very large offerings in order to cause the child to be made strong for his mother, and to make strong him that is under the knife likewise. Do not allow them to recognize the divine KA in the Swamp Land." Then spoke Tehuti unto the great gods who dwell in the Swamp-Land saying: "O ye nurses who dwell in the city of Pe, who smite fiends with your hands, and overthrow them with your arms on behalf of that Great One (Ra) who appeareth in front of you in the Sektet Boat, let the Matet* (Mantchet) Boat travel on. Horus is to you, he is counted up for life, and he is declared for the life of his father (Osiris). I have given gladness unto those who are in the Sektet* Boat, and the mariners (of Ra) make it to journey on. Horus liveth for his mother Isis, and he who is under the knife liveth for his mother likewise. As for the poison, the strength thereof has been made powerless. Verily I am a favored one, and I will join myself to his hour, the time of need, to hurl back the report of evil to him that sent it forth. The heart of Ra-Heru-Khuti rejoiceth. Thy son Horus is counted up for life, to make him to smite, and to repel from those who are above, and to turn back the paths of the Sebau fiends from him, so that he may take possession of the throne of the Two Lands. Ra is in heaven to make answer on behalf of him and his father. The words of power of his mother have lifted up his face, and they protect him and enable him to go round about wheresoever he pleaseth, and to set the terror of him in celestial beings. I have made haste in answering to these words." (* Boats of Ra in which he travels by day and by night)

56   And so Tehuti transferred the "fluid of life" of Ra, and as soon as this came upon the child's body, the poison of the scorpion flowed out of him, and he once more breathed and lived. When this was done Tehuti returned to the Boat of Ra, the gods who formed its crew resumed their rowing and the *Disk* passed on its way to make its daily journey across the sky.

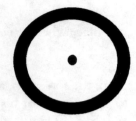

Above: The sundisk of Ra and Horus

The Sun is the symbol of Ra. It is the perfect symbol for cosmic consciousness (God), because it is all pervading and all powerful, while being impartial (shining on all) as the sustenance of all life.

The Moon, as the reflection of the Sun, is the perfect symbol of the human mind, because human consciousness is but a reflection of Cosmic Consciousness (God), the light of all consciousness and all existence.

At left: The world as the primeval matter which arose out of the deep dark ocean of space. In the theology of Abydos, it is Abydos, the city of Osiris, which is considered to be the first piece of land to have emerged out of the primeval ocean (Nu).

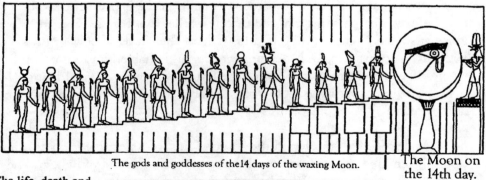

The gods and goddesses of the 14 days of the waxing Moon.

The Moon on the 14th day.

The life, death and resurrection of Osiris is ritualistically associated with the waxing and waning days of the moon cycle.

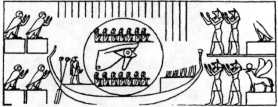

The gods and goddesses of the 14 days of the waning Moon.

57   The gods and goddesses in heaven who were amazed and uttered cries of terror when they heard of the death of Horus were made happy once more, and sang songs of joy over his recovery. The happiness of Isis in her child's restoration to life was very great, for she could again hope that he would avenge his father's murder and occupy his throne.

58   The final words of Tehuti comforted her greatly, for he told her that he would take charge of the case of Horus in the Judgment Hall of Anu wherein Osiris had been judged, and that, as his advocate, he would make any accusations which might be brought against Horus to recoil on him that brought them. Furthermore, he would give Horus power to repulse any attacks which might be made upon him by beings in the heights above, or fiends in the depth below, and would ensure his succession to the Throne of the Two Lands of Egypt.

59   Tehuti also promised Isis that Ra himself should act as the advocate of Horus, even as he had done for his father Osiris. He was also careful to allude to the share which Isis had taken in the restoration of Horus to life, saying, "It is the words of power of his mother which have lifted up his face and they shall enable him to journey wheresoever he pleaseth and to put fear into the powers above. I myself hasten to obey them. Thus, everything turned on the power of the spells of Isis who made the sun to stand still and caused the dead to be raised..."

THE INITIATION OF HORUS
(From the ancient text entitled The Virgin of The World)

60   Once Horus' health was restored, he began to grow in a short time. He began to ask questions about his origin, the nature of the universe, and of his purpose in life, and to these questions Isis gave him the following answers as his mother and spiritual preceptor. Thus begins the holy discourse of Isis to Horus, the first words of wisdom which lead Horus to immortality.

61   "O Horus, after the creation of the universe, fear and ignorance succeeded fear, and searching search incessant, and for so long as the Creator of the universals willed, did ignorance retain its grip on all. But when He judged it fit to manifest Him who He is, He breathed into the gods, the Loves, and freely poured the splendor which He had within His heart into their minds, in ever greater and still greater measure that firstly they might have the wish to seek for that which is

Above: Hathor-Isis suckling Horus, scene from the Temple of Denderah.

Isis nurses baby Horus:
The ancient Egyptian prototype of the mother and child which is popular all over Africa and can also be seen in Christian and Indian iconography with the birth of Jesus and Krishna, respectively. The mother is the first teacher; Isis not only raises Horus, but also initiates him into the mysteries of life and creation in order to enlighten him and make him strong for the battle of life.

86

real, next they might yearn to find, and finally have power to win success in the spiritual search as well. But this, my Horus, wonder-worthy son, could never have been done had that seed in them been subject to death, for that as yet had no existence, but only with a soul that could vibrate responsive to the mysteries of Heaven."

62   "Such was all-knowing Tehuti, who saw all things, and seeing understood, and understanding had the power both to disclose and to give explanation. For what he knew, he engraved on stone; yet though he engraved them onto stone he hid them mostly, keeping sure silence though in speech, that every younger age of cosmic time might seek for them. And thus, with charge unto his kinsmen of the gods to keep sure watch, he mounted to the stars."

63   "Tehuti returned to Heaven and invoked a spell on them, and spoke these words: 'O holy books, who have been made by my immortal hands, by incorruption's magic spells . . . free from decay throughout eternity, remain untouched and incorrupt from time! Become un-seeable, un-findable, for every one whose foot shall tread the plains of this land, until old Heaven does bring forth the proper instruments for you, whom the Creator shall call souls.' "

64   "Thus, O my son Horus, Tehuti brought the teachings of wisdom which were given to him by the God of All, and they are hidden in nature until the time when those who are ready to seek for their essential nature, those with true aspiration, seek with honesty and reverence."

66   "In the beginning there was just matter which had been emitted by God, devoid of that special essence which is called life. The Great God looked upon the world, but He, no longer willing that the world above should be inert, but thinking good to fill it full of breaths (living spirits), so that its parts should not remain immobile and inert, He thus began on these with use of holy arts as proper for the bringing forth of His own special work."

67   "For taking breath from His own Breath and blending this with knowing Fire-consciousness, He mingled them with certain other substances which have no power to know; and having made the two together, with certain hidden words of power, He thus set all the mixture going thoroughly, until out of the compost smiled a substance, as it were, far subtler, purer far, and more translucent than the things from which it came; it was so clear that no one but The Artist could detect it."

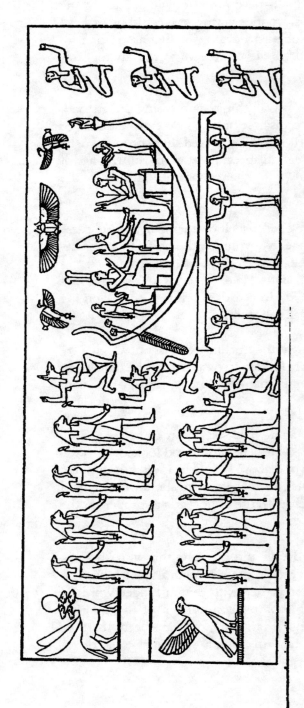

The bark of Osiris sailing over heaven, which is supported by four pillars, in the form of goddesses. On the right are three hawk-headed spirits, and on the left are:—1. Three jackal-headed spirits; 2. The eight primeval gods of Khemennu, frog-headed and snake-headed; 3. The four-headed ram of the North wind; and, 4. The Ram-headed hawk of the East wind.

'The one 'sailing in a Boat' sets before the mind the power that directs the world. As therefore, the Pilot, being apart from the ship, has the control of its rudders, so the Sun subsisting separately has control of the helms of all the world. And as the pilot from above at the stern, giving forth from himself the first brief beginning of the course, directs everything, so by an infinite priority of rank, the God from above, imparts without division from the first principles of Nature, the first-operative causes of motions. These things, therefore, and still more than these, are denoted by One Sailing in a boat.'

—Iamblichus, Egyptian Initiate (circa 250-330 A.C.E.)

88

68   "O Horus, these were the souls, created out of God's very being. In time they came to be conscious of themselves and looked up at the Father of All. Being sparks of their creator as sun rays are emanations of the sun, souls have the power to create due to their ability to know and use the mind."

69   "O Horus, this power became the source of pride and conceit. The souls thought themselves to be equals to The God, and as their punishment, were enclosed in watery encasements. This is the nature of human existence and it is the reason why human beings are a blend of what is physical and what is Divine."

70   "O Horus, then the Great God decreed that Love and Necessity should be the lords of life. Further, the Lord of All said: 'Know, all of you who are set under My un-aging rule, that as long as ye keep you free of sin, ye shall dwell in the fields of Heaven, but if some cause of blame for anything should attach itself to you, ye shall dwell in the place that Destiny allots condemned to mortal wombs.' "

71   "The Great God continued: 'If, then, the things imputed to your charge be slight, leaving the bond of fleshy frames subject to death, ye shall again embrace your origin in Heaven, and sigh no more; but if ye shall commit some greater sins, and with the end appointed of your frames be not advanced, no longer shall ye dwell in Heaven, nor even in the bodies of mankind, but shall continue after that to wander round in lives irrational.' "

72   "Thus speaking, Horus mine, He gave to all the gift of breath, and thus continued: 'It is not without purpose or by chance I have laid down the law of your transformings, but as it will be for the worse if ye do something unseemly, so for the better, if ye shall will what's worthy of your birth.' "

73   "The Great One continued: "For I, and no one else, will be the Witness and the Watcher. Know, then, it is for what ye have done heretofore, ye do endure this; being shut in bodies as a punishment.' "

74   "Thus continued the Lord of All: 'The difference in your rebirths, accordingly, for you, shall be as I have said, a difference of bodies, and their ultimate dissolution will be a benefit and a return to the fair happiness of former days.' "

75   "He continued: 'But if ye think to do something else unworthy of Me, your mind shall lose its sight so as to think the contrary of what is true, and take the punishment for benefit; the change to better things for infamous despite.' "

Above: Osiris as the creator who engenders Life Force energy into creation.

At left: Osiris as the "Bull of Heaven", carrying the mummy of the initiate on his back. (See also page 46)

76   "The Great God continued to speak, saying: 'But the more righteous of you who stand upon the threshold of the change to the diviner state shall among men be righteous kings and genuine philosophers, founders of states, and lawgivers, and real seers, and true herb-knowers, and prophets of the gods, most excellent, skillful musicians, skilled astronomers, and augurs wise, consummate sacrificers as many of you as are worthy of things fair and good.' "

77   "O my son Horus, after saying this the Great One returned to the original state and Tehuti oversaw the process as the souls entered into bodies."

The Mystical Secrets of Creation

78   "As this embodiment process occurred, the Great Earth Spirit arose and questioned Tehuti: 'What are these encasements which the souls are entering into?' Tehuti answered, 'Men!..' Then the spirit said: 'It is a daring work, this making man, with eyes inquisitive, and talkative tongue, with power henceforth to hear things even which are no concern of his, dainty of smell, who will use to its full his power of touch on every thing.' "

79   "The Earth Spirit continued: 'Have you, his generator, judged it good to leave him free from care, who in the future daringly will gaze upon the fairest mysteries which Nature has? Would you leave him without grief, which in the days to come will make his thoughts reach unto mysteries beyond the Earth?' "

80   "The Earth Spirit continued to speak, saying: 'Men will dig up the roots of plants, and will find out the juices' qualities. Men will observe the nature of the stones. Men will dissect not only animals irrationally, but they'll dissect themselves, desiring to find out how they were made. They will stretch their daring hands out into to the sea, and cutting self grown forests down will ferry one another over to lands beyond. Men will seek out as we the inner nature of the holy spaces which no foot may tread, and will chase after them into the height, desiring to observe the nature of the motion of the Heaven.' "

81   "The Spirit continued: 'These are yet moderate things which they will do. For nothing more remains than Earth's remotest realms; nay, in their daring they will track out Night, the farthest Night of all.' "

82   "The Spirit continued: 'Nothing have they, then, to stop them from receiving the initiation in the good of freedom from all pain, and, unconstrained by terror's grievous goads, from living softly out a life free from a care.' "

Above: Winged Isis

Oh benevolent Isis, who protected her brother Osiris, who searched for him without wearying, who traversed the land in mourning and never rested until she had found him. She who afforded him shadow with her wings and gave him air with her feathers, who rejoiced and carried her brother home.

From a Hymn to Isis

At left: Isis as the goddess Ament or Amentat.

Like Amun, Ament means "hidden". It is a specific reference to the female form as well as the land of Amenta, the hidden underworld or Tuat. Thus, Isis and Osiris together form the hidden recesses of creation, and therefore, both are considered to be the source of life which engenders creation.

83   "The Spirit continued: 'Then will they not gird on the armor of an over-busy daring up to Heaven? Will they not, then, reach out their souls, freed from a care, unto the primordial elements themselves?' "

84   "The Spirit continued to speak, saying: 'Teach them henceforth to long, to plan out something, where they have as well to fear the danger of its ill-success, in order that they may be tamed by the sharp tooth of pain in failure of their hopes.' "

85   "The Spirit continued: 'Let the too busy nature of their souls be balanced by desires, and fears, and griefs, and empty hopes.' "

86   "So continued the the Earth Spirit, saying: 'Let loves in quick succession sway their souls, hopes, manifold desires, sometimes fulfilled, and sometimes unfulfilled, that the sweet bait of their success may draw them into struggle amid direr ills.' "

87   "The Spirit continued: 'Let fever lay its heavy hand on them, that losing heart they may submit desire to discipline.' "

88   "Once again Tehuti rose up and proclaimed that the Supreme One had charged him as manager of these affairs. Tehuti decided that he would create an overseer to watch over every detail and impose the karmic laws of human existence."

89   "Tehuti then spoke, saying: 'Wherefore the overseer of His command will be the keen-eyed goddess of the All, Meskhenet, and I will skillfully devise an instrument, mysterious, possessed of power of sight, that cannot err, and cannot be escaped, whereto all things on earth shall of necessity be subject, from birth to final dissolution, an instrument which binds together all that's done. This instrument shall rule all other things of Earth as well humankind.' "

90   "He spoke and straightway in cosmic order, there began the differentiation of the up-to-then, black unity of all things... And Heaven shone forth above, decked out with all his mysteries. Earth, still a-tremble as the Sun shone forth grew harder, and appeared with all the fair adornments that bedeck her round on every side. For beautiful to God are even things which men think mean, in that in truth they have been made to serve the laws of God."

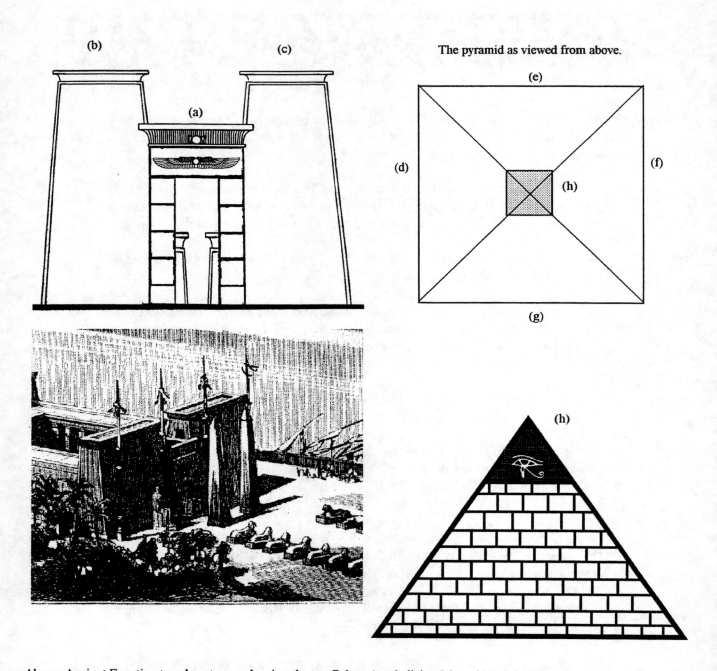

The pyramid as viewed from above.

Above: Ancient Egyptian temple entrance showing the two Pylons (symbolizing Isis and Nephthys) and the single opening (symbolic of Osiris).

The single opening (a) symbolizes non-duality and singularity of consciousness. Thus, on entering into the temple, there is a symbolic ritual-meditation leading toward a spiritual movement out of the world (duality - Isis and Nephthys, b-c) and into the shrine wherein the underlying oneness of the universe (Osiris) is to be explored and discovered. Thus the Supreme Spirit (oneness) expresses in creation through the principle of duality.

The four flags (⌐ ⌐ ⌐ ⌐) in the front of the temple symbolize creation or the four sons of Horus who sprout from the lotus which arises from the primeval ocean at the feet of Osiris (see cover). The mystical symbolism of the number four also refers to the four sides of the pyramid (d-e-f-g) which come together at the top (h) into one point, known as the *Eye of Horus*, and the four pillars of Heaven which support creation.

94

91   "And God rejoiced when now He saw His works a-moving, and filling full His hands, which hold as much as all surrounding space with all that Nature had produced, and squeezing tight the handful mightily.

92   "He said: 'Take (these), O holy Earth, take those, all-honored one, who are to be the mother of all things, and henceforth lack nothing!' "

93   "God spoke, and opening His hands, such hands as God should have. He poured them all into the composition of the world. And they in the beginnings were unknown in every way for that the souls who had been recently shut in prison, not enduring their disgrace, began to strive in emulation with the gods in Heaven, in full command of their high birth, and when held back, in that they had the same Creator, made revolt, and using weaker men as instruments, began to make there set upon each other, and range themselves in conflict, and make war among themselves."

94   "Thus strength did mightily prevail over weakness, so that the strong did burn and massacre the weak, and from the holy place, down they cast the living and the dead, down from the holy shrines, until the Elements in their distress resolved to go to God, their Monarch, to complain about the savage state in which men lived."

95   "The evil now being very great, the Elements approached the God who made them, and formulated their complaint in some such words as these."

96   "It was moreover Fire who first received authority to speak. He said: 'O Lord, Artificer of this new World, your name mysterious among the gods and goddesses, and up to now, revered by all mankind, how long have You, O Ultimate One, judged it right to leave the life of mortals without God?'

97   "He continued: 'Show now Thyself unto Thy World consulting Thee; initiate the savagery of life with peace; give laws to life; to righteousness give oracles; fill with fair hopes all things; and let men fear the vengeance of the gods, and none will sin.' "

98   "Fire continued: 'Should they receive due retribution for their sins, they will refrain henceforth from doing wrong; they will respect their oaths and no one any more will ponder sacrilege.' "

Osiris seated in judgment on a chair placed on the top of a flight of nine steps, on which stand the nine gods of his Company. The pig in the boat represents Set. In the right-hand corner stands Anubis. From a sarcophagus in the Louvre.

In Chapter 23, Utterance 6, the initiate describes his/her resolve in seeking liberation from the *Pool of Double Fire* (world, physical existence, state of duality). Through the force of will manifested in the ability to accomplish the *wish of the heart,* the initiate has *quenched* the heart which was agitated with desires, passions, etc., from involvement with the world of duality. Through force of will and a disciplined mind (heart), the initiate directs him/herself to identify with Osiris (physical manifestation of the nameless GOD) and thus becomes one with *That Being Who Is At The Top Of The Steps.*

> *"I am Osiris, Lord of Restau, I* (the initiate) *share with That Being Who Is At The Top Of The Steps. Due to the wish of my heart I have come here from the Pool of Double Fire; I have quenched these fires in myself."*

Note: The nine steps and nine gods represent the Ennead, the nine principles of creation and dissolution.

99   "He continued: 'Let them be taught to render thanks for benefits received that I the Fire, may joyfully do service in the sacrificial rites, that they may from the altar send sweet-smelling vapors forth.' "

100   "Fired continued to speak: 'For up to now I am polluted, Lord, and by the godless daring of these men, I am compelled to burn up flesh. They will not let me be for what I was brought forth; but they adulterate with all indecency my undecaying state.' "

101   "And Air too said: 'I also, Master, am made turbid by the vapors which the bodies of the dead exhale, and I am pestilential, and, no longer filled with health, I gaze down from above on things I ought not to behold.' "

102   "Next Water, O my son of mighty Soul, received authority to speak, and spoke and said: 'O Father, O wonderful Creator of all things, Spirit self-born, and nature's Maker, who through Thee does conceive all things, now at this last, command the rivers' streams forever to be pure, for that the rivers and the seas wash the murderers' hands or else receive the murdered.' "

103   "After came Earth in bitter grief, and taking up the tale, O son of high renown, thus she began to speak: "O sovereign Lord, Chief of the Heavenly Ones, and Master of the Wheels upon which this universe turns, You ruler of us Elements, O Sire of them who stand beside Thee, from whom all things have the beginning of their increase and of their decrease, and into whom they cease again and have the end that is their due according to necessity's decree, O greatly honored One, the godless rout of men does dance upon my bosom.' "

104   "Earth continued: 'I hold in my embrace as well the nature of all things; for I, as You didst give command, not only bear them all, but I receive them also when they're killed. But now am I dishonored. The world upon the Earth, though filled with all other things, has not a God.' "

105   "Earth continued to speak: 'For having nothing to fear, they sin in everything, and from my heights, O Lord, down they fall by every evil care. And soaking with the juices of their carcasses, I'm all corrupt. Hence am I Lord, compelled to hold in me those of no worth. With all I bear I would hold God as well.' "

106   "Earth continued: 'Bestow on me, if not Thyself, for I could not contain Thee, yet some holy emanation of Thyself. Make Thou the Earth more honored than the rest of Elements; for it is right that she should boast of gifts from Thee, in that she giveth all.'

Above: The Temple of Isis at Agilkia Island (Aswan) in Egypt, Africa.

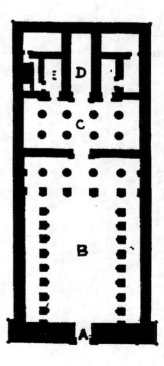

The ancient Egyptian temple basically consisted of three main sections which were preceded by the entranceway pylons (A). Several rooms that were used for various purposes were attached to the main sections. These sections were (B) the Court, (C) the Hypostyle Hall and (D) the Chapel (Holy of Holies). This format follows the system of the Trinity which among other things implies the teachings related to the three levels of religion, the three steps of spiritual study prescribed by the ancient Temple of Isis and the three ancient Egyptian initiatic education levels of aspirants.

107   "Thus spoke the Elements; and God, full-filling all things with the sound of His holy voice, spoke thus: 'Depart, ye Holy Ones, ye Children worthy of a mighty sire, nor yet in any way attempt to innovate, nor leave the whole of My World without your active service.' "

108   "He continued thus saying: 'For now another efflux of My nature is among you, and he shall be a pious supervisor of all deeds, judge incorruptible, of living men, and monarch absolute of those beneath the earth, not only striking terror into them, but taking vengeance on them. And by his class of birth, the fate he has deserved shall follow every man.' "

109   "And so the Elements did cease from their complaint upon the Master's order, and they held their peace; and each of them continued in the exercise of his authority and in his rule."

110   And Horus thereon said: "How was it, mother, then, that Earth received God's Emanation?" And Isis said: "I may not tell the story of this birth, for it is not permitted to describe the origin of thy descent, O Horus, son of mighty power, lest afterwards the way of birth of the immortal gods should be known unto men except so far that God the Monarch, the universal Orderer and Architect, sent for a little while thy mighty sire Osiris, and the mightiest Goddess Isis, that they might help the world, for all things needed by them."

111   "It is they who filled life full of life. It is they who caused the savagery of mutual slaughtering of men to cease. It is they who hallowed precincts to the gods, their ancestors, and spots for holy rites. It is they who gave to men laws, food, and shelter."

112   " 'It is they who will,' said Tehuti, 'learn to know the secrets of my records all, and will make separation of them; and some they will keep for themselves, while those that are best suited for the benefit of mortal men, they will engrave on tablet and on obelisk.' "

113   "It is they who were the first to set up courts of law, and filled the world with justice and fair rule. It is they who were the authors of good pledges and of faith, and brought the mighty witness of an oath into men's lives."

114   "It is they who taught men how to wrap up those who ceased to live, as they should be."

Above: The Pylons of the Temple of Isis at Agilkia Island (Aswan) in Egypt, Africa.

115   "It is they who searched into the cruelty of death, and learned that though the spirit which goes out longs to return into men's bodies, yet if it ever fails to have the power of getting back again, then loss of life results."

116   "It is they who learned from Tehuti that the surrounding space was filled with spirits, and engraved on hidden stones the hidden teachings."

117   "It is they alone who, taught by Tehuti in God's hidden codes, became the authors of the arts, and sciences, and all pursuits which men do practice, and givers of their laws."

118   "It is they who, taught by Tehuti that the things below have been disposed by God to be in sympathy with things above, established on the earth the sacred rites over which the mysteries in Heaven preside."

119   "It is they who, knowing the destructibility of human frames, devised the grade of prophets, in all things perfected, in order that no prophet who stretched forth his hands unto the gods should be in ignorance of anything, that magic and philosophy should feed the soul, and medicine preserve the body when it suffered pain."

120   "And having done all this, my son, Osiris and myself, perceiving that the world was now quite full, were thereupon demanded back by those who dwell in Heaven, but could not go above till we had made appeal unto the Monarch, that surrounding space might with this knowledge of the soul be filled as well, and we ourselves succeeded in making our ascent acceptable to Him. . . . for that God does in hymns rejoice."

121   "O mother," Horus said, "on me as well bestow the knowledge of this hymn, that I may not remain in ignorance."

122   And Isis said: "Give ear, O son! Now if you would, O son of mighty Soul, know anything besides what I have spoken, ask on!"

123   "Well you have, mother, explained all," said Horus. "But noble souls how they are born, you have not told me yet."

124   "As on the Earth, son Horus, there are states which differ one from the other, so also is it in the case of souls. For they have regions whence they start; and that which starts from a more glorious place, has nobler birth than one which does not so."

Above: The outer courtyard of the temple of Isis at Agilkia Island (Aswan) in
Egypt, Africa.

125   Horus asked: "O Divine Mother, how are male and female souls produced?" Isis answered: "Souls, Horus, son, are of the self same nature in themselves, in that they are from one and the same place where the Creator modeled them; nor male nor female are they. Sex is a thing of bodies, not of souls."

126   "That which brings it about that some of them are stouter, some more delicate, is, son, that particular 'air' in which all things are made. 'Air' for the soul is nothing, but the body which envelopes it is composed of earth and water, air and fire."

127   "As, then, the composition of the female ones has more of wet and cold, but less of dry and warm. Accordingly, the soul which is shut in a plasm of this kind becomes relaxed and delicate, just as the contrary is bound to be in case of males."

128   "For in their case there's more of dry and warm, and less of cold and wet, wherefore the souls in bodies such as these are sturdy and more active."

129   "And how do souls become intelligent, O mother mine?" And Isis answered, "The faculty of the intellect, my son, is swathed in wrappings. When these are dense and thick, the eye is dim; but when they're thin and light, then is the sight most keen. So is it also for the soul. For it as well has envelopes incorporeal appropriate to it, just as it is itself incorporeal. These envelopes are 'airs' which are in us. When these are light, thin and clear, then is the soul intelligent; but, on the contrary, when they are dense, thick and turbid, then vision and intuition is as in bad weather, the soul sees not at distance, but only things which lie about its feet."

130   "Please answer me O lady, mother mine! For what cause is it that when men still keep alive in long disease, their rational part of their very reason and their very soul at times becomes disabled?"

131   And Isis answered, "Of living things, my son, some are made friends with fire, and some with water, some with air, and some with earth, and some with two or three of these, and some with all."

132   "And, on the contrary, again some are made enemies of fire, and some of water, some of earth, and some of air, and some of two of them, and some of three, and some of all."

Above: Osiride columns of Ramesses II in Egypt, Africa.

Below: Line drawing of the Osiride columns.

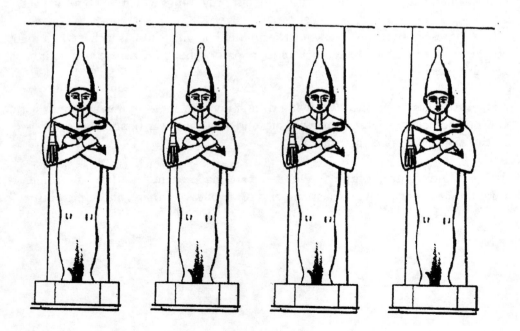

133 "For instance, son, the locust and all flies flee fire, the eagle and the hawk and all high-flying birds flee water, fish, air and earth, and the snake avoids the open air. Whereas snakes and all creeping things love earth, all swimming things water, winged things, air, of which they are the citizens, while those that fly still higher love the fire and have their habitat near it. Not that some of the animals as well do not love fire, for instance salamanders, for they even have their homes in it. It is because one or another of the elements does form their bodies' outer envelope."

134 "Each soul, accordingly, while it is in its body, is weighted and constricted by these four elements. Moreover, it is natural it also should be pleased with some of them and pained with others."

135 "For this cause, then, it does not reach the height of its prosperity; still, as it is divine by nature, even while wrapped up in them, it struggles and it thinks, though not thinking such thoughts as it would think were it set free from being bound in bodies."

136 Moreover, if these frames are swept with storm and stress, or of disease or fear, then is the soul itself tossed on the waves, as man upon the deep with nothing steady under him.

THE BATTLE OF HORUS (HERU) AND SET
(From the Greek text entitled: The History of Isis and Osiris, the
Fourth Sallier Papyrus and the Chester Beatty Papyrus)

137 Here begins the fight between Horus and Set. It began on the 26th day of the month of Tehuti, and lasted three days and three nights. It was fought near the Hall of the Lords of *Kher-aha* (Heliopolis-On) and in the presence of Isis.

137a When Horus became a young man and was fully trained by Isis in the mysteries of the soul and of the wisdom concerning the highest Divinity from which even Osiris, Isis and he, himself, originated, Osiris encouraged him to take up arms and establish truth, justice and righteousness (Maat) in the world by challenging Set, its current ruler. Horus called on the Ennead to act as judges in the question of the legality of Set's assumption of the throne after killing Osiris.

138 Shu was the first to give his judgment saying: "The throne rightfully belongs to Horus no matter how mighty Set might be. Justice requires that Horus be given

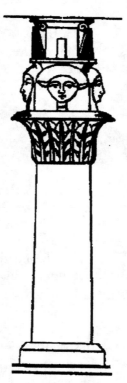

Above: The Hathor-headed Temple column.

the throne." Tehuti agreed with this, saying: "What Shu has said is a million times true!" Shu once again exclaimed: "The entire Ennead is in agreement, the throne belongs to Horus." Hearing this Isis began to rise up in joy and asked the northward wind to change its direction in order to carry the news to Osiris who is in the *Beautiful West.*

139   Then the King of the gods, Ra-Atum, spoke out thus disapprovingly: "Is the Ennead now making their own decisions?" Then Set moved forward and shouted: "How can this puny child claim the throne; let him challenge me in a personal contest and I will defeat him for all to see."

140   Tehuti once again spoke out with the words of reason, righteousness and justice: "What Set says is wrong; we all know this. How can the throne be given to Set when the rightful heir is alive here before us? Horus should be given the throne; aren't we all agreed on that?"

141   The Sun God, Ra, then said: "I am not in agreement with that." Having said this, the entire hall fell into a cold silence. The Ennead came up with the idea of calling Banedjed to judge the issues. He suggested that they send a letter to Neith, The Divine Mother. Tehuti immediately set about to write the letter in the name of the All-Lord. "As the King of Upper and Lower Egypt, beloved of Tehuti, I ask you how should we decide between these two who have been before the tribunal for eighty years?" Neith replied thus: "Give the throne to Horus, the son of Osiris. This is the correct way to justice. If you do anything else it will be injustice and you will suffer the consequences for your evil doings. I shall become angry and cause the sky to come crashing down upon you. Give Set two goddesses to attend on him and increase his wealth by a factor of two. Then you will have done what is correct."

142   Hearing this Ra became angry, saying: "This feeble child can not be given the throne of Egypt." Hearing this the gods and goddesses of the Ennead became angry themselves and Baba, the baboon god, spoke out: "The shrine of the Ra is empty; we do not take any further notice of you!" Ra, feeling bad to himself, covered himself and laid down on the ground.

143   The company of gods and goddesses asked Baba to leave since they feared that they had angered Ra. They feared that He might stop the revolutions of the Boat of Millions of Years and thus bring all creation to an end. They tried to talk with him but he refused to listen to them. He retired to his abode and refused to return to the court. The great god, Ra, was growing weary of the contest between

Scene from the battle of Horus and Set.
Horus spearing a hippopotamus fiend (form of Set) with the help of Isis.

They (Horus and Set) soon began the contest by transforming into large beasts. Isis tried to help by creating a harpoon with her magic. She could not distinguish between the two combatants but cast the harpoon into the waters anyway. She struck Horus in the side, who exclaimed in pain: "Mother, your harpoon has struck me, please let me go." Isis immediately released him and cast it again. This time she struck Set who exclaimed: "Isis, I am your brother. O sister why are you against me? What evil have I done to you? Please release me!"

From the battle of Horus and Set - Line 161

Horus and Set, and passed a day lying on his back in his arbor, and his heart was very sad, and he was alone.

144   Seeing this, the beautiful daughter of Ra, Hathor, decided to implement a plan to bring the Sun God out of his despondency and to encourage him to once again assume his place in the court. She began to dance around the court while stripping off her clothes. The gods and goddesses crowded around and began to laugh and applaud her artistic and passionate expression. After a while, this commotion attracted the attention of Ra, who returned to see what was going on. He saw the beautiful Hathor and began to come out of his negative mood. Hathor, lady of the southern sycamore, came and stood before her father, the master of the universe. She uncovered her vulva for his face, and the Great God smiled at her. .

145   Ra then returned to take his place among the Ennead and instructed Horus and Set to put forth their case so that the court may hear it again.

146   Again Set spoke out first: "The throne belongs to me. Who else but me protects the voyage of the Sun boat when the chaos serpents attach to it? Since I am the one who protects the existence of the gods, the throne should be given to me!"

147   Then Tehuti and Shu spoke out disapprovingly: "We cannot give the throne to an uncle when the rightful heir is standing right here before us!"

148   Horus finally spoke out and complained bitterly: "Will you take away my birthright with this injustice and do it right here in front of the Ennead?" Hearing all of this, Isis became exceedingly angry and complained incessantly until the Ennead promised to do justice to Horus.

149   Noticing that the Ennead was not supporting him, Set now became furious and threatened them all: "From now on I will strike any one of you down every single day, and I will not put forth my case in any court where Isis is allowed to enter into."

150   Ra agreed to this and decreed that they should all go to a special island and that Nemty, the ferryman, should not allow Isis across to join them there.

151   Using her special powers, Isis transformed herself into the form of an old lady and came to the shore where Nemty was. She told him that she needed to get across to the islands because she needed to carry food to the island for a young man who had been tending a herd for five days.

Above: Horus spearing a hippopotamus fiend (form of Set) with the help of Isis. In this picture Isis holds the Ankh and with upraised hand, lends her spiritual force to Horus.

152   "Here Nemty, I will give you this cake as payment for you to carry me across." Nemty replied: "Old woman, I am the divine ferryman and I have no need for your cake". Then Isis showed him a fantastic gold ring which she wore on her finger and said: "This great ring shall be yours if you carry me across". Nemty could not resist a bribe of this magnitude and agreed to carry her across.

153   Isis came upon the place where the court was. Set looked and he saw her as she approached in the distance. Thereupon she uttered a magic spell, and she changed herself into a maiden beautiful of limbs, and there was not the like of her in the entire land, and he was captivated with infatuation and passionate desire for her very much. Thereupon he rose, and he went over to sit down and ate bread with the great Ennead. He went to overtake her, and no one had seen her except him.

154   Thereupon she stood behind a tree, and he shouted to her saying, "I am here with you, beautiful maiden! How may I serve you" And she said to him, "My great lord! As for me, I was the wife of a herdsman of cattle, and I bore him a male child. My husband died, and the boy came to watch the cattle of his father. But one day a stranger came and sat down in the stables and said to my son, "I'll beat you up and take your cattle and kick you out!" Isis continued: "My greatest wish is for you to conquer him."

155   Set replied, "Is the cattle to be given to a stranger when the son of the father is yet alive? This would be a most blatant injustice and cannot be allowed."

156   At that moment Isis transformed herself into a kite and flew to the top of a tree. From there she shouted to Set: "Weep yourself. Your own mouth has said it, your own cleverness has given judgment. What more do you want?"

157   Set began to complain bitterly and became terribly upset: "This evil woman has tricked me". This attracted the attention of the Ennead who wanted to know what had happened. When he related the story of what Isis had done Ra exclaimed, "What she says is true. You have judged yourself so what will you do now?"

158   Set then set about to punish Nemty by cutting off his toes, and from that time on, he never looked upon gold again.

Above: A scene from the battle of Horus and Set. Horus spears Set who is in the form of a crocodile.

159   Then the Ennead returned and began to make preparations for the coronation of Horus. Even as he saw the crown being placed on the head of Horus, Set remained bitter and refused to admit that he had been defeated. He proposed to challenge Horus once more saying: "You may have the crown but you cannot rule until you beat me. I challenge you to a duel. Let us transform ourselves into hippopotami and engage in combat deep in the bottom of the river. Whoever comes to the surface first will be considered the loser."

160   With complete confidence, Horus agreed immediately to the challenge, and hearing all of this, Isis began to weep, because she feared that Set would kill her son.

161   They soon began the contest by transforming into large beasts. Isis tried to help by creating a harpoon with her magic. She could not distinguish between the two combatants but cast the harpoon into the waters anyway. She struck Horus in the side, who exclaimed in pain: "Mother, your harpoon has struck me, please let me go." Isis immediately released him and cast it again. This time she struck Set who exclaimed: "Isis, I am your brother. O sister why are you against me? What evil have I done to you? Please release me!"

162   Due to the pity and compassion she felt towards Set she freed him. In a passionate rage, Horus cut off her head and went off by himself in a frustrated state. In the mean time Tehuti replaced her head with that of a cow's. In the form of a black pig, Set found Horus while he was resting in an oasis contemplating his situation. Set then gouged out Horus' eyes and left him to suffer alone and dispirited. In pain and dejection, Horus spent the entire night reflecting on what had happened.

(The pieces of the eye of Horus)

163   Hathor found him and consoled him. She found a gazelle and took some of its milk, and took it to Horus. She spoke to him with the lovely sound of a celestial melody: "Uncover your eyes". Horus did as he was told, and she dripped the milk which was imbued with her healing force into his wounds.

Tehuti restoring to Horus the Udjat (Uatchit) Eye, 𓂀 , which Set had blinded.

163b   Also, it came to be that Tehuti came to Horus to restore his eyesight with his magical powers, great learning and possession of words of power.

THE EVIL OF SET
(From the Chester Beatty Papyrus)

164   Horus has now assumed the attributes of Amsu-Min or *"He who is the redeemer of his father"*. When Horus, fully healed, now returned to the Ennead, the two contendants went before the court of the Ennead again and Ra bade them both to end the quarreling and make peace. Set said to Horus, "Come, let us spend a happy hour at my place!" Horus answered, "Yes, with pleasure, with pleasure." When it was evening, the bed was spread for them and they lay down. During the night Set made his member stiff, and he made it go between the loins of Horus. Horus put his hands between his loins, and he caught the seed of Seth.

165   Horus returned to his mother, who had forgiven him for his act of uncontrolled passion due to frustration. Horus asked his mother Isis: "Come here, O Isis, my mother! Come and see what Set has done!" And he opened his hand, and he showed her the seed of Set. She cried out, seized her knife and cut off his hand, and she threw it into the water. But she took out another similar hand for him and replaced the one which had been cut off. Then she took a dab of sweet ointment and applied it to the member of Horus. She let it go stiff, having placed it in jar, and she made his seed run into it.

166   In the morning she took the seed of Horus to Set's garden. She said to his gardener, "Which herb is it that Set usually eats here with you?" The gardener replied, "He does not eat any herb here except lettuce." So Isis laid the seed of Horus on the lettuces.

167   Set came as he used to do every day, and he ate the lettuces as usual. He became pregnant with the seed of Horus. He went and said to Horus, "Come let us

Above: *Amsu*, *Min* or *Menu*, the ithyphallic (erect penis) form of Horus. Amun (hidden Supreme Being) is the source of the sexual energy which causes arousal and generation of life. This same sexual energy, when sublimated, is the power that Horus uses in the form of Amsu-Min to overthrow the fetters of Set (See *Egyptian Yoga: The Philosophy of Enlightenment* and the *Egyptian Book of Coming Forth By Day, Chapter 17*).

116

go so that I can contend with you in the tribunal." Horus said, "I will do so, indeed, I will do so."

168   Then they both went to the tribunal and stood before the great Ennead. They were told, "Speak concerning yourselves!" Set said, "Let me be given the office of ruler, for as to Horus, the same that stands here, I have performed an aggressive act on him."

169   The Ennead cried out aloud, and they belched and spat in the face of Horus. But Horus laughed at them, swore and said, "All that Set has said is false. Let the seed of Set be summoned that we may see from where it will answer."

170   Then Tehuti, lord of divine words, the scribe of truth of the Ennead, placed his hand on the arm of Horus, and he said, "Come out, you seed of Set!" And it answered him from the water in the waters. Then Tehuti placed his hand on the arm of Set, and he said, "Come out, you seed of Horus!" And it said to him, "Where shall I come out?" Tehuti said, "Come out of his ear!" and it said, "I who am divine effluence, shall I come out of his ear?" Then Tehuti said, "Come out of his forehead!"

171   And it came out as a golden disc on the head of Set. Set became extremely angry, and he reached out to lay hand on the golden disc. But Tehuti took it away from him, and he placed it as an ornament on his own head. Then he said, "Horus is in the right, and Set is in the wrong." Set swore an oath and said, "He shall not be given the office until we have sorted it out outside."

A Hymn to Min from the Stele of Sobk-iry:

I worship Min, I extol arm-raising Horus:
Hail to you, Min in his processional
Tall-plumed, son of Osiris,
Born of divine Isis.

Great in Senut, mighty in Ipu,

Isis

Set

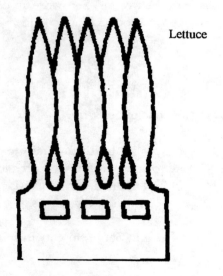

Lettuce

118

You of Coptos, Horus strong-armed,
Lord of awe who silences pride,
Sovereign of all the gods
Fragrance laden when he comes from Medja-land,
Awe inspiring in Nubia,
You of Utent, hail and praise.

172   Set demanded to be allowed one more chance to prove that he was worthy of the throne and that Horus was not. He said: "Let us both build ships of stone and race them down the Nile and whichever one wins the race shall wear the crown of Asar (Osiris)." Once again, Horus agreed to the challenge.

173   Set created a boat of stone and dragged it to the Nile but it sunk as soon as he put it into the water. Horus' boat was already in the water and it was floating because he had smartly made it out of wood and plastered it over to make it look like stone. When his boat sank, Set became furious and turned himself into a hippopotamus again, and struck Horus' boat which splintered to pieces. Horus began to attack Set with his spear, but stopped because the Ennead commanded him to do so.

174   In despair and frustration over the never ending saga between him and Set, Horus traveled north to seek advice from the Goddess Neith. At the same time Tehuti and Shu convinced the Ennead to send a letter to Osiris who now resided in the Beautiful West.

175   Osiris sent a letter back to the Ennead pleading with them to do what is correct. Horus, as the son of Osiris, should be the rightful heir to the throne. He was demanding to know why the Ennead was conspiring to take away the throne from his son. He asked them if they had forgotten that is was he who had brought wheat and barley to the world. All but two of them (the Ennead) agreed, because Horus, they said, was too young to rule. Then Ra became angry because he felt that Osiris was trying to tell him what to do, so he sent Osiris and arrogant letter in reply. Osiris then sent them a second letter.

Osiris began the letter sarcastically:

"How good are the actions of the Ennead! Justice has now sunk into the level of the underworld. Now listen to me, the land of the dead is replete of demons who fear no Goddess or God. If I were to send them

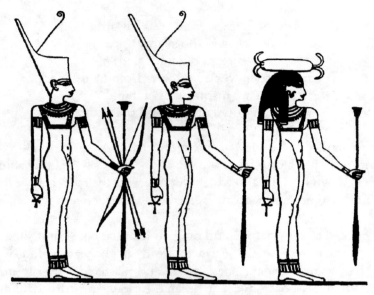

Above: The forms of the Goddess Neith.

Neith is the goddess of creation and war. Her attributes are the bow, shield and arrows. She is androgynous (neither male nor female), and was known to watch over Osiris' bier (ceremonial bed) when he lay dead, along with Isis and Nephthys.

Horus and his four sons, each armed with a knife, standing before Osiris and Serapis. The animal-headed man, with knives stuck in his body and bound by his arms to a forked stick, represents Set or Typhon, conquered.

120

out into the world of those who are living, they will bring back the hearts of the evildoers to the place where punishment is meted. Tell me, among you, who is more powerful than I? Even you, the Gods, must ultimately come at last to the Beautiful West!"

176   Following the receipt of Osiris' scroll (letter), the Ennead became afraid at what Osiris might do and they finally agreed that his wishes should be honored. Set was chained and brought into the court. Horus was crowned King of Egypt. Set accepted the decision and made peace with Horus. Ra unchained Set and decreed that he should remain with him in the sky as the Lord of Storms and the protector of the Barque of Millions of Years. All the gods and goddesses rejoiced.

176a   Horus defeated Set by becoming the *Ur-Uatchit*. The sacred form of Ur-Uatchit, the winged sundisk with two urei, symbolize the goddess Nekhebet on the right and the goddess Uatchit on the left. Thus it was decreed by Tehuti that the Ur-Uatchit should be seen decorating every temple as a protection of evil.

A HYMN TO OSIRIS
(From the Book of Coming Forth By Day)

177   A HYMN OF PRAYER TO OSIRIS. "Glory to Osiris Un-Nefer, the great god within Abydos, king of eternity, lord of the everlasting, who passeth through millions of years in his existence. Eldest son of the womb of Nut, engendered by Geb, the chief lord of the crowns of the North and South, lord of the lofty white crown. As Prince of gods and of men he has received the crook and the flail and the dignity of his divine fathers[1]. Let thy heart which is in the mountain of Amenta be content, for thy son Horus is established upon thy throne. You are crowned lord of Tattus[2] and ruler in Abtus[3]. Through thee the world waxeth green in triumph before the might of Neb-er-tcher[4]. He leadeth in his train that which is and that which is not yet, in his name Ta-her-seta-nef[5]; he toweth along the earth in triumph in his name Seker[6].

He is exceedingly mighty and most terrible in his name Osiris. He endureth forever and forever in his name Un-nefer[7]. Homage to thee, King of Kings,

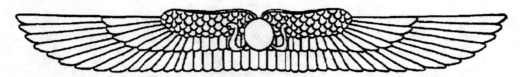

Above: An ancient Egyptian temple entranceway donning the Winged Sundisk of Horus, in Egypt, Africa.

'Horus defeated Set by becoming the Ur-Uatchit. The sacred form of Ur-Uatchit, the winged sundisk with two urei, symbolizes the goddess Nekhebet on the right and the goddess Uatchet on the left. Thus it was decreed by Tehuti that the Ur-Uatchet should be seen decorating every temple as a protection of evil.'

From the Osirian Resurrection Myth - Line 176a

It being of such a quality, God, who is author of all generation and production, and of all elemental forces, as being superior to them, immaterial and incorporeal exalted above the realm of nature and likewise begotten and undivided, entire of himself and concealed in himself, is supreme above all these and embraces them all in himself. And because he contains everything and gives himself to all the universe, he is made manifest out from them. Because he is superior to the universe, he is spread out over it by himself, and is manifested as separate, removed, high in the air and unfolded by himself above the forces and elementary principles in the world.

—Iamblichus, Egyptian Initiate (circa 250-330 A.C.E.)

Lord of Lords, Prince of Princes, who from the womb of Nut have possessed the world and have ruled all lands and Akert[8]. Thy body is of gold, thy head is of azure, and emerald light encircleth thee. O An[9] of millions of years, all-pervading with thy body and beautiful in countenance in Ta-sert[10]. Grant thou to the Ka of Osiris, the initiate, splendor in heaven and might upon earth and triumph in Neter-khert; and that I may, sail down to Tattu like a living soul and up to Abtu like a bennu (phoenix); and that I may go in and come out without repulse at the pylons of the Ṭuat[10]. May there be given unto me loaves of bread in the house of coolness, and offerings of food in Annu[11] , and a homestead forever in Sekbet-Aru[12], with wheat and barley therefor..."

It has come to a good ending in Thebes, the place of truth.

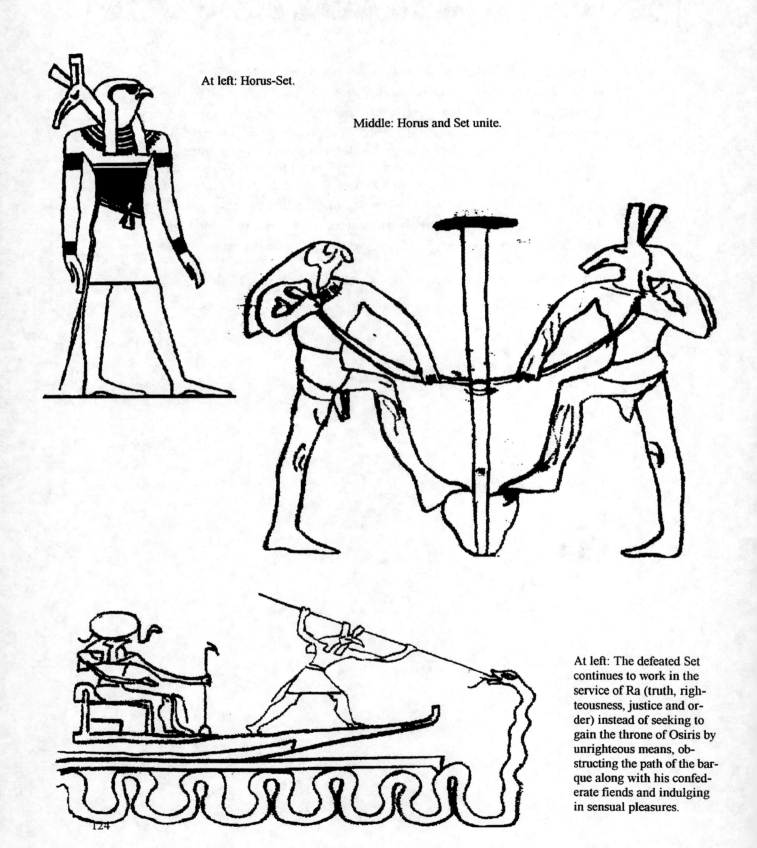

At left: Horus-Set.

Middle: Horus and Set unite.

At left: The defeated Set continues to work in the service of Ra (truth, righteousness, justice and order) instead of seeking to gain the throne of Osiris by unrighteous means, obstructing the path of the barque along with his confederate fiends and indulging in sensual pleasures.

124

Notes on the Hymn to Osiris

1- Osiris, as the night sun (the moon) was also the sun of Ra.

2- Tattu was the name of two towns in Ancient Egypt. In mystical terms it refers to being firmly established in the Netherworld. The Ancient Egyptian word *Tattu* refers to "steadfastness" or "stability" as well as the pillar of Osiris. This is also being referred to in the following line from the *Egyptian Book of Coming Forth By Day*, Chapter I: 13-15:

nuk Tetteti, se Tetteti au am-a em Tettetu Mesi - a em Tettetu
"I am Tetteti (steadfast), son of Tetteti (steadfast), conceived and born in the region of Tettetu (steadfastness)."

3- *Abtu* was the city which the Greeks called *Abydos*. It is also reputed to be the resting place of the body of Osiris.

4- Nebertcher literally means "All Encompassing Divinity" or "Supreme Being".

5- The One who draws the world, i.e. Ra, the Supreme Being, who causes the world to exist by drawing it along in the movement of the Barque of "Millions of Years".

6- Seker is the divine form of the Supreme Being (Osiris, Ptah, Tenen) as the night sun, symbolizing the period of death.

7- The "Beautiful Being" or the "Good Being", i.e. Osiris.

8- The country of which Osiris is the ruler. There was an Akert or burial ground on the western side of the Nile. This is where many important excavations have been conducted in recent times, uncovering the tombs of Kings, Queens and Nobles of Ancient Egypt.

9- A name of the sun god, i.e. Ra (Osiris).

10- A name of the underworld.

11- The city of the sun, the first city which emerged with the creation, thus, the abode of Ra and the Ennead.

12- A section of the astral world. It is part of the *Sekhet-hetepu*, where souls of the blessed reap and sow.

Gloss on The Ausarian Resurrection

The Mystical Themes and Teachings of The Osirian Myth.

Introduction

Gloss writing is a special form of writing which attempts to provide an explanation for a particular text or manuscript. It does not attempt to examine each individual line of a work but seeks to illuminate the most important themes and mystical implications being brought forth by a particular text. In this case I have also given an introduction to the process of practicing the teachings being espoused as well as an insight into the effects these practices will have in the human personality. For a more detailed study (commentary) of the teachings derived from the line by line examination of the Ausarian Resurrection Myth, the reader is referred to the companion book to this volume called *"The Mystical Teachings of The Ausarian Resurrection"*.

The Substratum of Creation

Maat, Hathor and Tehuti were not part of the Ennead, yet they played important roles in the Osirian myth. As stated earlier, the neters of the Ennead are Ra-Atum, Shu, Tefnut, Geb, Nut, Osiris, Isis, Set (Seth) and Nephthys. Hathor, Tehuti and Maat represent attributes of the Supreme Being as the very *stuff* or *substratum* which makes up creation. This means that they are the elements which the creative principle uses in the act of creation. This idea may be better understood through the following simile. Consider a lump of clay. The clay can be given several forms but the substratum of any form which the clay is given, be it a pot, plate, bowl, cup, etc., will always remain the same, clay. The composition of the clay does not change. In the same manner Hathor, Maat and Tehuti represent attributes of the Supreme Being which do not change regardless of the forms which objects in creation take. Therefore, they are the constant, absolute principles among all that is changing, chaotic, transient, and therefore illusory, in human experience as well as in creation. Hathor represents the force of spiritual energy which drives the entire universe. The relentless order and synchronicity of the planets and stars, as well as the order of events which occur in the life of every human being, is symbolized by Maat, and the light of consciousness which is the underlying characteristic of all sentient life is symbolized by Tehuti.

Uatchit and Nekhebet represent the dual aspect of creation, the "Two Lands" (Upper Egypt, symbolized by the Lotus plant and Lower Egypt, symbolized by the Papyrus plant). In a mystical sense they symbolize heaven and earth, spirit and matter. However, they also represent the subtle spiritual energy known as the Arat (Serpent Power), more commonly known by the name Kundalini. The Serpent Power is the Life Force energy which sustains life and promotes the desire for action in the human being. It operates through the subtle spiritual energy centers and is symbolized by the shaft which is intertwined by serpents in the staffs of Uatchit and Nekhebet, as well as the staff of Tehuti. The unity of these two principles, which are opposite poles of the same energy, is synonymous with Enlightenment and the absolute truth.

Hathor represents the Life Force energy of Ra. She is the power of Creation itself. Creation, the manifestation of the Divine Spirit, is seen as female, and the Soul of Creation, as male. Tehuti represents the mind of God. He represents the higher intellectual capacity of the mind when it is attuned to the Divine. Tehuti the messenger of God. Maat (Ma, Maa, Mayt) represents the very order which constitutes creation. Therefore, it is said that Ra created the universe by putting Maat in the place of chaos. Therefore, Creation itself is Maat. She is the mother of the universe. As such, the word *ma* has appeared in many languages from around the world in relation to the word mother. In Ancient Egypt Ma or Mut signifies mother. In India, *mata*; in English speaking countries it is *mother* or *mama*; in Spanish it is *mami*, or *madre*. Thus the principle of the universal mother has found its way into human language.

Creation without order is chaos. Consider what would happen if the elements (water, air, fire, earth) did not exist according to their set parameters. What would happen if water became flammable or if earth became gaseous? What would happen if the laws of gravity acted in reverse? There would be no consistency or order in the phenomenal universe and no way for life to exist. So Maat is the basis upon which Creation exists, and Creation is the mode in which the divine Supreme Being expresses Him/Her Self. Therefore, anything which impedes order, regularity and harmony is against Maat, Creation and God. Spiritual movement and spiritual practice are difficult in an atmosphere of unrest, agitation, disorder and turmoil. Likewise, anything which promotes order, peace, harmony, truth, justice, righteousness, etc., automatically promotes spirituality, divine awareness, spiritual wisdom and self-discovery.

God of God of the
Touch. Intelligence.

God of God of
Seeing. Hearing.

The gods of the Senses.

In a relief which was made for *Ptolemy IV* at Edfu, there is a depiction of the Barque of Creation which shows the King standing before the barque, with upraised arms, offering Maat to The God. At the Front of the boat is Heru-p-khart, Horus the Child, with a flail. Within the boat are Heru-merti (Horus of the two eyes implying the all encompassing divinity), Maat, Apuat, Shu, Hathor, Tehuti, and Neith. Behind the King, outside of the boat, stand the gods of the senses of *Hu* (Taste) and *Saa* (Touch, feeling and understanding). At the other end, also outside of the boat, stand the gods of the senses of *Maa* (Sight) and *Setem* (Hearing). Hu and Saa were known to serve as bearers of the Eye of Horus. They were also considered to be the tongue and heart of Osiris-Ptah. Thus, they represent the vehicles through which human beings can understand and espouse the teachings of moral and spiritual wisdom.

The positioning of the gods and goddesses is of paramount importance, because it points to the understanding that the neters within the boat itself are emanations of the Divine, while those outside of the boat are effects or reflections of the creative principles. Therefore, the occupants of the boat may be understood as *absolute attributes* of the Divine, while the characters outside of the boat may be understood as *relative manifestations* of the Divine in time and space. Just as sound, light and fragrances are emanations of the objects which project them, the senses are also emanations from the consciousness of the life forms which use them. The senses therefore, are relative, dependent on the particular animal and the level of sensitivity. They have no independent existence outside of the living being(s) who/which possess them. The information brought by them is processed with the use of the mind and intellect. Therefore, they are depicted as being outside of the boat. Furthermore, even the mind and intellect are relative. Spiritual sensitivity and wisdom varies from person to person. Thus, only the Spirit is absolute. The Spirit remains the same while the physical body, personality, intellectual capacity and level of sensitivity (of the senses) are relative, transient and variable. The mind, intellect, senses and ego-personality of a human being are all transient projections of the Spirit.

So from a mystical standpoint the picture symbolizes the human ego, in the form of the King and his senses, in the act of devotional meditation on the Divine, offering Maat, 𓐙, to The God, 𓃂, (Neter), in the form of Horus, The Child. Thus, living according to the principles of Maat and turning the senses and one's personal interest toward serving the Divine allow for one's spiritual movement to unfold. Saa is closely related to Tehuti, representing intelligence or higher intellect in the human being which gets close to the cosmic mind (Tehuti) through devotion to God. Maa (sight) is closely related to Maat as the clarity of vision which allows one to live by order, justice and righteousness, and not to fall under the pressure of egoistic desires and negative thoughts.

In addition to the senses, there are two more important abstract qualities through which the Divine expresses. These are Sekhem and Heh. Sekhem is energy or power though which the universe manifests. Heh, along with his counterpart Hehet, represent eternity. They are aspects of the primeval ocean, Nu. Thus, from the eternal emanates the temporal. The universe is itself composed of a divine, eternal essence which exists according to the law and order (Maat) of the Divine (Supreme Being). The qualities of humanity (egoism, mind and senses) arise from the Divine basis or substratum. They are expressions of the Divine, which when internalized, allow for self-discovery and the awareness of eternity when externalized, they promote time and space (temporal - egoistic) awareness.

The Cycles of Creation

The findings of modern science have corroborated the mystical teachings of Ancient Egypt and India. In both of these cosmological systems Creation and time are understood as being circular or cyclical. This means that time moves in a circle rather than in a line from point A to point B as it is usually conceptualized in modern society. Modern science has shown that two lines moving in opposite directions join in infinity. This seems like a contradiction or paradox. However, upon reflection, the mystical wisdom of the ancients sheds light on this great truth.

In the epic Ancient Egyptian story known as "The Destruction of Evil Men and Women" there is a passage where the God Ra decides to leave the earth because as he explains, he will not be regenerated until the next period or cycle of Creation begins:

> "And the Majesty of this God (Ra) said unto the Majesty of Nu, 'My members are weak and have suffered pain since primeval time, and I shall not recover until another period comes'".

The "period" referred to above is related to the cycle of Creation in which Ra emerges from the primeval waters and emanates Creation in the form of the Ennead. This implies that Creation has not occurred once but countless times. Creation is a cycle in which there is emergence and expansion which in human terms occurs over a period of billions of years, while from the perspective of God it occurs in a moment.

It is interesting to note here that the Hindu system of reckoning time envisions time as a cyclical movement instead of as a linear. It involves cycles of Creation which evolves over a period of millions of years and ends up where they began. These units of time are called Yugas. This system of regarding time as a recurring cycle as in a circle is similar to the Ancient Egyptian system described above. Along with this, a correlation may be made between the Hindu God *Rama* and the Ancient Egyptian God *Ra*. In Indian Mythology the Supreme Being, known as

Brahman or "The Absolute", becomes three creative principles. These principles are known as the Trinity of *Brahma*, *Vishnu* and *Shiva*. Vishnu is said to incarnate from time to time in order to sustain *Dharma* or righteousness. Like the Ancient Egyptian *MAAT*, Dharma represents, order, righteousness and justice. When chaos in the form of evil and unrighteousness threaten to destroy society, God incarnates in human form in order to show humanity the proper way to live. Vishnu has had many incarnations. Two of the most popular ones are Krishna and Rama. This is the concept of Avatarism and it is also to be found in Ancient Egypt with the incarnation of Osiris and Isis as well as the incarnation of Hathor.

Mystical Symbolism in the Characters of the Osirian Myth

Asar-Aset-Heru
(Osiris-Isis-Horus)

From a mystical standpoint, the Trinity of Osiris-Isis-Horus represents the movement of the Spirit as it manifests in Creation. As we have seen through the story as well as the iconography associated with them, in reality it refers to the deeper principles of human, as well as super-human, existence. Osiris becomes the silent Spirit who is the source and support of Creation in his names *Asar-Tua,* "Osiris, the Begetter" (in the Tuat), and *Osiris-Neb-Heh,* "Osiris, Lord of Eternity". Isis is the Creation itself. Horus is the dynamic manifestation of the Spirit (of Osiris) which moves in and interacts with Creation (Isis). Thus, Osiris expresses as Creation and as the dynamic forces within it. This teaching is also expressed in the idea of the Trinity concept and the birth of God into human form (Avatarism).

The three men who offer boons in the Annunciation Scene on page 66 represent the triune aspect of Creation which is the teaching behind the Trinity. This teaching refers to Creation itself as well as to human consciousness. Creation manifests as three aspects. This teaching is expressed in the Ancient Egyptian statement: "I was One and then I became Three", and "Nebertcher: Everything is Amun-Ra-Ptah, three in one." Nebertcher (Supreme Being, a name of Osiris) manifests as Amun-Ra-Ptah. In this teaching, Amun represents the witnessing consciousness, Ra represents the mind and senses, and Ptah represents matter and all physical manifestation. Therefore, the Trinity owes its existence to the one. Thus the three wise men bringing boons represent Creation (all that exists and the awareness of that existence) itself paying homage to its Creator. The realization of the underlying unity, the oneness behind the multiplicity of the Trinity, gives profound insight into the true nature of the Divine and the way to discover the Supreme Self. When you begin to understand that the underlying basis behind Creation, meaning your consciousness or identity, your senses and mind, your perceptions of the physical universe, is in reality the One Supreme Spirit, you begin to turn away from the world of ordinary human existence, to discover the Self within, and to *Know Thyself.*

131

Osiris
The Incarnation of the Higher Self
into the realm of time and space.

In the Osirian myth, Osiris is the son of Geb and Nut, who are in turn the offspring of Shu and Tefnut, who are themselves children of Ra. In another Creation myth of Osiris, it is said that Osiris uttered his own name, *Asar,* and thereby brought the world and all life within it into existence. This is the process of Divine incarnation whereby the Supreme Being becomes the universe. Osiris, *Lord of the Perfect Black,* is the personification of the blackness of the vast un-manifest regions of existence. Osiris is the essence of all things, and the very soul of every human being as the Higher Self, who, through ignorance, has become involved in the world, and struggles to regain its original state of perfection. Nephthys represents the lower nature of matter or the binding, fettering and condensing aspect which dulls the intellect and intoxicates the mind and senses. Therefore, the union with Isis symbolizes the achievement or striving for spiritual salvation or resurrection while the union with Nephthys symbolizes bondage, suffering and the cycle of births and deaths, known as reincarnation. Osiris symbolizes the fragmented ocean of consciousness which has been cut into pieces by the lower self. No longer is there the vast all-encompassing, all-knowing, all-seeing consciousness. The Divine has become limited in association with the human mind, body and senses, due to the desire to experience human feelings and egoistic sentiments. Instead of looking at the universe through the cosmic mind, the Divine now expresses Him/Herself through billions of life forms whose bodies, minds and senses are too limited to see the vastness of Creation.

Set (Seth)
The Lower Self.

Set represents the unbridled lower self of all human beings. His impulsiveness and reckless passionate pursuits are the ever present enemy of the aspirant or anyone else who is striving for control over the urges of the mind, body and senses. The lower self is represented by the desires of the mind which lure the soul into the varied situations of pain and pleasure in the world of time and space (the relative existence). These desires lead to a degraded mental capacity which manifests in the forms of selfishness, greed, hatred, anger, lust and other human failings. These faults or mental complexes are termed *fetters.* The fetters of the mind prevent the soul from discovering peace, harmony and oneness with the universe.

Isis
(Aset)
Love, Cosmic Consciousness and Wisdom.

In the temple of Denderah, it is inscribed that Nut gave birth to Isis there, and that upon her birth, Nut exclaimed: *"Ås"* (behold), *I have become thy mother"*. This was the origin of the name *"Åst"*, later known as Isis to the Greeks and others. It further states that she was a dark-skinned child and was called *"Khnemet-ankhet"* or the lady of love. Thus, Isis also symbolizes the "blackness" of the vast un-manifest regions of existence, Osiris. Her identification is also symbolized in her aspect as *Amentet*, the Ṭuat, itself. Therefore, Amentet (Isis) and the soul of Amentet (Osiris) are in reality one and the same. In her aspect as Amentet, Isis represents the subtle substance of nature, the astral plane.

The motherly love of Isis was instrumental in discovering and putting the pieces of Osiris' dead body back together. The two most important features which Isis encompasses are love and wisdom. Isis' undying love and devotion to Osiris transcended her loss of him twice. Her love also caused the resurrection of her son, Horus, as well. This divine devotion led her to discover the pieces of Osiris' dead body. This is the devotion of the initiate which leads him or her to the Divine. All that is needed is a deep, ardent love for the Divine.

In her name, *Rekhat*, Isis also represents *rekhit* or wisdom. She is the patroness of all *rekht* or Sages. Isis represents the kind of wisdom which transcends all intellectual knowledge. She is at the same time, Creation (Amentet), and the ultimate reality of that Creation. Thus, it is said that she veils herself and that "no mortal man has unveiled her". The wisdom of Creation or knowing Isis in her full essence means becoming one with her in consciousness. When this unity occurs, one transcends ordinary human consciousness, so in this sense, no worldly human can discover her. The wisdom of Isis refers to that profound understanding of the essence of the Divine which is devoid of any kind of ignorance in reference to the transcendental Self. This wisdom is the intuitional realization which comes from pondering the nature of the Divine. Pondering implies repeated reflection and meditation on the Divine, trying, with sincerity and humility, to understand and become one with the Divine.

Isis is also a healer. She healed the body of Osiris even after it had been dismembered into several pieces. As a goddess she assists all those who pray to her, bestowing health and well being. She manifests in the form of love, motherhood, valor, devotion to God and intuitional realization of the Higher Self, Enlightenment.

Osiris and Isis were worshipped throughout the ancient world. In the first century B.C.E. Isis was one of the most popular goddesses in the city of Rome. Her temples were filled with altars, statues, laves, obelisks, etc., brought from Egypt, and orders of priestesses were endowed in order to perform the "Mysteries of Isis" and other Egyptian miracle plays in the great temples of the Eternal City. From Rome, the cult of Isis spread to Spain, Portugal, Gey, Gaul, Switzerland, and by way of Marseilles, to north Africa. In a manner similar to which Isis was identified with many other goddesses in Egypt and Nubia, in foreign lands she was given the attributes of other goddesses such as Selene, Demeter, or Ceres, Aphrodite, Juno, Nemesis, Fortuna, Panthea, etc.

In the *Golden Ass* of Apuleius of Madura, Isis says to Lucius:

"The whole earth worships my godhead, one and individual, under many a changing shape, with varied rites, and by many diverse names. There the Phrygians, first-born of men, call me "mother of the gods that dwell in Pessinus"; there the Athenians, sprung from the soil they till, know me the Rhamnusian, but those on whom shine the first rays of the Sun-god as each day he springs to new birth, the Arii and the Ethiopians and the Egyptians, mighty in ancient lore, honour me with my peculiar rites, and call me by my true name of "Auset (Isis), the Queen"."

Nephthys
(Nebt-het - "The Lady of the House")
Nature, Worldly Consciousness and Death.

Nephthys is the sister of Osiris and Isis. She represents the gross aspect of nature and the natural phase of life called death. Nature is what the Spirit impregnates with its life giving essence. Therefore, nature (Nephthys) is the recipient of Osiris' seed (spirit). According to natural law, anything that is born must be subject to the laws of nature and ultimately die. In his

Above: Isis and Nephthys

134

original form, detached from nature, Osiris was timeless, immortal, and untouched by the passions and frailties of human nature. As an incarnation of the Divine, Osiris becomes intoxicated with nature, his own Creation, and becomes associated with it through intercourse with Nephthys. Osiris, as a symbol of the human soul, is a stark example of the fate of human existence. His situation embodies the predicament of every individual human being. This is why the Ancient Egyptian Pharaohs and all initiates into the mystery of Osiris are referred to as Osiris and Horus, and are considered to be the daughter or son of Isis. Just as Osiris became intoxicated with His own Creation, so too the human soul becomes involved with nature and thereby produces an astral body composed of subtle elements, and a physical body composed of an aggregate of gross physical elements (water, earth, fire, air) which exist within Shu (ether-space).

There is deep mystical symbolism in the images and teachings surrounding the Triad or Osiris, Isis and Nephthys. In the temples of *Denderah*, *Edfu* and *Philae*, there are sculptured representations of the Mysteries of Osiris. These show *The Osiris* (initiate) lying on a bier (ritual bed), and Isis and Nephthys, who stand nearby, being referred to as the "two widows" of the dead Osiris. Isis and Nephthys are depicted as looking exactly alike, the only difference being in their head dresses: Isis ⌁, Nephthys ⌁ or ⌁. However, the symbols of these goddesses are in reality just inverted images of each other. The symbol of Nephthys is the symbol of Isis when inverted ⌁➔⌁. Therefore, each is a reflection of the other. Thus, it can be said that both life and death are aspects of the same principle.

The bodies and facial features of Isis and Nephthys are exactly alike. This likeness which Isis and Nephthys share is important when they are related to Osiris. As Osiris sits on the throne (see cover), he is supported by the two goddesses, Isis and Nephthys. Symbolically, Osiris represents the Supreme Soul, the all-encompassing Divinity which transcends time and space. Isis represents wisdom and enlightened consciousness. She is the knower of all words of power and has the power to resurrect Osiris and Horus. Nephthys represents temporal consciousness or awareness of time and space. She is related to mortal life and mortal death. This symbolism is evident in the sistrums which bear the likeness of Isis on one side and of Nephthys on the other, and the writings of Plutarch where he says that Isis represents "generation" while Nephthys represents "chaos and dissolution". Also, in the hieroglyphic texts, Isis is referred to as the "day" and Nephthys as the "night". Isis is the things that "are" and Nephthys represents the things which will "come into being and then die". Thus, the state of spiritual Enlightenment is being referred to here as Isis, and it is this enlightened state of mind which the initiate in the Osirian Mysteries (*Asar Shetaiu*) has as the goal. The Enlightenment of Osiris is the state of consciousness in which one is aware of the transient aspects of Creation (Nephthys) as well as the transcendental (Isis). Isis represents the transcendental aspect of matter, that is, matter when seen through the eyes of wisdom rather than through the illusions produced by the ego. So, an enlightened personality is endowed with dual consciousness. To become one with

Osiris means to attain the consciousness of Osiris, to become aware of the transcendental, infinite and immortal nature (Isis) while also being aware of the temporal and fleeting human nature (Nephthys).

In the *Book of the Dead* (Chap. xvii. 30), the initiate identifies with Amsu-Min and says:

> *"I am the god Amsu (or Min) in his coming forth; may his two plumes be set upon my head for me."* In answer to the question, *" Who then is this?"* the text goes on to say, *"Amsu is Horus, **the avenger of his father**, and his coming forth is his birth. The plumes upon his head are Isis and Nephthys when they go forth to set themselves there, even as his protectors, and they provide that which his head lacketh, or (as others say), they are the two exceedingly great uraei which are upon the head of their father **Tem,** or (as others say), his two eyes are the two plumes which are upon his head."*

The passage above provides an exact idea about the true nature of Isis and Nephthys. Nephthys is associated with the life which comes forth from her death in Isis. They are complementary goddess principles which operate to manifest life-death-life or the cycle of birth-death-rebirth known as reincarnation. Another important teaching presented here is that Isis and Nephthys are identified as the "the two exceedingly great uraei". They are the two forces of the Serpent Power known in India as Kundalini. The Serpent Power refers to the Life Force energy which manifests in the physical human body in the form of two opposites. In Ancient Egyptian mythology and yoga these two opposites are known as "Uatchit and Nekhebet" or "Isis and Nephthys" or "The Two Ladies". In India they are known as "Ida and Pingala". The opposites also refer to the solar pole and the lunar pole or the active and passive nature of the energies. In reality the energy is the same. It originates from the same source but it manifests as opposite due to the polarization it assumes. Thus, it may be seen as male and female. The Serpent Power energy resides at the base of the spine and when aroused through spiritual evolution (practice of yoga) it courses through the body, finally reaching the crown of the head and re-unites into its original oneness; the poles dissolve, leaving oneness of consciousness or enlightenment. (see Egyptian Yoga Guide Book 12 for more on the Serpent Power)

Horus
(Heru)
The Rebirth of the Spiritual Life - Aspiration for Freedom, the New Life of the Resurrected Soul.

Horus represents the union between Spirit (Osiris) and Creation (Isis). However, unlike Anubis, who also represents the union of Spirit and Matter, Horus represents the higher aspect of this union because Isis is the embodiment of wisdom and truth while Nephthys is the embodiment of nature and the grosser physical elements. In this aspect Horus represents the subtle spiritual realization of spirit and matter united and seen as one.

Horus is the rebirth of the Spirit. This rebirth is not a physical birth from the womb, but a rebirth of the mind. No longer is there interest in worldly pursuits which are empty and shallow. Instead, there is a burning desire to face and conquer the lower self and regain the original glory and freedom of knowing and becoming one with the Higher Self. This is symbolized by Horus regaining the throne of Upper and Lower Egypt. In doing so, he has regained mastership of the higher and the lower states of consciousness. Thus, Horus represents the union and harmonization of spirit and matter, and the renewed life of Osiris, his rebirth.

HERU (Horus) is the God of Light. Before Horus is victorious, he is a symbol of the "Dual Nature of Humankind". Horus in this aspect represents the opposite forces that are within each of us, the animal nature (passionate behavior as demonstrated by cutting off Isis' head) and the Divine. Therefore, the real battle is within each of us and not in the outer world of time and space.

Both Horus and Ra utilize the symbol of the hawk, 🦅, an animal which is swift and possesses sharpness and clarity of vision. Thus, the symbol of the hawk refers to the quality of a highly developed intellectual capacity to see what is real, true and abiding versus that which is false, fleeting and illusory. It is because of this quality of discriminative intellect that Anubis is considered as an aspect of Horus. The principles of mystical spirituality as represented by Isis, Maat and Tehuti (order, justice, peace, love, contentment, righteous action, study and reflection on the teachings, meditating on the Divine, etc.) are leading toward the truth while the egoistic values of society, as represented in the character of Set (greed, hatred, anger, lust, restlessness, etc.), lead to falsehood, pain, suffering, disappointment and frustration.

The picture of Set-Horus (page 124) shows us that the "enemy" or foe of truth (MAAT) is inside each of us. Set, the symbol of evil, is actually a part of Horus that must be conquered and sublimated. In this aspect, Set represents the "Beasts" or "Demons" we must conquer: ignorance, passions, desires, restlessness of the mind, temptation, lust, greed, depression, insecurity, fear and pain. Only in this way can the "God of Light" inside us shine through.

137

Anubis
(Anpu)
Discernment and Discriminative Knowledge of
What is Real and What is Not Real.

Anpu (Anubis) is the son of Osiris and Nephthys. He is the embalmer of the deceased (spiritual aspirant) and symbolizes the trained intellect of the aspirant, who is dead to the wisdom of divine reality and hopes to be resurrected (to discover divine reality). This implies the ability to discipline one's mind and body so as to not get caught up in the illusions or emotions of the mind. When the mind and its wavelike thought vibrations are under control, the way is open to spiritual realization in an atmosphere of peace and harmony. This peace and harmony do not necessarily imply an outer situation of calm. It does imply an inward peace which comes from understanding the implications of the wisdom teachings. Anubis represents the dawn when darkness turns to light. He watches over the balance (scales) in the hall of judgment of the *Book of Coming Forth By Day* with extreme diligence, and in the aspect of *Apuat*, he is the *Opener of the Ways* who leads souls to the *Elysian Fields in the Great Oasis*. Therefore, his great quality of *discriminative knowledge* allows the aspirant to *diligently* watch the mind in order to promote thoughts which are divinely inspired (*Shemsu Hor* - follower of Horus), instead of those which are egoistic (Setian) and tending toward nature and its perils (life, death, pain, pleasure, etc.). Anubis, as the son of Nephthys and Osiris, is therefore, a combination of gross nature (Nephthys) and the Spirit (Osiris).

It is Anubis who leads souls to the abode of the Supreme Being in the *Book of Coming Forth By Day* by constantly urging them to awaken from the dream of the world process and its illusions. Thus, Anubis should be considered as the original *Angel of Death.* The reliefs and hieroglyphs of *Anubis sitting atop the ark containing the inner-parts of Osiris* are found at the entrance or purification area of the burial chamber (chest or Ark) of the initiate, 🏺. In the *Book of Coming Forth By Day*, it is stated that Anubis appointed the *Seven Spirits, the followers of their lord Sepa*, to be protectors of the dead body of Osiris.* Sepa is the name of the chief of the Seven Spirits who guarded Osiris, and *seven* is the number of spiritual energy centers in the subtle spiritual body (Serpent Power - Kundalini Chakras). Anubis is an aspect of Horus, and Horus is the Higher Self. Therefore, the true enlightener of the Self is the Self. In this manner, it is your innermost Self who is enlightening you through your desire to practice spiritual discipline.

Horus and Set
The Struggle between the
Higher and the Lower Self - Purification.

The struggle between Horus and Set is the struggle of every human being to control the mind with its erratic desires, longings, unfulfilled expectations and disappointments. This struggle is not avoidable by anyone who is not enlightened. Some people succumb under the weight of the lower self and its desires for fulfillment. This is a pathetic condition which those people have allowed to develop due to their own indulgence in the sensual desires of the body, and also due to their ignorance of their true divine nature which is buried deep within, under the weight of the egoistic thoughts and unconscious ignorant feelings. When aspiration arises, the practice of Maat ensues until spiritual sensitivity is perfected. This process of virtuous living based on spiritual principles (Maat) serves to cleanse the heart (mind) of the impurities of the lower self and place the aspirant on the road to victory (enlightenment). When the determination to pursue the Divine arises, the struggle becomes a holy war against ignorance and illusion within one's consciousness. If this process is not understood as a struggle to overcome anger, hatred, greed, bigotry, jealousy, etc. within one's self, the energy of the struggle becomes directed to the world outside of oneself in the form of political, religious, social, ethnic, gender, etc., conflicts.

Tehuti
Reason - Link to the Higher Self.

The struggle between Horus and Set does not end with either destroying the other. Horus pursues the path of reason seeking counsel with the wisdom of Tehuti. Wisdom follows the exercise of reason and reason follows the practice of studying, questioning, reflecting and inquiring into the nature of truth. Set, the lower self, refuses to abide by the decree of wisdom but he is eventually sublimated through his own humiliation and ignorance. In the end, when the aspirant is aligned with all divine forces, the lower self can no longer struggle. The overwhelming force of the Divine pushes the lower self into a position of service rather than of mastership. This is its rightful place.

The Eye of Ra and The Eye of Horus

There are several Ancient Egyptian myths relating to the "Eye". One tells that the Eye left Ra and went into Creation and was lost. Ra (Divine Self) sent Tehuti (wisdom) to find the Eye (individual soul) and bring it back. It was through the *Magic* (wisdom teachings) of the god Tehuti that the Eye realized who it was and agreed to return to Ra. Upon its return, however, it found that Ra had replaced it with another. In order to pacify it, Ra placed it on his *brow* in the form of a *Uraeus serpent, where it could rule the world.* One variation to the story holds that the Eye left Ra and went to Nubia in the form of a Lioness or a Lynx (Hathor, in her aspect as destroyer of evil and unrighteousness). When Ra heard this, he sent the Nubian god, *Ari-Hems-Nefer* (a form of Shu), and Tehuti to bring the Eye back. They took the form of baboons (symbol of wisdom) and soon found the Eye near the Mountain of the Sunrise, where Osiris was born. The Eye refused to leave because it learned to enjoy its new existence. It was destroying those who had committed sins (plotted against Ra) while on earth. Tehuti worked his magic on the Eye and brought it back to Ra. Another variation of the story holds that Ra sent *Shu* and *Tefnut* in search of the Eye. The Eye resisted, and in the struggle, shed tears, and from the tears grew men. This is a clever play on words because the word for "tears", **Remtu,** ⬭ 𓆣 𓄿 𓏏 𓍿 𓏥, (that fell from the eyes of Ra) and the word for "men", **Reth** or **Rethu,** ⬭ ══ 𓀀 𓀁 𓏥, have similar sounds in Ancient Egyptian language.

The relationship of "tears" to "men" symbolizes the idea that humankind is the expression of the desire of the Divine Self to have experiences in the realm of time and space. Further, "tears" are a symbol of human experience. It implies that human experience is a sorrowful condition because consciousness has degraded itself to the level of gross, limited human experience in the form of an individual ego as opposed to the expansive, limitless Self. This contraction in consciousness is what allows the ego to emerge as an individual and distinct personality out of "nowhere", just as a dream personality emerges out of "nowhere". Instead of knowing itself as the immutable soul, the soul sees the ego and the world of time and space as the reality. This development would be like the ocean forgetting that it is the ocean and believing itself to be one of the waves. Therefore, instead of seeing itself as encompassing all the waves, it is concerned with its transient experience, as an individual wave, and with comparing itself to other waves.

Life is "sorrowful" from the standpoint of wisdom because even conditions that appear to be pleasurable are in reality setting the individual up for disappointment and frustration later on, because no positive situation can last indefinitely. Also, the pursuit of worldly pleasure and pain sets up mental impressions that will survive the death of the body and lead the soul to further incarnations in search of fulfillment. Therefore, the Sages say that *all life is painful to the wise.* This is why Yoga philosophy emphasizes going beyond both pleasure *and* pain in order to transcend the bondage to time and space. This can be accomplished by turning away from the world which is illusory and seeking to discover the Self.

The masses of people who do not have spiritual sensitivity put up with the world and its ups and downs due to lack of reflectiveness. Having been taught from their youth by family and society to look for happiness in the world, they do not know any better. Through the development of wisdom and reflection, the aspirant can develop an intuition which transcends pleasure and pain move beyond the world of ordinary human experience as a source of happiness. The following Ancient Egyptian teachings highlight the idea of the sorrowfulness of ordinary human experience and urge the aspirant to live according to the teachings of virtue and wisdom in order to avoid the sufferings of life.

"As joy is not without its alloy of pain, so neither is sorrow without its portion of pleasure."

"Grief is natural to the mortal world, and is always about thee; pleasure is a guest, and visiteth thee by thy invitation; use well thy mind, and sorrow shall be passed behind thee; be prudent, and the visits of joy shall remain long with thee."

"Good things cease to be good in our wrong enjoyment of them. What nature meant to be pure sweetness, are then sources of bitterness to us; from such delights arise pain, from such joys, sorrows.

"Those who give away their treasure wisely, giveth away their plagues: they that retaineth their increase, heapeth up sorrow."

Through the story of the Eye, very important mystical teachings are being conveyed. The Eye, *Udjat*, is a symbol of intuitional vision. Also, it represents the desire of the Divine to go into itself (Creation) and the subsequent forgetfulness that ensues. The resistance of the Eye to return to the divine abode is a symbol of the predicament of ordinary people who, through ignorance and intense desire, detest the idea of even considering the spiritual values of life because their hearts (minds) are consumed with passion. They are consumed with the desire to experience the pleasures of material existence. Having created the universe in itself, the Supreme Being sent its Eye (consciousness) into Creation. Consciousness then became "lost" in Creation and became the souls of human beings and all life forms, forgetting its true Self. The Eye, lost in Creation, is the human soul which is caught up in the cycle of birth-death-birth (reincarnation) due to forgetfulness and distraction (ignorance of its true nature). The Supreme Being (Ra) sent out its messenger of wisdom (Tehuti) in the forms of *Metu Neter* (ancient scriptures of wisdom) and *Sbai* (spiritual preceptor-Guru) to instruct the Eye in reference to its true nature. Having "remembered" who it was in reality, the Eye then returned to its rightful place.

The same teaching of the Eye is to be found in the story of Horus and Set where Set (ego) tore out Horus' Eye. It is Tehuti who restored the Eye through the power of magic (wisdom teaching). In this context, the whole teaching of wisdom which Tehuti applies (*Hekau* -Magic) to the Eye causes it to remember its essential nature and its glory as the Eye of Horus. Upon its return, the Eye provided Horus with the strength of will he needed to overthrow Set. This story mythologizes the journey of the human soul and its eventual redemption wherein it achieves the sublimation of the ego and attains to *Self-realization*.

In this aspect, the plight of the Eye and its subsequent restoration through the teachings of Tehuti, the transmitter of wisdom, embodies the principle of the teacher-disciple relationship though which spiritual knowledge is transmitted. We saw this same principle in the Initiation of Horus by Isis and it may be found in the Gnostic Christianity with the teachings of Jesus to his disciples and the story of Thecla as well as in the Indian Vedantic principle of the Guru-Disciple relationship such as Krishna and Arjuna and Vasistha and Rama. Tehuti is the master teacher who initiates the aspirant on the spiritual path of wisdom. In teaching others, the priest or priestess assumes the role of Tehuti. Tehuti is the *Guru* of the Eye. In Hinduism, this process is immortalized in the epics, the *Bhagavad Gita* and the *Yoga Vasistha Ramayana* scriptures. In these two scriptures, two aspirants are reminded of their divine essential nature by the Gurus who are themselves, one with the Divine Self. Gradually, they are led to realization of the Self through a process which involves the classical teachings of Yoga (wisdom, reflection and meditation). These texts are highly recommended for any serious student of Yoga scriptures.

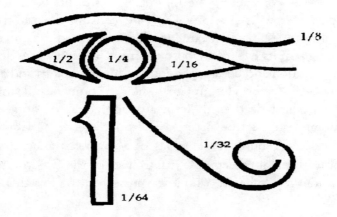

When Horus' eye (the moon) was torn out and thrown away by Set, the god Tehuti, who presides as the moon (see verse 8) found it and using the formula below, turned it into the Moon. When the parts of the Eye of Horus are added up, it gives the answer 63/64 which approximate the whole number 1. One is the number which symbolizes oneness, wholeness, all sight, all knowing, the Supreme Being, The Absolute. As long as the soul is involved in creation (matter), there will remain some small separation between the individual BA and the Universal BA, the ONE. In order to become completely unified, merged into infinity, the individual soul of the enlightened person dissolves into the Universal Soul at the time of death; this is complete ONENESS with the divine. The missing part of the Eye of Horus, 1/64, is added by Tehuti through magic.

Thus through the magic of Tehuti (wisdom), the parts (representing our consciousness) may be reconstituted to wholeness. Tehuti is an aspect of Ptah, the Cosmic Mind. In this aspect Tehuti symbolizes the higher consciousness (mind) of those humans who are attuned to the Universal (Cosmic) Mind.
Thus Tehuti speaks:

> *"I came seeking the Eye of Horus , that I might bring it back and count it. I found it (now it is) complete, counted and sound, so that it can flame up to the sky and blow above and below..."*

Therefore, through the Eye (vision, consciousness) of Tehuti (wisdom), the Eye of Horus (inner vision) may be brought back to its original place, that it may attain the heights of heaven and achieve control over the spiritual domain (above) and the realm of matter (below). Tehuti is the God who brings MAAT (truth, righteousness, justice). Thus, through wisdom and righteousness our original condition may be restored. The name for the Eye of Horus may be pronounced as *"Wedjat", "Udjat" or "Utchat"* meaning: *"the whole or restored one"* and also *"that which protects."*

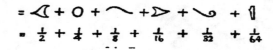

$$= \text{◁} + \text{O} + \text{⌒} + \text{▷} + \text{↶} + \text{╎}$$

$$= \frac{1}{2} + \frac{1}{4} + \frac{1}{8} + \frac{1}{16} + \frac{1}{32} + \frac{1}{64}$$

When the parts of the Eye of Horus (Udjat, left eye) is added up, the result is 63/64 which approximate the whole number 1. As long as the soul is involved in creation (matter), there will remain some small separation between the individual BA and the Universal BA, the ONE.

In the Pyramid of Unas, the Eye of Tehuti is called *"The Black Eye of Horus."* In the same text is said to Unas:

> *"Thou hast seized the two Eyes of Horus, the White Eye and the Black Eye and thou hast carried them off and set them in front of thee and they give light to thy face."*

In the saga of the struggle of Horus and Set, the most central issue is the return of the Eye to its rightful place in the "brow" of Horus. This event is synonymous with the resurrection (redemption) of the soul of Osiris (soul-initiate-aspirant), when he was killed by Set (ignorance-pride-ego). While the scriptures speak about two eyes (right and left), they are both indeed refering to the same inner spiritual vision which allows a human being to transcend the egoistic vision of life. Thus, through the restoration of spiritual vision (discovering the Eye of intuitional understanding) a human being (Osiris) is *resurrected.*

The ego in a human being is what leads him or her into positive or negative situations and also makes a person susceptible to either pain or pleasure, adversity or prosperity, in life. The Eye of intuitional vision protects one from any and all adversity and injury because once one attains intuitional vision, the light of understanding vanquishes all negative thoughts, fears and desires in the human heart which could lead a person to situations of pain and sorrow. Also, it nulifies all negativity from outside (from people or nature) which might seek to cause harm to a person either in thought, word or deed. Therefore, an enlightened human being (Sage, Saint) is beyond the pain and sorrow of life because he or she has transcended the ego itself.

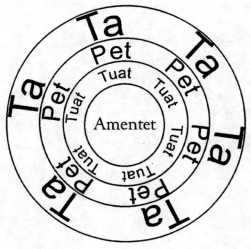

At left: A two dimensional schematic drawing of the Tuat.

OSIRIS AND THE ṬUAT

The Ancient Egyptian concept of Creation includes three realms. These are the TA, ⸻ Ⅱ (Earth), Pet, ⌐∘∘ (Heaven), and the Ṭuat ★🐍▭ ⌒◿ (the Underworld). Ṭuat is pronounced with the "Ṭ" sounding as a "D" in much the same way as the "Tao" of Taoism is pronounced "Dao". The Ṭuat is the abode of the gods, goddesses, spirits and souls. It is the realm where those who are evil or unrighteous are punished, but it is also where the righteous live in happiness. It is the "other world", the spirit realm. The Ṭuat is also known as Amenta since it is the realm of Amen (Amun). The Ṭuat is the realm Ra, as symbolized by the sun, traverses after reaching the western horizon, in other words, the movement of Ra between sunset and sunrise, i.e. at night. Some people thought that the Ṭuat was under the earth since they saw Ra traverse downward, around the earth and emerged in the east, however, this interpretation is the understanding of the uninitiated masses. The esoteric wisdom about the Ṭuat is that it is the realm of the unconscious human mind and at the same time, the realm of cosmic consciousness or the mind of God. Both the physical universe and the astral plane, the Ṭuat, are parts of that cosmic consciousness.

The Ṭuat represents Creation itself. As such it is composed of seven sections known as *Arits* or "Mansions". They may be thought of as rooms within rooms or dimensions within dimensions or planes of existence within successively higher planes of existence. These seven sections relate to the Seven Hathor Cows which are sired by Osiris in the form of Apis the *Bull of Amenti*, and they relate to the seven energy centers or levels of psycho-spiritual evolution of every human being, known as the *Serpent Power* or *Life Force Energy*. It is necessary to pass through all of these levels in order to reach the Supreme Abode. For this to be possible, the initiate must possess certain special knowledge about the passageways. Each passageway is guarded by a gatekeeper and a herald. They ask the initiate questions, and if answered correctly, they announce the new arrival and allow passage. The

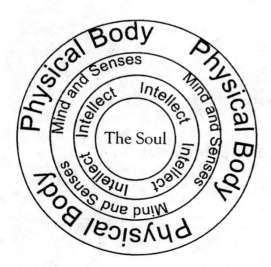

At left: A two dimensional schematic drawing of the mystical interpretation of the levels of human consciousness. Notice that they correspond to the levels of creation and that the soul is equated to the supreme abode of the Spirit (Amentet).

The intellect, mind, senses and physical body constitute the ego-personality of a human being. The soul is eternal while the ego is transient and perishable. The ego is therefore a limited and temporary expression of the soul.

145

special knowledge consists of spiritual wisdom gained from the study of spiritual scriptures blended with meditative experience (the second and third levels of religious practice). Of course, spiritual studies and meditative experiences are only possible when life is lived according to virtuous principles (Maat).

There is a special realm within the Ṭuat. This is the abode of Osiris as well as the ultimate destination of those who become enlightened. It is the realm of Supreme Peace. It is known as *Sekhet-Aaru*, or in other times, as *Amentet*. Amentet is a reference which unites the symbolism of Osiris with that of Amun (Amen) because *Tet*, 𓊽, refers to the Tet or Djed Pillar of Osiris. The Tet symbolizes the awakened human soul which is well "established" in the knowledge of the Self. *Tettetu*, 𓊽𓊽𓏤𓂋𓐍, refers to the abode of Osiris. This is what the following line from the *Egyptian Book of Coming Forth By Day*, Chapter I: 13-15, is referring to:

$$\text{[hieroglyphs]}$$

nuk Tetteti se Tetteti au am - a em Tettetu mesi - a Tettetu
"I am steadfast, son of steadfast, conceived and born in the
region of steadfastness."

This special realm is shrouded in the deepest darkness and it is untouched by the myriad of cries, dismemberments and sufferings of unrighteous souls (the enemies of Ra) as well as the cries of happiness of the righteous souls who are experiencing heavenly or pleasurable conditions according to their good deeds of the past. This part of the Ṭuat is composed of seven *Arits* or Halls. It transcends time and space as well as the mind and thoughts. It is absolute existence. The rest of the Ṭuat as well as the physical world is relative reality. In this special realm, there is no growth of any kind. There is no birth, no death and no passage of time, just eternity. This is the meaning of the following hekau-utterance from *The Egyptian Book of Coming Forth By Day*, Chapter 125:1-17:

> The Osiris, the scribe Ani (initiate), whose word is truth, saith: "I have come unto thee. I have drawn close to you in order to experience thy beauties. My hands are extended in adoration of thy name of "MAAT" (Truth). I have come. I have drawn myself to the place where the cedar tree existeth not, where the acacia tree does not put forth shoots, and where the ground neither produces grass nor herbs. Now I have entered into the place of hidden things, and I hold converse with the god Set.... Osiris, the scribe Ani, has entered into the house into the House of Osiris, and he has seen the the hidden and secret things which are therein....

That which is the place where nothing grows is the place of absolute stillness. It is a region that is devoid of forms or mental concepts of any kind. It is the primeval or celestial waters from which Creation arises. It is the place which is "hidden" from that which is in motion, the relative reality. Therefore, it is hidden to those whose minds are in constant motion due to desires, cravings, emotional attachments, greed, etc. That which is relative or temporal emanates out of that which is absolute and eternal. The relative reality emanates from this hidden place of stillness. It is to this place of stillness where one must go and have "communion" with God. When this occurs, that which is hidden is revealed.

This deepest and most dark realm of the Ṭuat is Osiris, Himself, and this is why Osiris is referred to as the "Lord of the Perfect Black" and is often depicted as being black or green of hue. It is also why Nut, Isis, and Hathor are also described as "dark-skinned"*. They are emanations from this realm of blackness which is described as a void or "*nothingness*" in the hieroglyphic papyrus entitled *The Laments of Isis and Nephthys*. This notion of nothingness is akin to the Buddhist notion of *Shunya* or the "void", which refers to the area of consciousness which is devoid of mental concepts and thoughts. When there are no thoughts or forms in the mind, it is calm, expansive and peaceful. When there are thoughts in the mind, the mental awareness is narrowed and defined in terms of concepts. If the mind is confined to these concepts and narrow forms of thought, then it is confined to that which is limited and temporal. If it eradicates its desires, cravings and illusions, then it becomes aware of the innermost reality and realizes its connection to the entire cosmos. Thus, the teaching of the Ṭuat (Amentet, Re-Stau, etc.) gives insight into the nature of the human mind. It is a description of the mental landscape, its demons (everything that leads to ignorance and mental agitation), and gods and goddesses (who represent the positive thoughts, feelings and the way to discover the abode of the innermost Self, everything that leads to peace, harmony and wisdom). Therefore, the task of a spiritual aspirant is to eradicate the concepts, agitation, desires and cravings in the mind and to discover the "hidden" innermost reality which is Hetep (Supreme Peace), eternal and pure. (*from an inscription in the temple of Denderah, Egypt)

From a higher level of understanding, the Ṭuat is the unconscious mind and Osiris is that level which transcends the thinking processes... its deepest region. It is the level of consciousness that is experienced during deep dreamless sleep. Therefore, it is the "Hidden" aspect of the human heart, and thus, it is also known as Amun.

Another very important teaching in reference to the Ṭuat or "Beautiful West" comes from the following Hymn to Amen-Re.

"Amen-Re who first was king,
The god of earliest time,
The vizier of the poor.
He does not take bribes from the guilty,
He does not speak to the witness,
He does not look at him who promises,
Amun judges the land with his fingers.
He speaks to the heart,
, He judges the guilty,
He assigns him to the East,
The righteous to the West."

The previous hymn instructs us in the wisdom that those who are judged by God to be unrighteous will not attain the coveted goal of reaching the abode the of Supreme Divinity. Instead they will be directed toward the "East". This is a clear reference to reincarnation. The "East" implies the dawn and a new life for the sun in the form of Khepri. In effect, it symbolizes the rebirth of the sun through Nut. Reincarnation is the continuous cycle of birth-death and rebirth into a new body which the soul undergoes over a period of millions of years until it is purified enough to discover and return to its original source, the Supreme Divinity. In ancient times, the Greek historian, Herodotus, recorded that the Ancient Egyptians were the first to understand and teach the wisdom in reference to reincarnation. Therefore, in order to reach the West, it is necessary to be pure of heart which implies having lived according to the principles of Maat as well as having developed reverence and devotion toward, and wisdom about, the Divine. This implies that one has lived life based on studying, reflecting, meditating and practicing the spiritual teachings.

The Characters of the Osirian Myth as
Psycho-spiritual Stages of Human Evolution.

The main characters in the Ausarian Resurrection Myth may be seen as Psycho-spiritual stages which every human being must pass through on the journey towards spiritual enlightenment. Beginning with its incarnation as the soul of Osiris, the soul becomes intoxicated and deluded by nature, and the ignorance of reality sets in wherein the base qualities of the mind are experienced. These qualities are exemplified by the character of Set. From Set at the lowest level, the psycho-spiritual awareness develops through Anubis-Maat, Horus-Hathor and Min, until it discovers and unites with the absolute, transcendental reality Osiris-Isis.

The Struggle of Horus and Set and the Impartial Supreme Self

It is notable that Ra, the Supreme Self, the Creator of the universe and father of the gods and goddesses, the one who *stands in his boat of Creation on the pedestal of Maat*, should object to Horus' coronation as the rightful heir to the throne. Upon closer reflection, this seemingly contradictory event in the epic myth (beginning with Hekau-Verse 140) reveals important mystical teachings in reference to the nature of the Self.

It must be remembered that both Horus and Set are Ra's children. Both of them have emanated from Ra and therefore, both of them are part of Ra. Therefore, even though Set represents evil and has even committed murder, he is recognized as being part of the Supreme Being who has the innate potentiality to realize his own divinity and to change his life for the good instead of for evil and selfishness. Thus, it is not conceivable that God should want to allow those who are unrighteous to lead the world, but the intention, through the process of the struggle of life, is to transform evil into good.

Horus, on the other hand, is unproved and young. Although he is the rightful heir to the throne by birthright and has been taught the mysteries of the universe and trained in the magical powers by Isis and Tehuti, he is still not worthy of leadership. True leadership is not a right which can be given by blood relation, filial relation or book learning. It is a right which is acquired through hard work in self-development. The struggle of life (as symbolized by the struggle of Horus and Set) is the proving ground for Horus in which his divine qualities are drawn out. In a real sense, Creation is set up to provide every individual with struggles, through which opportunies arise for the person to rise above the pettiness of the ego in order to discover the sublime nature of the inner self and its infinite powers. If there were no struggles for a human being to face, there would be no achievement and no enlightenment.

In spiritual terms, Horus' ascendance to the throne is a metaphor of spiritual enlightenment. Spiritual enlightenment cannot occur until there is a struggle between the Higher Self and the lower self. Thus, Ra's refusal to accept Horus was part of a plan to provide for the development of Horus' and Set's spiritual consciousness. In the life of every spiritual aspirant there are struggles, conflicts and challenges which afford him or her the opportunity to choose the path of enlightenment or the path of egoism. When the path of enlightenment is chosen (controlling anger, forgiveness, chastity, introspection, purity in thoughts, virtuous action, truthfulness, universal love, detachment, etc.), the ego begins to subside and spiritual consciousness blossoms. When the path of egoism is chosen (anger, hate, greed, lust, mental unrest, pleasure seeking, excessive extroversion, attachment to material objects and love which is limited to family, craving for fame, arrogance, disrespect, etc.), then the soul becomes more and more bound to the ignorance which leads it to experience intensified situations of disappointment, anguish and reincarnation. Thus, when the ego is intensified, bondage to ignorance is intensified. When the ego is being controlled through the process of spiritual discipline (living life on the basis of spiritual principles), the struggle of good and evil and truth and falsehood leads to spiritual enlightenment and an expansion of consciousness, leading to freedom from the bonds of ignorance and mortal consciousness.

This hekau also points to the fact that no matter how evil a being appears to be, there is always the innate possibility for attaining spiritual enlightenment if there is sincere application to spiritual disciplines. If there is a sincere desire to atone for the sinful behavior of the past, there is opportunity for Self-discovery. When this Self discovery begins to occur, the ignorance which led to sinful behavior becomes eradicated and the personality which committed the sins in the past becomes transformed by the forces of Isis (wisdom) and Maat (virtue). The light from the Self has only been dimmed by the heaviness of the impurities of the heart. Once the impurities are cleansed, the true, divine personality, the Higher Self, emerges.

Osiris-Nephthys
(Spirit and Nature)

The relationship between Nephthys and Osiris gives deep insight into the innermost desires of the human heart. Nephthys is the very embodiment of nature. As such, she is devoted to Osiris, because Osiris (Supreme Being, the Spirit) is the source and cause of all phenomenal existence (nature). Thus the desire of Nephthys to unite with Osiris in reality represents the innermost desire of the soul in every human being to unite with God. Osiris is the embodiment of the Self (the Spirit), and it is the innate nature of the Spirit to unite with Nature. Thus nature and the Spirit are in love with each other, and nowhere is this better expressed in Ancient Egyptian iconography than in the images of Geb and Nut, through the mythology surrounding their union and separation. This relationship between

150

Nature and the Spirit is also paramount in the Tantric symbolism of Hindu mythology in the form of Shiva (God, the Spirit) and Shakti (Nature). This is the cause of the proliferation of the myriad forms of life on earth and throughout the universe. Nature is the form or outer expression and the Life Force within nature is an expression of the Divine Spirit.

In this respect, the union between Osiris and Nephthys cannot be seen as an illicit or adulterous relationship. It is to be understood as the symbol of the Soul (Osiris) in every human being which has become intoxicated, as it were, by the promise of human experience. It is a union which occurs based on the innermost urges of the heart, however, it is a movement based on ignorance of the truth about one's true identity. When the intellectual capacity for reason in a human being is clouded by ignorance, the desires of the ego hold sway over the feelings, thoughts and actions of the soul. Thus, the desire to unite with the Self, instead of being understood as a need to discover (unite with) the Higher Self, becomes degraded into a movement towards indulgence in sexuality as an attempt to unite with another person or the acquisition of material possessions in order to possess (unite with) them. This movement becomes the source of negative qualities such as jealousy, envy, greed, vanity, conceit and narcissism. Based on the erroneous idea, propagated by society, that life is to be lived for the purpose of indulging in sexual desire, amassing wealth and possessions, and gaining fame, people constantly seek to engender situations which are considered prosperous in the form of sensual pleasures and egoistic indulgences which only lead to more psychological pain and disappointment, as well as to physical and mental agitation and depletion. The relationship between Osiris and Nephthys represents the delusion of the mind which leads to infatuation with the transient forms of nature and which creates mental unrest and weakness of will. These are the gross expressions of dullness in the human mind which oppose the movement towards spiritual enlightenment. They lead toward death and dismemberment of consciousness, rather than toward wholeness and completeness.

Set
(Slave to the Lower Self)

Set represents the human condition wherein a person is under the control of his/her ignorant mind, senses and ego. This is the most degraded state of human existence. The lower self and its qualities hold sway over the mind and every aspect of the person's life. The qualities of Set develop in a person when there is dedication of one's thoughts to worldly or material goals and towards selfish pleasures and self-centeredness. This is symbolized by his marriage to Nephthys (earth, death, decay, etc.). Throughout the story, Set's desire for Isis is also expressed. Like Nephthys' desire for Osiris, Set is desirous of Isis, but this desire is of an impure nature. Set does not want Isis for who she is, but as a possession to be held and experienced in the gross way as one might possess property or chattel.

Set's intellect, being clouded by the pressure of desire, renders him powerless against the strategies of Isis and he ultimately fails in all his attempts to possess her. Discovering Isis can only be achieved by putting the desires of the lower nature in a subordinate position and developing an increasing understanding of the higher reality beyond the egoistic desires, feelings and thoughts of the lower self.

Set's attempted assault on Horus is also an expression of the same movement of the distorted desire to unite with the Higher Self (Horus). As an expression of his uncontrolled pride, vanity, conceit, and ignorance, Set is compelled to do whatever is necessary to achieve his object of desire. The movement in ignorance (Set) is a metaphor for the soul which is beset and overpowered by egoism and desires of the lower nature. Negative thoughts deplete one's willpower and the ability to reason clearly. The negative thoughts, those based on ignorance, desire, greed, hatred, lust, etc., are vices or fetters which bind the soul to negative experiences. The ego constantly seeks to impregnate, as it were, the unconscious mind, with selfish desires. If the ignorance is strong enough and the mind is weakened by the negative desires, it will be susceptible to the negative thoughts which become implanted as seeds of desire. However, if the mind is nurtured by self-knowledge and wisdom, it can capture the seed of negativity and neutralize it, while at the same time establishing the seeds of understanding, love, and spiritual energy. This is the deeper significance of the sexual struggle between Set and Horus. Set, the ego, is to be impregnated with virtue in the form of positive feelings, self-knowledge, devotion towards the Divine, righteousness, universal love, contentment, peace, etc. The end result of this impregnation is the spiritualization of the ego as symbolized by the emergence of the sundisk of Horus on Set's brow. Spiritualization of the ego implies that the ego becomes aware of the deeper roots of its own existence. It becomes humble as the discovery emerges that it is only a reflection of the true Self. Self-knowledge and wisdom (Isis) cannot be achieved by brute force or egoistic schemes. It requires a movement toward self-control, inner reflection, study of the teachings, peacefulness, self-lessness, honesty, truthfulness, and devotion towards the Divine.

The desire for objects and situations for the purpose of deriving happiness from the world of human experience is the source of all negative qualities in a human being. The inability to satisfy the desires leads to anger and hatred towards the person or situation which is perceived to be the obstacle toward achieving the object of desire. This flaw in the character of Set was evinced in his negative attitude towards Horus, Isis, Osiris, and anyone else who tried to come between him and the throne of Egypt. Every human being desires to discover the inner reality, to create a heaven as it is experienced in the innermost reaches of the heart. When the desire for self-discovery and creativity becomes degraded in a human being, it expresses as an abnormal desire for sex and sensual pleasures which can be gained through personal relationships, possessions and social acclamation. When the desire of self-discovery is understood and the proper practice of yoga is promoted, the desires for sex and material possessions naturally assume their proper place in life. Once it is understood that the happiness which one experiences through relationships or acquiring objects is only a small fragment of the happiness of Enlightenment, the practice of yoga assumes priority in your life. Under these conditions, life can become more harmonious, peaceful and productive. The soul engenders a movement towards expansion and creativity in consciousness rather than a desire for procreation and the pleasures of the senses. Expansion in consciousness implies the discovery, in greater and greater degrees, that the higher reality, the spiritual essence within, is greater, abiding and more fulfilling than the transient pleasures of the mind and senses. This is the mystical process of sex sublimation.

When society is governed by the desires of the lower nature, disharmony and criminality are engendered. These desires, based on ignorance and lack of reasoning, allow feelings of racism, sexism and egoism to flourish. In this condition, people come to feel they are individuals who have a right to own property and people, as well as to hurt others who are "below" them as measured by physical strength, wealth or fame. Further, it engenders a feeling that others, as well as nature, are objects for one's own egoistic aims. Then it becomes possible to damage, maim, kill or destroy whatever is in the way of one's acquiring or dispossessing others from (stealing) the object of desire. When society is based on the principles of spiritual truth, the lower nature is sublimated and it evolves into a great tool for spiritual and material achievements in the forms of the arts, which stirs and inspires the heart, as well as great accomplishments in science which benefit all life, and leadership, both secular and non-secular, which brings out the best in humanity by promoting opportunities for all to discover their full potential in an atmosphere of caring, understanding and universal love.

Consider the following. When you desire some object or situation and you develop attachment towards that thing, you are actually allowing that thing to control you. Many people learn that they can only feel happy if they get something they desire. Therefore, if they can't get it, there is anger and frustration. If per chance they do succeed, they develop greed and want more. Both succeeding and failing leave the mind in a state of agitation, and when there is mental agitation, there cannot be clarity of vision or spiritual awareness, but only egoism and the struggle to fulfill one desire after the next. Thus, when there is no mental peace, there is no real peace. Therefore, what most people consider to be rest, pleasure and relaxation is in reality a modified form of mental agitation which temporarily creates the feeling of satisfaction or contentment, but which soon after leads the person on a new quest to satisfy a new desire. From a mythological standpoint, sin is to be understood as the absence of wisdom which leads to righteousness and peace and the existence of ignorance which leads to mental unrest and the endless desires of the mind. Sin operates in human life as any movement which works against self-discovery, and virtue is any movement towards discovering the essential truth of the innermost heart. The state of ignorance will end only when the mind develops a higher vision. It must look beyond the illusions of human desire and begin to seek something more substantial and abiding. This is when the aspirant develops an interest in spirituality and the practice of order, correctness, self-improvement and intellectual development. These qualities are symbolized by MAAT, and Anubis is the symbol of the discerning intellect which can see right from wrong, good from evil, truth from untruth, etc.*For more on the teachings of Tantrism, the role of sexuality in spiritual life, see the *Egyptian Yoga Guide Book #3, Egyptian Tantra Yoga: Sexual Energy and The Evolution of Human Consciousness.*

Anubis
(Sheti - Saa - Maat)

Sheti, ⬭ ⌣ ⤵ ⸗, means "Spiritual discipline or program, to go deeply into the mysteries, to study the mystery teachings and literature profoundly, to penetrate the mysteries". Saa, ▤⊠*, refers to the quality of the developing intellectual ability which begins to understand the nature of Divine reality. It implies the study of the wisdom teachings and an increasing understanding of their deeper meanings as well as an emphasis on practicing the spiritual values of life and controlling the mind and senses. This stage also implies the practice of virtuous deeds which will serve to purify the mind by allowing it to feel useful and positive while promoting harmony in the environment and society. Such a lifestyle of virtue, righteousness and order is presided over by MAAT. Anubis is an aspect of Horus and embodies the initial qualities of spiritual aspiration. The Ancient Egyptian spiritual texts have given ten qualities which are essential for spiritual initiation. Anubis is a primary deity representing qualities 1, 2, 3, 9 and 10 while Horus represents 4, 5, 6, 7, and 8. *(for more on Saa, see the book *The Keys to The Mysteries* by Dr. Muata Ashby)

(1) "Control your thoughts",
(2) "Control your actions",
(3) "Have devotion of purpose",
(4) "Have faith in your master's ability to lead you along the path of truth",
(5) "Have faith in your own ability to accept the truth",
(6) "Have faith in your ability to act with wisdom",
(7) "Be free from resentment under the experience of persecution" (Bear insult),
(8) "Be free from resentment under experience of wrong" (Bear injury),
(9) "Learn how to distinguish between right and wrong",
(10) "Learn to distinguish the real from the unreal."

A spiritual aspirant or initiate may be defined as: anyone seriously seeking spiritual development who chooses to enter (be initiated) into a lifestyle directed toward spiritual realization rather than perishable worldly attainments.

Anubis is often related to the dog or jackal deity. The jackal deity has two aspects, *Anubis* and *Apuat*. Anubis is the embalmer, the one who prepares the initiate, the *Shti* (one who is in his coffin-the body). As a neophyte, the initiate is considered to be dead (a mummy) since he/she does not have conscious realization of the transcendental reality beyond the ego-personality. He or she is an ordinary mortal human being in consciousness. At this stage the aspirant must be prepared through virtue and physical purification to receive the teachings, because without this preparation, the highest teachings would fall on deaf ears. The next aspect is *Apuat, The opener of the Ways*. In this context Anubis represents vigilance and the constant practice of discrimination and watchfulness (mindfulness) over the ego-self. Apuat represents the development of intuitional realization which unfolds within the human heart in degrees. Gradually, through the practices of discrimination and watchfulness, the ego-self becomes effaced and reveals the true self as one with Osiris.

Anubis represents: "Control of the thoughts", "Control of one's actions", and "Devotion of purpose", "Learning how to distinguish between right and wrong," "Learning to distinguish the real from the unreal". Anubis is solely devoted to Osiris, and as such, represents the process of concentration and oneness of vision which lead to Divine awareness.

Anubis also implies dispassion and detachment from worldly desires. This should not be misinterpreted as a pathetic development. Detachment from the world implies a keen understanding that the world and all objects in it cannot bring happiness to the soul, because they are transient and fleeting. Since the essence of all objects is the Self, in detaching from objects you are merely detaching from the reflection of the Self and attaching to the real Self behind the objects. From the perspective of spirituality, the act of detaching from objects does not mean simply giving up objects. Rather, it means you now have a more profound way of seeing and understanding objects. You now have deeper insight into the true nature of the object; it is this understanding which allows you to detach from objects. You understand they are temporal creations from the source of all existence, your very own heart, as in a dream, and therefore are not abiding realities that can or should be possessed or owned.

In the beginning it may be painful to leave the worldly attachments to seek a higher reality in much the same way that it is painful for a child to leave the warmth and safety of home. However, when the child spends time in school or goes out into the world, he or she begins to outgrow the need for constant attachment to childish thoughts and needs. Once the new reality is discovered, the old fears and attachments are transformed in a normal human being. The period of experiencing pain ends in time and the joy of freedom and the possibility of exploring the world overpowers the pain of loss. In spiritual evolution, the wisdom teachings and mystical practices lead to decreasing dependency upon worldly attachments. This movement engenders an expansion in consciousness and a unique form of inner peace, called bliss. The movement in detachment from worldly objects and egoistic values allows the mind to develop will power, clarity of thinking and devotion toward the Divine. Clarity of thinking promotes intellectual knowledge which in turn leads to intuitional wisdom and spiritual realization.

The qualities of Anubis assist in the spiritual movement since an intellectual grasp of mystical philosophy is necessary for progress on the spiritual path. However, intellectual sophistication, sharpness and subtlety are only a means and not an end in itself. Spiritual evolution necessitates a transcendental movement beyond the level of the ordinary human intellect (the level of the mind and senses).

Knowing something intellectually is like learning a subject in school. You can learn about certain facts from books but what do you really know? You may learn about China but is it the same as visiting China and experiencing the sights, sounds and smells for yourself? Intellectual knowledge is like learning about China from the book whereas transcendental knowledge is like visiting China. Intellectual knowledge is indirect knowledge. True knowledge comes from direct experience. The object of the teachings is to lead the aspirant to first understand the teachings, and then to experience their truths.

Modern science (Quantum Physics) tells us that the universe is not solid matter but energy in different states of vibration or order. Therefore, what the mind and senses perceive is not nature in its true form. The Sages and Saints of old have maintained this same teaching for thousands of years. This principle is the source of all spiritual philosophies and all ideas about the afterlife and the spiritual realms. The Sages hold that when an individual leads himself or herself to cleanse the mind from its erroneous ideas based on ignorance and worldly impressions gathered from the body, mind, and senses, a new transcendental reality becomes evident. The difference in spiritual evolution between intellectual knowledge and transcendental knowledge is that transcendental knowledge (to Know Thyself) requires going beyond one's ordinary egoistic impressions, thoughts, and ideas about oneself, as well as transcending the senses. This is possible through the practices of virtuous living (according to Maat), studying the wisdom teachings and through meditation. It is one thing to learn about the Ṭuat but it is another thing to go there and experience it. However, the Ṭuat is a realm which transcends ordinary concepts of time and space, which are concepts of the human mind. Therefore, no location can be given for the Ṭuat. It can only be discovered when the mind is rendered subtle and devoid of impurities. Thus Sages and Saints have enjoined several disciplines for cleansing the mind and body so as to allow spiritual awareness to unfold. These disciplines form the basis of yoga practices and religious rituals as well as meditation. In this sense *The Book of Coming Forth By Day* is a collection of rituals designed to turn the mind's attention away from worldly distractions, thereby allowing the soul to behold the transcendental truth.

Horus-Hathor
(Righteous action - Virtue - Spiritual Power and Sexual Energy.)

Horus embodies the following principles of Initiation: "Have faith in your master's ability to lead you along the path of truth", "Have faith in your own ability to accept the truth", "Have faith in your ability to act with wisdom", "Be free from resentment under the experience of persecution" (Bear insult), "Be free from resentment under experience of wrong" (Bear injury). Horus developed faith in his master, Isis. Even after being slighted by the Ennead and after being insulted by Set, Horus was able to go beyond the egoistic feeling of resentment. He steadfastly pursued Maat, righteousness, and thus was able to succeed in the end.

Horus represents the state of consciousness wherein there is awareness of the underlying unity of spirit and matter. Having been nurtured by Isis (study of the wisdom teachings) and encouraged by Osiris (experience of communion with the Divine through meditation), the soul's latent divine qualities and boundless power emerge. This stage implies an attenuation of the negative qualities and an unfoldment of the divine glory in the human heart. At this stage the soul becomes associated with Hathor, the power of the Divine, and is able to act heroically in all areas of life in order to succeed against evil in the form of inimical personalities and adverse situations, but more importantly, in the face of negative thoughts and feelings.

Hathor represents the power of the Sun (God), therefore, associating with her implies coming into contact with the boundless source of energy which sustains the universe (God). This movement implies performing actions which are in accord with Maat, with the mental clarity of Anubis, and backed up by the wisdom of Isis. When actions are in line with Divine Will (Maat), there are boundless positive resources and energies which unfold. When there is unrighteousness, mental unrest, anxiety and ignorance, depletion of energy occurs. Therefore, making contact with Hathor implies the development of inner harmony which engenders clarity of vision that will lead to the discovery of what is righteous and what is unrighteous. A mind which is constantly distracted and beset with fetters (anger, hatred, greed, lust, selfishness, etc.) cannot discern the optimal course in life; it becomes weak willed and unrighteous thoughts and actions result. Unrighteous actions lead to adverse situations, and adverse situations lead to pain and sorrow in life.

The principle of sexuality is another important element in the symbolism of Hathor. She does not represent promiscuity or vicarious sexual pleasure, but the very purest form of sexual energy. Sexual energy is the source of all forms of creative action. It impels all life to move, to create. The question is whether this movement will be towards progress and positive development or degradation and de-evolution. Sexual energy is the most basic instinct in human nature. It is engendered from the primordial need of the soul to unite and make itself whole. When the energy is led by ignorance, such as in the case of one who is not aware of the deeper essence of the Self within, the energy externalizes and becomes refracted or distorted, as it were, and the person seeks to unite, sexually with others, or with objects by possessing them. However, this form of activity cannot bring inner satisfaction because it is fleeting and limited. Therefore, when the sexual energy is sublimated by first gaining a deeper understanding of it, and then by controlling and harnessing it, this force can be directed towards the process of spiritual discovery, wherein the lower nature composed of sexual desires gives way to a higher form of love for the Divine. Thus the lower self is led to unite with its own true source, the Higher Self.

This process of sex sublimation involves the control of sexual energy, and its direction towards an integrated development of mind, body and spirit, wherein the emotional and intellectual faculties of the mind are gradually expanded to encompass all creation. This is why Hathor represents the principle of sexual energy and the principle of destruction at the same time. Used in the proper way, sexual energy destroys evil and ignorance while at the same time bringing the highest experience of peace and inner fulfillment. When used in an improper way, sexual energy destroys the physical constitution by depleting its vitality, will power, reasoning ability and the ability to experience true mental peace. Overindulgence in sexuality leaves the mind longing for more pleasure, and the pursuit of pleasure clouds the intellect and agitates the unconscious, engendering more thoughts and desires. The inability to fulfill these desires leads to frustration and spiritual stagnation.

As old age advances, the mind which has not discovered a deeper reality beyond the values of the masses, which stress sexual prowess, worldly enjoyments, financial wealth and social popularity, is left in a state of frustration and despair, because none of these can be maintained as the body moves closer to death. At the time of death the deep feelings of unrest and ignorance in the unconscious mind are carried forth into the afterlife and become the basis for experiencing hellish conditions. Therefore, it is wise to develop a movement in life which leads to the discovery of a deeper, more stable essence in life which is not dependent upon the transient nature of life in the phenomenal universe, but which transcends it. When true peace, inner awareness and fulfillment are discovered in life, these qualities are carried forth and become the basis for experiencing heavenly conditions. This is the purpose yoga and mystical spirituality, and it is the ideal in a society which is based on the principles of MAAT.

The *Menit* (menat) necklace is a distinctive ornament of the Ancient Egyptian goddess. The Ancient Egyptian word "Menit" is synonymous with "Hathor", and its root is the Ancient Egyptian word for "nurse". It is held to be the combination of the male and female generative (sexual) energies. So it is the goddess who transmits the Life Force energy to the initiate. This energy arouses a movement toward spiritual aspiration and self-discovery leading to Enlightenment.*

*For more on the teachings of Tantrism, the role of sexuality in spiritual life, see the *Egyptian Yoga Guide Book #3 Egyptian Tantra Yoga: Sexual Energy and The Evolution of Human Consciousness.*

Min
(Self-control - Sex-sublimation)

In the *Book of the Dead* (Chap. xvii. 30), the initiate identifies with Amsu-Min and says:

> *"I am the god Amsu (Min) in his coming forth; may his two plumes be set upon my head for me."* In answer to the question, *" Who then is this?"* the text goes on to say, *"Amsu is Horus, the avenger of his father, and his coming forth is his birth. The plumes upon his head are Isis and Nephthys when they go forth to set themselves there, even as his protectors, and they provide that which his head lacketh, or as others say, they are the two exceedingly great uraei which are upon the head of their father Tem, or as others say, his two eyes are the two plumes which are upon his head."*

Min is the aspect of Horus in the form of the victorious savior (vindicator) of his father's honor. Hathor is his companion and female aspect, whose passion and restorative influence provides healing and strength to allow Horus to continue the struggle against Set. Both of them represent the idea of aroused and sublimated sexual energy.

The passage above also shows that Isis and Nephthys are the forces of life and death which manifest the power of Amsu (Horus).

The state of "Horus-Min" consciousness, when Horus is victorious, is the goal of all spiritual efforts. It is the ultimate objective of all spiritual-religious traditions. It means being triumphant over ignorance in the form of egoism and the fetters of Set (anger, hatred, greed, lust, selfishness, desire, elation, depression, conceit, etc.). At this stage, there is no possibility for the lower nature to sway the mind of a person. Now the lower self is like a slave to the Higher Self. The freedom from the fetters allows the mind experience boundless *Sekhem*, Life Force energy-power, and to be at peace *Hetep,* ▵. This peace and harmony allows the mind to see beyond the veil of ordinary human consciousness, in effect, to behold the Divine Self, Osiris.

Osiris-Isis
(Pure spirit - Absolute - Transcendental - Supreme Self)

Ancient Egyptian mysticism expresses the true nature of every human being as composed of a soul, an astral or subtle body and a physical body. The Soul (the Self) is singular and pure. Therefore, it is likened to a dot. The soul seemingly develops a mental process and through this process, a form of ignorance or forgetfulness of its true nature develops. The soul becomes submerged, as it were, in the sea of thoughts and impulses from the mind and senses. It remains as a latent witness in the deep unconscious level of the mind. It is caught in the powerlessness produced by the web of ignorance it has spun for itself. Through the mind and senses, it experiences the universe, life, death, happiness, sadness, etc. However, in reality, the soul is never touched or affected by the occurrences of life, but nevertheless it experiences them as being real and compelling. The belief in mortal existence as being real prevents it from discovering the deeper, transcendental reality, therefore, the soul travels on a journey which involves many experiences of birth, life and death as well as the myriad of experiences which occur in dreams and in the after death state (Heaven or Hell).

Osiris

(The Immortal Self)

Isis   Nephthys

(Life)   (Death)

The mystical teaching outlined above is the reason why every human being is referred to as Osiris. The innermost Self of every human being is none other than the Supreme Self who has assumed the form of all living and non-living things. The highest task of every life form is to throw off the veil of ignorance and to discover the Higher Self within. The picture of Osiris, Isis and Nephthys in the inner shrine (see cover) is a mystical representation of human existence. Osiris is accompanied by Isis and Nephthys, who, as previously discussed, represent life and death, respectively. However, Osiris, while encompassing them, at the same time also transcends them. In other words, they are emanations of him, but in reality, this expression of duality in the forms of Isis and Nephthys is only a projection of himself. In reality Osiris, the Soul, is essentially one and whole. Even while appearing to be dual, transient and constantly moving and changing, the innermost reality of the Soul is oneness, constancy, uniformity and peacefulness. Therefore, while it appears that there are three principles (Osiris-Isis-Nephthys), in reality there is only one being, one consciousness, in existence. This Transcendental Self is also known as *Nebertcher* or "The All Divinity". This singular Supreme Being has caused an image (the universe) to appear in the vast ocean of consciousness (the Tuat), just as a movie projector causes an image to project upon the surface of a screen. In the same way, the experiences of birth, life, death, success, failure, etc. are produced by every individual and these experiences do not touch or affect the innermost Self, the Soul, of an individual. However, just as a person can become lost in the action of a movie and identify with a character who is experiencing happiness or sorrow in the movie performance to the extent that they themselves become temporarily happy or sad, the human soul forgets its true nature and sees itself as an individual entity cut off from the rest of the universe. It has become lost in the experiences of human life. However, regardless of the depths of ignorance which the soul may reach, it is possible for every individual to undo the web of confusion in the human heart through the process of yoga.

Osiris and Isis are in reality one entity. The Self (Osiris) and the wisdom of its own self (Isis) are in reality one and the same. When the individual soul transcends the state of Horus, having lived life based on Maat, having acquired the wisdom of Isis and having vindicated Osiris, having become enlightened as to the Divine Self within, there is complete and absolute union with the Divine Self, the underlying reality behind all physical and non-physical existence as well as the innermost reality of the human heart at the time of the death of the physical body .

What is The *Pert em Hru?*

The teachings of mystical spirituality are contained in the most ancient writings of Egypt, even those preceding the Dynastic or Pharaohnic period (5,500 B.C.E.- 300 B.C.E). All of them contain some portion of the Osirian myth and refer to the religious practitioner (be they male or female) as "The Osiris". The most extensive expositions of the philosophy may be found in the writings which have in modern times been referred to as "The Egyptian Book of the Dead."

"The Book of the Dead" was originally known as "Rw Prt M Hrw" or "Ru Pert em Heru" by the Ancient Egyptians, which is translated as: "The Utterances for Going Forth into the Light." In Egyptian mythology, Heru (Horus) not only means "Light", but also "Day". Day implies the light of knowledge and spiritual enlightenment as opposed to the darkness of ignorance and human degradation. In fact, Day and Light are two of the most important attributes of the gods Horus and Ra, who represent the the highest potential of every human being. This symbolism is reinforced by the fact that both Horus and Ra utilize the symbol of the Hawk, 🦅, an animal which is swift and possesses sharpness and clarity of vision, and the same symbol of the hawk is used to refer to the human soul. Thus, the text is directed toward enlightening the human soul as to its true nature, allowing one to become aware of his/her deeper Divine essence. Therefore, the title may also read more accurately as "The Book of Coming Forth By Day" or "The Guide for Becoming Horus".

The writings were named "The Egyptian Book of the Dead" by modern Egyptologists. These Egyptologists had obtained them from the modern day dwellers of the area of north-east Africa who had found them buried with the remains of the Ancient Egyptian dead. In the interest of simplicity, consistency and accuracy, the name "Egyptian Book of Coming Forth by Day" will be used throughout this text. More importantly, with respect to the goal of attaining Enlightenment, the use of title "Egyptian Book of Coming Forth by Day" over "The Egyptian Book of the Dead" has far reaching psycho-mythological, and hence, psychospiritual implications. The word "Day" represents, light, knowledge and rebirth while the word "Dead" brings images of decay, destruction and finality. In addition, in the Ancient Egyptian system of yoga and religion, there is no death, only a transformation based on one's actions, thoughts and innermost consciousness while living in the physical world.

The *Pyramid Texts* and the *Book of Coming Forth By Day* are similar in scripture and purpose. In fact, the origins of the latest versions of the *Book of Coming Forth By Day*, which were composed toward the end of Ancient Egyptian civilization, can be traced to the earliest versions. The *Pyramid Texts* are hieroglyphic writings contained in the pyramid tombs of the Kings of the early dynastic period (5,000 B.C.E.). The *Pyramid Texts* and the Books of Coming Forth By Day are collections of utterances and rituals, originally recorded in hieroglyphic scripture and later on in hieratic, demotic and Coptic scripture. They were designed to lead the initiate to transform his/her consciousness from human to divine by purifying the mind with wisdom about Pa Neter (The God), the Transcendental Supreme Self, and the neters (divine forces in the universe). Each of these constitute major treatises of Ancient Egyptian mystical philosophy, and together they constitute an advanced, holistic system of spiritual development, comparable to the Yoga-Vedanta philosophy of India. All of these have as their main purpose, to effect the union of the consciousness of the individual human being with the transcendental Self, the Supreme Being.

Over the long period of time (over 5,000 years) of the Ancient Egyptian dynastic civilization which lasted over 5,000 years, the teachings presented in the *Book of Coming Forth By Day* evolved from simple principles to a collection of utterances often referred to as chapters or spells. Due to invasions, political conflicts and corruption in the late history of Ancient Egypt, the original teachings became corrupted as they were edited, re-written and added to by priests and priestesses who were not aware of the original teachings of certain symbols and mystical teachings. Current Egyptological scholarship reckons the total number of chapters or utterances which are to be found in all of the surviving Books of Coming Forth By Day to be 192. However, different papyri contain different amounts of chapters and some contain newly composed chapters. For example, the Turin Papyrus contains only 165 chapters out of the possible 192. So there is no one late version of the *Book of Coming Forth By Day* which contains the entire collection of utterances or which presents them in a completely correct manner as to order or content, though it is possible to trace the teachings given in the earlier times to the utterances presented in the later texts. Some of these later texts, especially those containing chapters 1, 17, 23, 30b, 64, 82, 83, 125, 137a, 174, 175, 177 and 178, along with their vignettes, serve as exegesis (clarification, elucidation) for the earlier texts. The earlier texts, specifically those relating to the founding myth of Osiris-Isis-Horus and the Pyramid Texts which constitute the earliest known versions of the rituals of Coming Forth By Day, are the most important sources for deriving the true essence and practice of Shetaut Asar-Aset-Heru.

Christianity and The Osirian Religion

If you have practiced or studied Christianity, you will have noticed many similarities to the Osirian Mystery. Some of the most important similarities are the virgin birth of a savior, the persecution of the child who was born to be the rightful heir, the torture, murder and subsequent resurrection of the savior and the ritual of the Eucharist.

In much the same manner that Jesus was born of a "virgin birth", Horus was also. Unlike an ordinary human conception which occurs when a woman's egg is fertilized by the man's sperm, Horus was conceived by Isis when she received the spirit of Osiris. Osiris' body was dead, but the love and devotion of Isis brought him back to life and then she was able to draw the spiritual seed which engendered the birth of Horus. Thus Horus represents the union of the spirit of God with Creation itself.

Like Jesus, Horus was forced to flee his homeland in order to seek safety from the murderous ruler (king) who wanted to remain as the undisputed monarch for life. The torture, passion and death of Osiris is paralleled by that of Jesus. Symbolically they both represent the human soul which incarnates into human form and experiences suffering and death at the hands of egoism, in the form of Set and his associates in the case of Osiris, and Pontius Pilate, the Roman governor and their associates in the case of Jesus.

One reason for the similarities between Christianity and the Osirian religion is that early Christianity developed in Ancient Egypt. This is evinced by the writings of the Christian and Jewish Gnostics who lived in Ancient Egypt and followed the Ancient Egyptian mystery teachings, incorporating them into the developing beliefs of Judaism and Christianity.

According to ancient Jewish tradition, the Ark of the Covenant was a portable wooden chest which was adorned with gold. It contained the two stone tablets on which the Ten Commandments, given to Moses by God, had been inscribed. The

Ark was held as the most sacred shrine of ancient Israel since it symbolized God's covenant with the Jewish people. Only the high priest was allowed to look upon it; no one else could touch it. King Solomon built a tabernacle to house the Ark, but it was destroyed in 586 BCE, and there are no further records of the original Ark remaining. In today's synagogues, the Holy Ark is a recess or closet in which the sacred scrolls of the congregation are kept. The Ancient Egyptian religion of Osiris also used an Ark. It was used to keep the pieces of the body of the dismembered Osiris. There are many surviving pictures and sculptures of the Egyptian Ark which often show Anubis sitting on it in the form of a guardian. The measurements given for the Ark are similar in all respects to the stone chest which may still be seen in the "Kings Chamber" of the Great Pyramid in Egypt. The stone chest was used for initiation rites and meditation exercises in Ancient Egypt. The "Coffined One" (the initiate assuming the place of Osiris) would be led to achieve greater and greater levels of Enlightenment through the use of special wisdom and meditation techniques, along with controlled cosmic forces harnessed by the pyramid itself.

Having fascinated scholars ever since their discovery in 1945, the 52 Gnostic texts found at Nag Hammadi, Egypt, which date back to the time of the biblical Jesus have redefined the manner in which the social climate during the time of Jesus is being viewed. Up to the time of their discovery, it was known that many sects of Christian groups existed in ancient times throughout Asia Minor and in the city of Alexandria in Lower Egypt. These groups were considered to be outcasts and heretics by the Roman Catholics. It was also known that the early councils of the Roman Catholic Bishops had altered, edited and even omitted from the Bible, many existing scriptures of the time whose proponents had also claimed to be inspired by Jesus. By the time the Roman Catholic Church had compiled and canonized the scriptures which would make up the present day Christian Bible, these works had undergone many revisions and changes. The Nag Hammadi texts contain many teachings or sayings attributed to Jesus in the Bible. Therefore, the Nag Hammadi texts clearly show that early Christianity developed in Ancient Egypt prior to its spread to Asia Minor, Greece and Rome. Thus, the Nag Hammadi texts are perhaps even more important than the Dead Sea Scrolls because they contain detailed expositions of the philosophy of Christian Gnosticism and display a link to Ancient Egyptian Mysticism. In the same way that the Ancient Egyptian initiate is directed to become one with Osiris, the Christian Gnostic Egyptian texts direct the Christian mystic to "become one" with the Father and to thereby discover the "Kingdom of Heaven". This is a very important distinction between Gnostic Christianity and the Orthodox Christianity of Roman Catholicism. While the orthodox (in Christianity as well as in other religions) seek to discover God, there is always a separation between God and the worshiper. There is an expectation that God will be found sitting on a throne somewhere as a loving Father waiting to embrace the child. This distinction may be noted between orthodox Islam and Sufism as well. In mystical religion, the objective is to discover and become one with God or the Divine, to discover that the innermost reality within the human

Below: The ancient
Egyptian Eucharist using
bread, wine and incense.

"This is the Flesh itself of
Osiris"

From the *Egyptian Book of
Coming Forth By Day*
(Book of The Dead)

The Sem Priest Offering bread.

The Sem priest presenting a white vessel of wine.

The Sem priest presenting a ball of incense.

heart is the object of one's spiritual search, to realize that God is not a personality
but the essence of all that exists. This is the underlying message of the Eucharist
ritual of the Christian Mass, and it was this same ritual which was at the heart of
the Osirian Mystery many thousands of years prior to the advent of Christianity.

The Christian Eucharist and the Osirian Mystery

The Eucharist or Christian sacrament also originated in the Osirian mystery of
Egypt. The ritual of consuming bread and wine as the body of the dead and
resurrected savior can be found in the early Ancient Egyptian Pyramid Texts (5,500
B.C.E.). It also became popular in many other cults and mystery traditions prior to
its practice in the Christianity. According to Hippolitus, a writer on the Naasenes,
a group who were considered to be Christian heretics (groups with doctrines
opposing the orthodox Christian church), he states that *"the ineffable mystery of the
Samothracians, which is allowable"* only for *"the initiated to know"* was exactly the same
proclaimed by Jesus Christ in the Eucharist ritual where he stated: *"If ye do not drink
my blood, and eat my flesh, ye will not enter the Kingdom of Heaven"*. Hippolitus states
that according to the Naasenes, this ritual of flesh and blood was called *Corybas* by
the *Phrygians* as well as the *"Thracians who dwell around Haemus."*

165

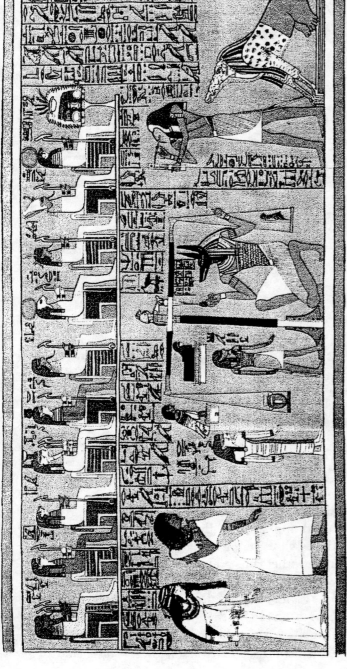

166

The Judgment Part One: "The Weighing of Words"

The purification of the heart and the determination of the individuals karmic destiny.

The Scene of the weighing of the heart from The Papyrus of Ani (Book of Coming Forth By Day of Ani).

The Weighing of Words implies an examination of one's conscience, not just the thoughts of the conscious mind, but the deep rooted convictions, desires, emotions, attitudes, intentions and motives in the unconscious and the actions which they prompted during the course of life.

Shai and Renenet are found in the judgment scene in the Hall of MAAT wherein Tehuti records the result of a person's deeds and level of spiritual understanding. The hands of Tehuti are the goddess "SHAI" which means "fate" or "destiny" and the goddess "RENENET" which means "Fortune and Harvest." The implication is that we reap (harvest) the result of our actions (destiny) according to our level of wisdom. Thus, we ourselves are the determiners of our own actions, the judge of our own actions and the determiners of our own fate and fortune or the fruits we will reap for those actions. Therefore, one's own actions will determine one's fate, which is carried out by Meskhenet. This is the first record of the teachings of Karma (The total effect of a person's actions and conduct during the successive phases of his existence). The decree may be that a soul will reincarnate, live an astral existence in the Field of Reeds of the Tuat (Heaven), be punished by being subject to the fiends in the Tuat, return to the world of the living (physical world) or move forward, meet and become one with Osiris in the innermost shrine. Those who are enlightened and have come to understand their oneness with Osiris go to rejoin Him in the *Beautiful West* (the Land of the Setting Sun- Ra) also known as Amenta, and become one with Him. When you succeed in cultivating an intuitive intellect (*Saa*) which understands the nature of creation and the oneness of all things in the one "Hidden God", then you will achieve *Saa-Amenti-Ra*, the intelligence or knowledge of the Amenti of Ra, the hidden world. Those who do not achieve this level of spiritual realization are subjected to the various experiences which can occur in the Tuat.

The Weighing of Words

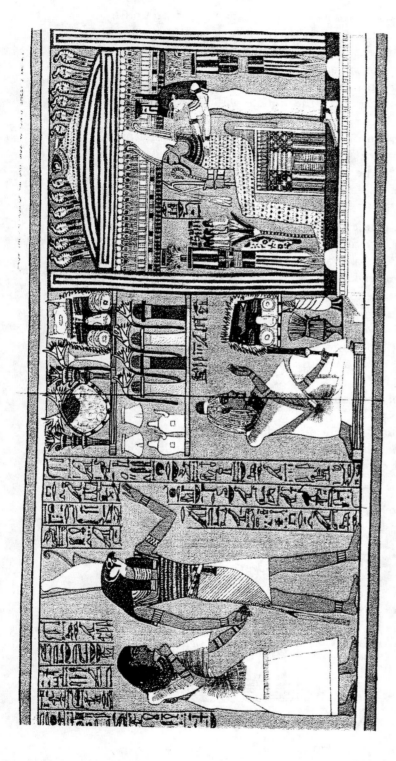

The Judgment Part Two: Osiris (the initiate) meets Osiris (the Supreme Self)
The Scene from the Innermost Shrine From The Papyrus of Ani (Book of Coming Forth By Day of Ani).

The initiate speaks: "There is no sin in my body. I have neither told lies nor acted with deceit; make me one of those favoured beings who are in thy train."

Having been found to be "Maa-kheru" ("True of Words"-innocent - righteous) by the 42 gods and goddesses in the Hall of MAATI, Horus then leads the initiate into the presence of Osiris where he/she kneels and declares that he/she is innocent of all wrong doing. When spiritual discipline is perfected, the true Self within is revealed, and Osiris is discovered as the innermost Self. This event is depicted in the meeting of the Osiris (the initiate) and Osiris (The Supreme Being) in the innermost shrine. It symbolizes the ultimate spiritual realization of the supreme truth of one's own existence.

Over 5,500 years before the Christian era, the Egyptian Mystery Religion of Osiris incorporated an elaborate system for mental, physical and spiritual transformation through the use of ritual worship of the Divine (Yoga of Devotion). The process is well described in the Ancient Egyptian Pyramid Texts and the Egyptian Books of Coming Forth By Day. This ritual worship centers around the figure of Osiris, who represents the all-encompassing Divine Self. Through continued ritual offerings to Osiris and the identification of the initiate with Osiris as the true recipient of the offerings, the initiate is gradually united with Osiris (the Supreme Divinity-Higher Self). Thus, a system of Ritual Identification where the aspirant understands that he/she is really worshipping his/her own Higher Self is established. This is the true intent of the Eucharist ritual. There are hundreds of instances of bread and wine offerings in the *Ancient Egyptian Pyramid Texts* and *Books of Coming Forth By Day*. The following utterances (hekau) highlight the offering process and the ritual identification of the initiate with Osiris, and with the other Gods and Goddesses. These lines, taken from various segments throughout the Pyramid Texts and the Book of Coming Forth By Day, are only a partial sampling. They show the gradual realization of the initiate that the gods are in reality aspects of him/herself and are to be recognized and sublimated in order to achieve harmony and inner peace.

"I am Osiris...I am The Great God, the Self-created One, Nun...I am Ra...I am Geb...I am Atum...I am Osiris...I am Min...I am Shu...I am Anubis...I am Isis...I am Hathor...I am Sekhmet...I am Orion...I am Saa...I am the Lion... I am the young Bull...I am Hapi who comes forth as the river Nile..."

Through the practice of ritual identification with the Divine, the aspirant engenders a state of consciousness which develops into a mystical union with the Divine. The Christian Eucharist clearly symbolizes the ritual identification of the

Osiris Mer-àt-f of the town of Hep (Apis).   Under the bier are the seven crowns of the god.
Dendérah

Nehas-t 〰️🏠🔼▲ | ⎯ 👁️

"resurrection" or "spiritual awakening".
(Osiris rising from the tomb)

Christian practitioner with Christ. However, the mystical experience necessitates the dissolution of the ego. This is the time when the Christian follower is supposed to dissolve, in consciousness, into the Christhood state of mind or consciousness. The ritual identification of the aspirant is of paramount importance because this very idea is at the heart of the myth which is being played out in the ritual. If this understanding is absent, the ritual will not have the desired effect. With this understanding, the true name of the follower of Christianity is Christ, the true name of the follower of Vaishnavism is Vishnu, the true name of the follower Vedanta Philosophy is Brahman, the true name of the follower of Buddhism is Buddha, and the true name of the follower of the Osirian Mysteries is Osiris. The same process is applied to the worship of female deities (Isis, Kali, etc.). In Indian Yoga, the practice of identification with the Divine is called *Ahamgraha Upashama*, which means that the worshiper meditates and affirms that he or she is the Divinity and not the individual ego. Hence, the Upanishadic texts prescribe the mantra *Aham Brahma Asmi*, "I am the Absolute Supreme Being", or the aspirant may use one of the other names of God such as *Krishna* or *Rama* in the male (father) aspect or *Kali*, *Saraswati* or *Durga* in the female (mother) aspect.

In much the same way as the Christian follower is exhorted to accept the bread and wine as the body and blood of Christ, the Ancient Egyptian initiate was continuously told to accept offerings in the form of bread, fruit, wine, beer, vegetables, etc., which represented Osiris and the Eye of spiritual consciousness. Perhaps the most important offering an initiate must accept is the Eye of Horus which represents the power of intuitional vision, the memory of the true Self which is one with the Divine. The Eye is the most powerful weapon the initiate has against the forces of evil (ignorance about the true Self) because it represents knowledge of the true Self or enlightenment which occurs when the Arat (Serpent Power or Kundalini) energy-consciousness rises through the energy centers of the spiritual body (Pillar of Osiris) and reaches the sixth energy center in the forehead, also known as the *Third Eye*, symbolized by the serpent in the forehead. In this sense, the Eye of Horus is the highest offering given to the initiate who is exhorted to accept the Eye which was stolen and damaged by Set (egoistic acts and identification with the ego-self, also known as the Tree of Knowledge of Good and Evil which takes the soul away from God). The following selections from the Egyptian Pyramid Texts illustrate the significance of the Eye and its identification with the offering of wine and bread.

From the Ancient Egyptian Pyramid Texts:

Utterance 28
   O Osiris Unas, Horus has given you his Eye; provide your face with it.
   O Osiris Unas, take the Eye of Horus which was wrested from Set and which you shall take to your mouth, with which you shall split open your mouth—
   WINE.

Osiris, Isis and Nephthys

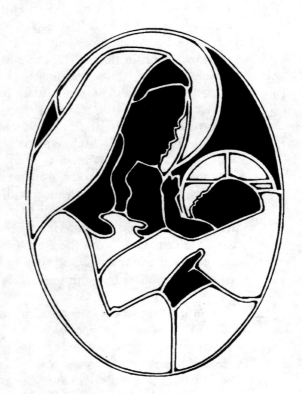

At left: Isis protecting Osiris

Above: The Madonna and child

Utterance 51
O Unas, take the Eye of Horus which you shall taste— CAKE.
Utterance 89
O Osiris Unas, take the Eye of Horus which Set has pulled out—A LOAF.
Utterance 93
O King, take this bread of yours which is the Eye of Horus.

From the Christian Bible:

Matthew 26:
26. And as they were eating, Jesus took bread, and blessed [it], and broke [it], and gave [it] to the disciples, and said, Take, eat; this is my body.
27 And he took the cup, and gave thanks, and gave [it] to them, saying, Drink ye all of it;
28 For this is my blood of the new testament, which is shed for many for the remission of sin.

The Eucharist is the central rite of the Catholic mass or church service. It re-enacts the Last Supper when Christ gave his disciples bread, saying, "This is my body," and wine, saying, "This is my blood." This sacrament is also known as the Holy Communion. However, there has been a controversy over what the communion is supposed to be since the rise in prominence of the Orthodox Roman Catholic Church. At the Lateran Council in 1215, a doctrine called *Transubstantiation* was defined. It stated that there is a change in substance of the Eucharist elements after the consecration. This means that the substance of bread and wine changes to Christ's actual body and blood, respectively. This doctrine is opposed by that of *Consubstantiation* which holds that after the words of consecration are uttered in Communion, the substances of bread and wine remain, along with the body and blood of Christ.

The important idea in the ritual of the Eucharist is that identification should go beyond rituals, prayers, austerities and penances. Identification implies a complete absorption into the Divine which completely excludes the ego self. Some mystery cults such as that of Osiris and Attis went further in amplifying the identification of the initiate with the death, dismemberment and resurrection of the deity by having the initiate lay in a coffin for a period of time (meditation) and then rise up in triumph over death. The stigmata is another effect of strong psychic identification with the passion of Jesus, however, if the identification with the passion of the deity is not transcended, the experience remains at the level of the senses, mind and intellect. Even these still fall under the heading of egoism. What is required is that these be transcended and for the initiate to enter into an expanded consciousness as a result of the experience in the ritual. Thus, the Eucharist ritual was a long standing ceremony which Christianity adopted from Egyptian religion. It was first practiced in the mysteries of Osiris and later in those of the Pythagoreans, Dionysus, Essenes, Mithras, and Attis who were initiated into the Osirian mysteries.

The ritual of eating the body and blood of the dismembered, reconstituted and resurrected deity needs to be understood for its profound symbolic meaning. Whether or not actual bread or some other symbol is used is less important than the understanding of the underlying significance of the wisdom teaching behind it. When the world is understood as being composed of differently arranged atoms which are themselves composed of energy as modern physics has proven, the idea of consuming any kind of substance assumes a strong spiritual meaning. In this sense, keeping the metaphysical understanding in mind, every time food is consumed, the process should be viewed as an Eucharistic ritual, because all substances are composed of the same underlying essence. This essence may be called Osiris, God, Brahman, Buddha, Amen, or energy. Therefore, every meal that is consumed is a communion with the Divine. Every breath is a communion as well because the body is consuming the necessary nutrients of life and in turn transferring its own essence into the environment. The environment itself is the body of God, the Divine Self. With this understanding, it is easy to understand that the body is constantly in communion with the ocean of energy for its survival. When there is conscious communion with that ocean as being one with it, then there is communion of the highest degree.

Opening The Mouth of The Osiris (the Initiate)

Nehas-t 〜〜〜▱⟊◥▬ | 🔻 👁

signifies: "resurrection" or "spiritual awakening".

The Ancient Egyptian ritual of the *Opening of the Mouth* is very important in *The Book of Coming Forth By Day*. After having declared oneself innocent of breaking any of the precepts of Maat and exercising knowledge of the Self (having become enlightened as to the existence and inner workings of the Ṭuat and one's innate divine power over the lower nature); the initiate can affirm that he or she is *Maak-heru* (true of speech, virtuous and righteous, without sin). After having successfully passed the test of the scales of Maat by being found devoid of anger, hatred, greed, desire for worldly pleasures, discontent, restlessness, etc., the initiate is clear to proceed on the spiritual journey as depicted in the figure entitled *Judgment Scene, Part One* (page 166). Now the way is clear to enter the innermost shrine and to become one with the Supreme Divinity as depicted in the figure entitled *Judgment Scene, Part Two* (page 167). Thus, scene one represents the second stage of yoga and religious practice which includes purification (eradication of gross mental and physical impurities), reflection on the teachings of Maat and Shetai (hidden mysteries of the Divine Self). Scene two represents the final stage of yoga and religious practice, self-discovery and unification with the Divine.

The body or *Shet-t* (mummy) is where the soul focuses its dynamic existence in time and space. Ordinary human existence is symbolized by the mummy. The mummy is the condition of spiritual dormancy which is embalmed by Anubis in preparation for the practice of the mysteries. This preparation involves the development of mental discipline, and the faculty of discernment between the real and unreal, virtuous and vicious, spiritual and mortal, wisdom and ignorance, etc. This teaching is symbolized by the mummified (bandaged) figure of Osiris (the soul). The bandages represent the fetters which bind the soul. The most important bandage is the 𓊨𓏏𓏏𓏥 ⟶, *Saiu Set* (fetters of Set). These were the bandages placed over the mouth of the mummy. These fetters are most important to The Osiris (the initiate or The Ausar), because the mouth symbolizes the memory or awareness-level of consciousness of the initiate. If the mouth is bound, there is no memory of the true Self. This means that the human being has no awareness of the deeper spiritual reality, only the reality of mortal existence.

Thus, Set, the uncontrolled, selfish ego, is limiting or constricting the expansion of consciousness in the mental process of an unenlightened human being. For this reason, there are hekau in *The Book of Coming Forth By Day*, Chapter 23, *Opening the mouth of Osiris Ani*, directed towards opening the mouth. Once again it is wisdom itself in the form of Tehuti, and the Divine Self in the form of Ptah-Osiris who accomplish the lifting of the fetters of ignorance (loss of memory of the true Self). The initiate affirms that the bonds (fetters) which were placed on his mouth by Set (egoism, desires, individuality, selfishness, etc.) have been removed by Ptah, Tehuti, Atum and Shu:

> ...*Be opened my mouth by Ptah, untied the bandages, twice, which are upon my mouth by the god of my town. Come then, Tehuti, filled and provided with hekau, untie the bandages, twice, of Set (which) fetter my mouth...*
> "*My mouth has been opened by Ptah, Tehuti (wisdom) comes with magic, and the fetters of Set which obstructed my mouth are destroyed.*"
>
> *Chap. 23, Lines 1-2*

The mind and body are essential elements of spiritual practice, because it is within them that spiritual discipline can be performed. They are the *Holy Land* to be cleansed, sanctified and discovered. In a figurative sense then, the human mind is the heart of the shrine of the body, the holy of holies or innermost section of the temple where divine realization occurs. When spiritual discipline is perfected, the true Self or *Shti* (he who is hidden in the coffin) is revealed and Osiris is discovered as the innermost Self. This event is depicted in the meeting of the initiate and Osiris in the innermost shrine. It symbolizes the ultimate spiritual realization of the supreme truth of one's own existence.

Isis and the Wakening of the Soul

Isis is the true heroine of the epic Ausarian Resurrection story. She not only causes the resurrection of Osiris, but the resurrection of Horus as well. With respect to her relationship to Set, Isis represents his real nemesis. Even though the struggle of the story seems to manifest as a battle between Set and Horus, in reality it is between Set and Isis. At every turn, Set's schemes and desires are thwarted by Isis and in the end, he loses the struggle to be the king, no matter what he tries to do. Thus, it is underlying presence of the Spirit (Osiris) and the cunning wisdom of Isis which enables Horus to be victorious over Set. It is this same aspect of intellectual development (as represented by Isis) which enables a spiritual aspirant to discover the increasingly subtle levels of the teachings in order to defeat Set in the form of ignorance, selfishness, egoism and brutishness within his/her own personality.

In reference to the iconography surrounding Isis in the spiritual struggle against Set, there is one important artifact which was used at the time of uttering prayers and meditations. This is the *sistrum*. The sistrum is commonly known as the rattle of Isis or Hathor (both are aspects of the same goddess principle). The sistrum consists of a handle surmounted by a metal hoop through which four pieces of metal rods are set. When shaken, the rods hit against the loop and cause a distinctive sound. The sistrum was produced in two forms. The second form incorporated the figure of the *Naos* or shrine (Holy of Holies) of the goddess instead of a loop. Plutarch, the ancient Greek writer, wrote about the sistrum and its spiritual significance:

The sistrum also shows that existent things must be shaken up and never have cessation from impulse, but as it were, be wakened when they fall asleep and die away.

For they say they turn aside and beat off Typhon [Set] with sistra, corruption binds nature fast and brings her to a stand, frees her and raises her from death by means of motion. Now the sistrum has a curved top, and its arch contains the four [things]. For the part of the cosmos which is subject to generation is circumscribed to the sphere of the moon, and all [things] in it are moved and changed by the four elements - fire and earth and water and air.

And on the arch of the sistrum, at the top, they put the metal figure of a cat with a human face and at the bottom, below the shaken things, the face sometimes of Isis and sometimes of Nephthys, - symbolizing by the faces, generation and consummation, for these are the changes and motions of the elements.

The Ancient Egyptian name of the sistrum is *skhem* or *sesheshet*. The goddess or priestess who holds and plays the sistrum to the Divine is known as *Neter sesheshet*. The *hoop* is a symbol of the *world-encircling* orbit of the moon. The sistrum often has two faces of Hathor. The two faces of Hathor represent Isis and Nephthys or life and death, respectively. The four metal rods represent the elements, but also the four spiritual energy centers of the spiritual body known as the pillar of Osiris. The human body, the energy which causes it to live and the subtle substance which composes the thoughts in the human mind, are all made up of minute particles of the elements. The mystical meaning of the shaking up of the rattle refers to the shaking up of human consciousness from the evil of ignorance and complacency which leads to spiritual stagnation and the development of evil (sinful-Setian) flaws in the human character (anger, hatred, greed, selfishness, lust, elation, depression, etc.). This process further relates to awakening the mind to the futility of trying to satisfy the desires of the lower nature, the fallacy of vanity and egoism, and the fleeting nature of happiness which is gained through and is dependent on worldly attainments or achievements. Further, the sistrum refers to realizing the transient and relative nature of human existence and the discovery of a higher vision wherein the Divine is to be recognized and experienced. It means, moving from ignorance to true knowledge, and from the pain of human suffering to the glory of divine inspiration and abiding happiness.

The sistrum may be likened to the *Conch* in Indian mystical symbolism, and the hand held Buddhist prayer wheel, as they are used for the same purpose, to "churn the ethers" in order to stir up the latent spiritual energies which lead to spiritual enlightenment. Other cultures may use bells, cymbals or other hand held objects to accomplish the same effect.

Incorporating the Osirian Rituals into your Life.

As explained earlier, rituals associated with religious practices can have a strong effect on transforming the mind when the deeper mystical implications are understood. The actual practice of the rituals presented in the *Book of Coming Forth By Day* represent intensive exercises and affirmations toward developing divine awareness. However, it is possible to follow important rituals on a daily, monthly and yearly basis which will allow you to incorporate the teachings into your everyday life. The following are some suggestions in this direction.

In the mysteries of the *Book of Coming Forth By Day*, every spiritual aspirant assumes the name of Osiris as part of his or her previous name. This ritual establishes a close bond between the aspirant and the Divine Self as described above. Thus, constant remembrance of this important identification should be exercised as often as possible.

The observance of the moon cycle is important because it follows the passion of Osiris. In this manner, a monthly reckoning of one's feelings and desires can be monitored and kept at the forefront of one's awareness while at the same time practicing reflection and remembrance of the teachings. The waning period symbolizes the destruction of Osiris by the evil of Set. Therefore, there should be a

175

special effort to control the passions and desires of the mind and body during this time. This movement is promoted by studying, reflecting and meditating on the teachings and making a conscious effort to control the lower impulses by practicing humility and selflessness, and exercising order and harmony in one's surroundings. In this manner Set is controlled in anticipation of the sublimation of Set which will occur at the pinnacle of the waxing period of the moon. When the darkened moon is facing earthward, it is called the "new moon". The other phases of the moon include crescent, half or first quarter, gibbous (more than half but less than fully illuminated: the gibbous moon.), and full. The moon wanes, through gibbous to half (last quarter) and back to new. The time of the waxing symbolizes the growth and life experiences of Osiris, and the waning period symbolizes the dismemberment of Osiris. The new moon symbolizes the resurrection of of Osiris, and the full moon symbolizes the radiant light of Horus as the reincarnated spirit of Osiris. Thus, the cycle of the moon is a daily and monthly reminder of the passion of Osiris which is synonymous with the experience of every human being and therefore it is a wonderful way to practice daily awareness and remembrance of the divine play of spirit and nature as well as the positive and negative elements within the human heart.

One important correlation between Jesus and Horus is the date of the celebration of the holidays surrounding them. The birthday of Horus in Ancient Egypt was December 25. This day follows the winter solstice (around Dec. 21st.) when the sun begins to rise again towards its summit, which it reaches at the summer solstice which occurs around June 21st. This is significant since the birthday of Jesus was changed from January 6 to December 25 by Christian authorities, long after the advent of Christianity. The solstices point to another factor which is the six months of rising and the six months of lowering in the effect of solar energy on the earth.

Isis and Sirius

Another significant correlation between Ancient Egyptian and modern Christian mythology is the Christian myth surrounding the Three Kings who traveled to the site of the birth of Jesus. The star Sirius was held to be specially important in Ancient Egyptian culture and religion, because its rising announced the coming of the New Year and the flooding of the Nile river which was the source of all sustenance.

The name Sirius comes from the Greek *Seirios*, "scorching". It is the brightest star in the sky, situated in the constellation, Canis Major and is also known as *Sothis*. It is located at a distance of 8.7 light years (51 trillion miles) from our earth, which makes it one of the closest and brightest stars. Also, she (Sirius) is visible from all over the earth. Sirius consists of a binary star system which includes Sirius and Sirius B. Sirius B is a white dwarf star which the Dogon* peoples of West

Africa knew of for many hundreds of years. It was rediscovered in 1862 by an American astronomer. The largest known stars are called supergiants with diameters that may be more than 400 times that of our sun. The small stars which are known as white dwarfs may have diameters of 0.01 times that of our sun. *(See the book *Egyptian Yoga: The Philosophy of Enlightenment* by Dr. Muata Ashby)

Many Ancient Egyptian temples were constructed in such a way that the light of Sirius reached the inner chambers. The Ancient Egyptian name of Sirius is *Sept*, △⌂✶, or *Sopdu*. Its symbols are related to Isis, and are sometimes used in her name, ✶◯⌂♌♒, or to refer to her. There are three stars in the Orion constellation which point almost directly to Sirius which rises in the eastern sky. Sirius is associated with Isis, the mother of Horus. Thus, the Three Kings in the Christian myth relate to the light of the three stars in the constellation which travel toward the rising light of salvation which is being born on the winter solstice (Horus), from the goddess Isis, who is the prototype of Mary, the mother of Jesus. In modern times, the star Sirius is still held in high regard by the Dogon nation of Mali in Africa. Sirius is a companion star to our sun. Our solar system and Sirius revolve around each other and both revolve around the universe. One myth surrounding Sirius is that human souls originate there and return there after death.

From a mystical perspective, the three stars refer to the Trinity principle which pervades the entire system of Ancient Egyptian mythology. The Supreme Being, *Nebertcher*, is known as the one who expresses as three, ⊞⊟⬭⌁ 🜁🜂🜃🜄🜅🜆🜇, "I became from God one, gods three". Three here refers to the three states of consciousness (waking, dream and dreamless deep sleep), the modes of operation of human mind (subject, object and the relationship between the two*), and the three modes of creation (consciousness, mind and matter or Heaven, Ṭuat and Earth). The triad or Trinity emanates from the singular source or essence of Creation, the Supreme Being, who is transcendent of the three. Thus, *one* symbolizes God, the Supreme, transcendental Divinity, and the *three* symbolize the multiplicity of Creation which is at all times sustained by divine will. Thus, the three follow the one. This principle of the *three* is also present in the annunciation scene from the temple of Luxor, Egypt, and was assimilated into the mythology of Jesus Christ as the Three kings who went to see the new born child, Jesus. (*see the Egyptian Yoga Guide Book Series for more information)

New Year's Eve is an especially important time in reference to the mysticism of Sirius. A little known fact about Sirius is that on New Year's Eve Sirius rises to the apex of the meridian above the earth and can be seen directly above from anywhere in the world at the midnight hour. Thus, Sirius marks the beginning of a New Year as well as the continuing cycle of life which reminds us of the glory and precision of the universe. In this aspect Sirius is a supreme example of Isis in her aspect as Maat, the universal order of Creation. Therefore, this time offers a great opportunity to reflect upon the attributes and teachings of Isis, Horus and Maat. As the segment below from the Ancient Egyptian Pyramid Texts explains, the rising of Sirius and the birth of the New Year is synonymous with the resurrection of the initiate, who is Osiris, and whose spiritual seed rises in the form of Horus, the vindicator, the new life.

"Horus brings Set to you[1], he has given him to you, and he has bowed down under you, for your strength is greater than his. Horus has made it possible for you to enclose for yourself all the gods within your embrace for Horus has loved his father in you[2], Horus will not allow you to be troubled, Horus will not be far removed from you, Horus has protected his father in you, you being alive as a living beetle, that you may be permanent in Mendes[3].

Isis and Nephthys have waited for you in Asyut because their Lord is in you in your name of 'Lord of Asyut; because their god is in you in your name of 'Canal of the God'; they worship you, do not be far from them. Isis comes to YOU rejoicing through love of you; your seed issues into her, she being ready as Sothis. Har-Sopd has issued from you in his name of 'Horus who is in Sothis'; you have power through him in his name of 'Spirit who is in the Dndrw-bark'. Horus has protected you in his name of 'Horus the son who protects his father"[4]. (Pyr. 1632-1636)

1- The initiate as Osiris.
2- The soul within every human being is Osiris.
3- Mythical tomb of Osiris, the Supreme Abode.
4- Amsu-Min.

CONCLUSION

The struggle between Horus and Set represents the struggle in every human being between the lower self and the Higher. It occurs in the human mind at the conscious, subconscious and unconscious levels. Your goal is to subjugate or sublimate your lower self (Set) and allow your Higher Self (Horus) to assume control of your life. When this happens you transcend all human frailties and are not subject to the forces of nature. Death will not exist for you and your consciousness cannot be fragmented as was Osiris', because you will have transcended the mind and its duality, swinging between Horian and Setian thoughts.

Two of the most important reliefs in the entire series of symbols are to be found on page 124. The first picture, Horus-Set, leads us to understand that Horus and Set are not two separate individuals, but two aspects of the same character. The entire story of the Resurrection hinges on this very point. It mystically symbolizes the plight of every human being who is struggling to conquer his or her lower nature and to become the master of his/her own life.

The second picture, Horus and Set Unite, is the next most important relief because it symbolizes the union of Horus and Set which is a mystical code for the lower and Higher Self in the individual human being. It means achieving inner harmony and peace with the universe, the culmination of the Ancient Egyptian injunction: *Know Thyself*. Set is not a devil or an evil force to be destroyed. He is the principle of the uncontrolled, untrained ego, with its rampant desires and selfish thoughts. Thus, in order to conquer Set, it is necessary to control the impulses of the lower Self. This is accomplished by allowing oneself to be be nurtured and protected by Isis, which means listening to the mystical stories and myths, studying the wisdom teachings through the initiation process and practicing Maat or leading a life based on virtue, order, correctness, justice, balance and peace.

When Set is controlled and sublimated, it is a wondrous force which can be directed towards what is positive, real and true in life. This movement brings true peace and happiness in life which is abiding, rather than the fleeting desires and impulses which lead to disappointment, frustration, pain and sorrow. The sublimation of Set is symbolized by the picture where he is made to assist in the travels of the barque of Ra (page 124). Instead of being the leader of the fiends who constantly try to promote chaos by impeding the movement of Ra, he is made to serve the Divine by clearing the path so that the barque may pass freely. This is a mystical metaphor of human life. The ego (Set) gets in the way of one's divine movement, divine awareness and inner mental peace, or the true way in which life should be led in order to receive divine inspiration, strength and will to cope with and succeed in life. When Set is controlled, the divine energy flows freely, providing inspiration and positive feelings and experiences in life as well as a feeling of closeness to the Divine. Thus, the goal of spiritual life is to develop selflessness and self-control. This implies control over the passions, emotions and desires of the body, mind and senses which constitute the Setian lower nature in a human being.

We close with two prayers. The first constitutes Chapter 157 of *The Ancient Egyptian Book of Coming Forth By Day*. The second is the declaration of righteousness in the Hall of MAATI.

> Isis came, she stopped at the town and sought out a hiding place for Horus when he came out of the marshes ... awoke in a bad state and painted his eyes in the god's ship. It was commanded to him to rule the banks, and he assumed the condition of a mighty warrior, for he remembered what had been done, and he engendered fear of him and inspired respect. His great mother protects him and erases those who come against Horus...
> ...a matter a million times true!

> I am pure. I am pure. I am Pure.
> I have washed my front parts with the waters of libations, I have cleansed my hinder parts with drugs which make wholly clean, and my inward parts have been washed in the liquor of Maat.

How to study the wisdom teachings:

It is important to understand that spirituality need not be and should not be reserved for a particular time on a particular day. With this understanding, it should be easy for you to understand now that every time you eat anything you are consuming matter whose essence is God. Every time you breath you are communing with the universe. Every time you interact with the objects of the world or with other living beings you are in holy communion with God, who is in reality your very Self and the innermost Self of everything else.

Another important aspect of ritual is the study of the teachings. Every day, a portion of the myth is to be read and reflected upon so as to engender an ever deepening understanding of the meaning and practice of the myth.

There is a specific technique which is prescribed by the scriptures themselves for studying the teachings, proverbs and aphorisms of mystical wisdom. The method is as follows:

The spiritual aspirant should read the desired text thoroughly, taking note of any particular teachings which resonates with him or her.

The aspirant should make a habit of collecting those teachings and reading them over frequently. The scriptures should be read and re-read because the subtle levels of the teachings will be increasingly understood the more the teachings are reviewed.

One useful exercise is to choose some of the most special teachings you would like to focus on and place them in large type or as posters in your living areas so as to be visible to remind you of the teaching.

The aspirant should discuss those teachings with others of like mind when possible because this will help to promote greater understanding and act as an active spiritual practice in which the teachings are kept at the forefront of the mind. In this way, the teachings can become an integral part of everyday life and not reserved for a particular time of day or of the week.

The study of the wisdom teachings should be a continuous process in which the teachings become the predominant factor of life rather than the useless and oftentimes negative and illusory thoughts of those who are ignorant of spiritual truths. This spiritual discipline should be observed until inner spiritual Enlightenment is attained.

When reading the devotional texts, strive to develop a feeling of surrender to the Divine Self within you. Allow your feeling to rise as you read the texts in such

The "Doubles" of Ani and his wife drinking water in the Other World.

a way that you become more and more exalted and more and more in tune with your inner feelings.

As you study the spiritual texts on your own, you may discover many utterances which resonate with your mind. Concentrate on these and use them in your daily practice. Never forget that the utterances are speaking about you, and not about some far off God who lives millions of miles away. Nebertcher, God, is within you, therefore, the teachings are speaking about and for you alone.

With this understanding, you can spiritualize your life through the knowledge that God is everywhere. The universe is a majestic Temple in which every movement and sound is a holy affirmation of the Divine. Wherever you go, whatever you do, whatever thoughts appear in your mind, whatever occurs in the world of time and space, you should realize these as passing, transient and illusory waves in the ocean of primordial consciousness which you are. As waves rise and subside, so too, all of the various thoughts and objects in the world are merely waves of energy in different configurations, which are born, grow and will someday die, only to once again become a part of the primordial pool of matter from whence they came. All the while you must be the observer, the detached watcher, who is awakening from the long dream of time and space. This is your dream. You are essentially God and therefore, you are the immortal essence of this ocean of consciousness.

Meditation on
The Ausarian Myth:

A Journey to the Ṭuat

Meditation on the Ausarian Resurrection*

Before practicing the following meditation, it would be auspicious to follow the procedure described below.

In the beginning, the mind may be difficult to control. What is needed here is perseverance and the application of the techniques described here. Another important aid to meditation is ritualism. You should observe a set of rituals whenever you intend to practice meditation. These will gradually help to settle the mind even before you actually sit to practice the formal meditation. They are especially useful if you are a busy person or if you have many thoughts or worries on the mind. First take a bath. Water is the greatest cleanser of impurities. In ancient times the Temple complex included a sacred lake for bathing. Practitioners of yoga would bathe before entering the temples and engaging in the mystery rituals.

Once you have bathed, put on clothing which you have specifically reserved for the practice of meditation. This will have a strong effect on your mind and will bring meditative vibrations to you because the clothing will retain some of the subtle essence of the meditation experience each time you use them. The clothing should be loose and comfortable. We recommend 100% Cotton or Silk because it is a natural material which will allow the skin to breath. Keep the clothing clean and use the same style of clothing for your meditation practice.

When you are ready, go to your special room or corner which you have set aside for meditation. Take the phone off the hook or turn off the ringer and close the door behind you, leaving instructions not to be disturbed for the period of time you have chosen or practice meditating when there is no one around to disturb you (4-6am). When you sit for meditation, light a candle and burn some incense of your choice, and then choose a comfortable position, maintaining your back straight, either sitting on the floor in the cross-legged posture (Lotus), sitting in a chair with feet on the floor or lying on your back on the floor in the corpse-mummy pose (without falling asleep). If possible, use a sistrum, bell or other noise making device before and after uttering the following prayers.

Next, invoke the assistance of the deity or cosmic force which removes obstacles to your success in spiritual practice. Anubis is the deity which leads souls through the narrow pathways of the Tuat. Therefore, request the assistance of Anubis, who represents the discriminative intellectual ability so that you may *"distinguish the real from the unreal"*.

"O Apuat (Anubis), opener of the ways, the roads of the North, O Anpu, opener of the ways, the roads of the South. The messenger between heaven and hell displaying alternately a face black as night, and golden as the day. He is equally watchful by day as by night."

"May Anubis make my thighs firm so that I may stand upon them".

"I have washed myself in the water wherein the god
Anpu washed when he performed the office of embalmer and bandager.
My lips are the lips of Anpu".

Next, invoke the presence of Isis-Maat who is the embodiment of wisdom and inner discovery of the Divine. Isis (Aset) is the mother of the universe, and she herself veils her true form, as the Supreme Transcendental Self. This "veil" is only due to ignorance. Therefore, pray for Isis to make her presence, which bestows instant revelation of her true form. This "unveiling" is a metaphor symbolizing the intuitional revelation of the Divine (Enlightenment) in your mind. Isis is in your heart and only needs to be revealed. However, she can only reveal herself to the true aspirant, one who is devoted to her (the Self) and her alone. Isis says: *"I Isis, am all that has been, all that is, or shall be; and no mortal man has ever unveiled me."* The invocatory prayer to Isis is:

"Oh benevolent Aset, who protected her brother Asar, who searched for him without wearying, who traversed the land in mourning and never rested until she had found him. She who afforded him shadow with her wings and gave him air with her feathers, who rejoiced and carried her brother home.

She who revived what was faint for the weary one, who received his seed and conceived an heir, and who nourished him in solitude while no one knew where he was. . . . "

"I am the hawk (Heru) in the tabernacle, and I pierce through the veil."

Then remember your Spiritual Preceptor, the person who taught you how to meditate. Thank them for their teaching and invoke their grace for success in your meditation.

> "I have faith in my master's ability to lead you along the path of truth".

> "The lips of the wise are as the doors of a cabinet; no sooner are they opened, but treasures are poured out before you. Like unto trees of gold arranged in beds of silver, are wise sentences uttered in due season."

Next, utter some invocatory prayers such as the Hymns of Osiris to propitiate the benevolent presence of the Supreme Being. Visualize that with each utterance you are being enfolded in Divine Grace and Enlightenment.

A Hymn To Osiris

"Glory to Osiris Un-Nefer, the great god within Abydos, king of eternity, lord of the everlasting, who passeth through millions of years in his existence. Eldest son of the womb of Nut, engendered by Geb, the chief lord of the crowns of the North and South, lord of the lofty white crown. As Prince of gods and of men he has received the crook and the flail and the dignity of his divine fathers. Let thy heart which is in the mountain of Amenta be content, for thy son Horus is established upon thy throne. You are crowned lord of Tattu and ruler in Abtu. Through thee the world waxeth green in triumph before the might of Neb-er-tcher. He leadeth in his train that which is and that which is not yet, in his name Ta-her-seta-nef; he toweth along the earth in triumph in his name Seker.

He is exceedingly mighty and most terrible in his name Osiris. He endureth forever and forever in his name Un-nefer. Homage to thee, King of Kings, Lord of Lords, Prince of Princes, who from the womb of Nut have possessed the world and have ruled all lands and Akert. Thy body is of gold, thy head is of azure, and emerald light encircleth thee. O "An" of millions of years, all-pervading with thy body and beautiful in countenance in Ta-sert. Grant thou to the Ka of Osiris, the initiate, splendor in heaven and might upon earth and triumph in Neter-khert; and that I may sail down to Tattu like a living soul and up to Abtu like a bennu (phoenix); and that I may go in and come out without repulse at the pylons of the Tuat. May there be given unto me loaves of bread in the house of coolness, and offerings of food in Annu, and a homestead forever in Sekhet-Aru, with wheat and barley therefor..."

188

Close here by reciting the auspicious hekau-mantras for commencing your meditation practice. The prayers should be recited four times. This quadruplicate format is a symbolic way to propitiate the divine forces which control the four quarters of the phenomenal universe and the heavenly realms. There are four directions which the mind is aware of (East, North, West and South) in the physical plane as in the astral. The prayer is directed toward the purification of the mind and body which will allow your spiritual practice (movement) to be unobstructed on earth as well as in heaven. It is a propitiation to the Divine that you should not be confined to the temporal world of time and space, and physical body and ego-self consciousness, so that you may go beyond the ignorance of ordinary human existence and thereby discover the truth of your true nature as one with the Supreme Self. As you utter the following words of power, visualize that you embody the qualities of the neters in the Ausarian Myth. See their virtues becoming your virtues and gain insight into their way. This is the deification of your personality, invoking your power within to transform yourself into a neter.

dua Asar

Adorations to Osiris

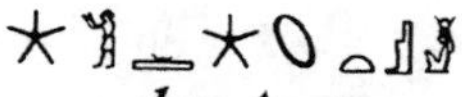

dua Aset

Adorations to Isis

dua Heru

Adorations to Horus

dua Het-Hor

Adorations to Hathor

dua Anpu

Adorations to Anubis

dua Tehuti

Adorations to Tehuti

Nuk pu Anpu, Nuk pu Anpu, Nuk pu Anpu, Nuk pu Anpu,
I am Anubis, I am Anubis, I am Anubis, I am Anubis

Nuk pu Maat, Nuk pu Maat, Nuk pu Maat, Nuk pu Maat
I am Maat, I am Maat, I am Maat, I am Maat

Nuk pu Aset, Nuk pu Aset, Nuk pu Aset, Nuk pu Aset
I am ISIS, I am ISIS, I am ISIS, I am ISIS

Nuk pu Heru, Nuk pu Heru, Nuk pu Heru, Nuk pu Heru
I am Horus, I am Horus, I am Horus, I am Horus

Nuk pu Asar, Nuk pu Asar, Nuk pu Asar, Nuk pu Asar
I am Osiris, I am Osiris, I am Osiris, I am Osiris

Nuk ab, Nuk ab, Nuk ab, Nuk ab
I am Pure, I am Pure, I am Pure, I am Pure

Now relax in silence for a few moments. Allow the utterances to resonate in your mind and become a witness to whatever you see in your mind's eye. Take several deep breaths, and with each one, feel your body becoming lighter and more relaxed.

For the next five minutes, take deep breaths and hold them for five seconds. As you do so, visualize that Life Force energy from the universe is pouring into your body. This is the Hathor breath for replenishing and accumulating mental energy. Feel revitalized and renewed.

Visualize that your body is rising up into the air, above the clouds and into space. Now visualize that you are in an astral plane. It is a dark realm, but it is not empty. Visualize that your body is made of pure light and there are stars all about you. Experience the vast expanse of your surroundings and feel at ease in the realm. Relax every muscle in your body and discover the peace and joy of expansion.

Now take flight by simply willing yourself to move up and away. Travel to the far reaches of this plane. Visit the stars and the planets. There are worlds, galaxies and universes which expand to infinity. Behold the beauty and majesty of the Divine. Now relax and allow the feeling of joy, immortality, infinity and eternity to permeate every part of you.

Now see in the distance, a dark realm. It is the darkest place you have ever seen.

No light emanates from or reaches this place. Nothing grows there. Come closer to this place and look into it. There is nothing to be seen but you feel a strange affinity to this place. It is beckoning to you, calling your soul to enter. You cannot explain it but somehow it feels warm, loving and complete. You attempt to go in but something prevents you, even as a glass door permits you to look within but not to enter.

What prevents you from entering is your ego. The deepest, darkest realm is the abode of the Supreme Self and none other can exist there. So if you wish to enter into the presence of the Divine, you will need to discard all notions of separation and all notions of individuality.

When you say "*I am Osiris,*" who is the "I"? You must forget the "ego-I" now and be Osiris. Therefore, allow the mind and its thoughts of separation, worries, anxieties, etc. to subside as you discover the essence of who the "I" is referring to, deep down. Leave the mind behind; its thoughts cannot help you now. Feel and experience the silence of the quiet mind and allow yourself to melt into the cosmic mind. Reflect thus: This vast universe, these stars, this body, all this is me; I am the universe. I am the gods and goddesses. I am the Divine Self! Become one with the peace and emptiness. Now there is only awareness, pure consciousness. No thoughts reach you; this is perfect being. Now you are entering into the realm of absolute darkness, the realm of Osiris.

Remain in this place of peace and tranquillity for as long as you like. When you are ready, gently return to normal body consciousness and slowly move your limbs as you rise. Paying your respects to the neters with upraised hands, utter the closing words of power and leave the meditation area feeling that divine grace has fallen upon you and will be with you throughout the rest of your day.

Om Asar Aset Heru,
Om Asar Aset Heru,
Om Asar Aset Heru,
Om Asar Aset Heru,

As you commune more and more with the Divine, your awareness will increase gradually and you will achieve greater and greater control of your thoughts, emotions, mind and senses, until you are in complete control and experience abiding spiritual awareness. This is the state of Enlightenment.

May you discover the glory of Meditation!

INDEX

Absolute, 18, 28, 160, 169
Africa, 18, 134, 162, 177
Air, 97, 103
Albert Einstein, 27
Alexandria, 164
Allah, 18, 28
Amen, 28, 81, 145, 146, 148, 172
Amenta, 65, 121, 145, 166, 188
Amun, 26, 27, 28, 63, 131, 145, 146, 147, 148
Amun-Ra-Ptah, 26, 27, 131
Ancient Egypt, 7, 8, 18, 19, 23, 24, 25, 26, 27, 28, 29, 30, 31, 33, 35, 36, 37, 63, 125, 128, 130, 131, 135, 136, 139, 140, 141, 145, 148, 150, 154, 159, 160, 161, 162, 163, 164, 165, 168, 169, 172, 174, 176, 177, 178, 179, 180
Ancient Egyptian Pyramid Texts, 24, 165, 168, 169, 178
Ani, 27, 35, 146, 166, 167, 173
Annunciation, 131
Anu (Greek Heliopolis), 27, 31, 75, 79, 85
Anubis, 32, 33, 53, 57, 59, 65, 67, 136, 137, 138, 154, 155, 156, 157, 164, 168, 173, 186, 187, 189, 190
Arabia, 55, 57
Arjuna, 142
Ark of the Covenant, 163
Asar, 25, 119, 132, 135, 187, 189, 190, 191
Aset, 25, 57, 133, 187, 189, 190, 191
Asia Minor, 18, 164
Attis, 171
Being, 26, 27, 31, 89, 125, 127, 141, 177
Bhagavad Gita, 36, 142
Bible, 36, 37, 164, 171
Bishops, 164
Book of Coming Forth By Day, 35, 36, 67, 121, 138, 157, 161, 162, 163, 166, 167, 168, 172, 173, 175, 180
Brahma, 131, 169
Brahman, 18, 28, 131, 169, 172
Buddha, 21, 28, 169, 172
Buddhist, 147, 175
Buto, 65, 83
Carl Jung, 25
Catholic, 164, 171
Chakras (see energy centers of the body), 138
Chester Beatty Papyrus, 105, 115
China, 32, 156

Christ, 169, 171
Christhood, 169
Christianity, 18, 27, 28, 163, 164, 165, 169, 171, 176
Church, 164, 171
Company of gods and goddesses, 28, 31
Consciousness, 18, 19, 21, 133, 134, 141, 154, 159
Coptic, 162
Cosmogony, 31
Creation, 18, 23, 26, 27, 31, 33, 41, 51, 91, 127, 128, 129, 130, 131, 132, 133, 135, 136, 139, 141, 145, 147, 149, 163, 177, 178
Dead Sea Scrolls, 164
Death, 57, 67, 71, 81, 134, 138, 160, 179
December, 176
Deism, 18
Demotic, 35
Detachment, 155
Dharma, 131
Diodorus, 55
Discipline, 7
Dogon, 176, 177
Durga, 169
Earth, 91, 93, 95, 97, 99, 101, 145, 177
Easter, 67
Eastern mystical philosophy, 28
Egyptian Book of Coming Forth By Day, 24, 36, 41, 125, 146
Egyptian civilization, 25, 30, 37
Egyptian religion, 171
Egyptian Yoga, 7, 19, 25, 27, 136, 154, 159, 177
Elements, 95, 97, 99
Enlightenment, 7, 21, 23, 24, 25, 27, 128, 133, 135, 153, 159, 162, 164, 177, 181, 187, 188, 191
Ennead, 31, 32, 34, 36, 51, 77, 105, 107, 109, 111, 113, 115, 117, 119, 121, 125, 127, 130, 157
Essenes, 171
Ethiopia, 55
Ethiopian priests, 55
Eucharist, 24, 163, 165, 168, 171
Evil, 43, 81, 115, 130, 169
Eye of Horus, 129, 139, 142, 143, 144, 169, 171
Eye of Ra, 28, 49, 139
Eyes of Horus, 144
Fear, 81

Fish, 75
Gaul, 134
Geb, 32, 41, 43, 51, 53, 73, 75, 79, 121, 127, 132, 150, 168, 188
Gnostic, 142, 164
Gnostic Christianity, 142, 164
Gnostics, 163
God, 18, 19, 21, 25, 26, 28, 29, 33, 35, 41, 45, 47, 49, 51, 55, 63, 81, 87, 89, 91, 93, 95, 97, 99, 101, 107, 109, 119, 128, 129, 130, 131, 133, 137, 143, 145, 147, 148, 149, 150, 151, 157, 163, 164, 165, 168, 169, 172, 177, 178, 181, 183
God of Light, 137
Goddess, 18, 25, 77, 99, 119
Goddesses, 26, 168
Gods, 26, 63, 121, 168
Good, 125, 141, 169
Great Pyramid, 164
Great Spirit, 18
Greece, 18, 164
Guru, 142
Hathor, 28, 32, 33, 35, 36, 43, 45, 47, 49, 51, 109, 113, 127, 128, 129, 131, 140, 145, 147, 157, 158, 159, 168, 174, 189, 190
Hawk, 81, 161
Health, 43
Hearing, 107, 109, 129
Heaven, 87, 89, 91, 93, 95, 101, 145, 160, 166, 177
Hekau, 30, 35, 142
Hell, 160
Hermetic, 35
Herodotus, 148
Heru, 25, 33, 63, 105, 136, 161, 187, 189, 190, 191
Heru (see Horus), 25, 33, 63, 105, 136, 161, 187, 189, 190, 191
Hetep, 147, 159
Hidden God, 166
High God, 25, 26, 28
Hindu, 18, 28, 130, 151
Hindu mythology, 28, 151
Hinduism, 142
Holy Land, 173
Holy of Holies, 29, 174
Horus, 14, 18, 25, 26, 27, 28, 32, 33, 34, 35, 36, 37, 41, 53, 63, 65, 67, 71, 73, 75, 77, 79, 81, 83, 85, 87, 89, 91, 99, 101, 103, 105, 107, 109, 113,

115, 117, 119, 121, 129, 131, 133, 135, 136, 137, 138, 139, 142, 143, 144, 149, 150, 152, 154, 157, 159, 161, 163, 167, 169, 174, 176, 177, 178, 179, 180, 188, 189, 190

Ibis, 49

Ida and Pingala, 136

Identification, 21, 168, 171

India, 27, 29, 32, 35, 55, 57, 128, 130, 136, 162

Indian Yoga, 169

Indus, 57

Initiate, 172

Intellectual, 156

Isis, 14, 18, 25, 27, 28, 29, 32, 33, 34, 35, 36, 37, 41, 51, 53, 55, 57, 59, 61, 63, 65, 71, 73, 75, 77, 79, 81, 83, 85, 99, 101, 103, 105, 107, 109, 111, 113, 115, 117, 127, 131, 132, 133, 134, 135, 136, 137, 142, 147, 149, 150, 151, 152, 157, 159, 160, 161, 163, 168, 169, 174, 176, 177, 178, 179, 180, 187, 189

Islam, 28, 164

Israel, 164

Jehovah, 18

Jesus, 28, 142, 163, 164, 165, 171, 176, 177

Jesus Christ, 165, 177

Jewish, 163, 164

Jnana Yoga, 29

Joseph Campbell, 28

Judaism, 28, 163

Justice, 105, 119

Ka, 83, 123, 188

Kali, 169

Kamit, 33

Kamit (Egypt), 33

Karma, 166

Khepri, 148

Khu, 30

Kingdom, 21, 28, 164, 165

Kingdom of Heaven, 21, 28, 164, 165

Kings Chamber, 164

Kmt, 33

Know Thyself, 21, 131, 156, 179

Knowledge, 138, 169

Koran, 36

Krishna, 28, 131, 142, 169

Kundalini, 7, 21, 127, 136, 138, 169

Learning, 155

Liberation, 21

Life Force, 127, 128, 136, 145, 151, 159, 190

Listening, 29

Lotus, 127, 186

Love, 7, 19, 21, 89, 133

Maat, 21, 32, 36, 41, 51, 71, 105, 127, 128, 129, 130, 137, 139, 146, 148, 149, 150, 154, 156, 157, 161, 172, 178, 179, 180, 190

MAAT, 33, 131, 137, 143, 146, 154, 158, 166

MAATI, 167, 180

Magic, 139

Manetho, 25

Manu, 75

Matter, 136

Matthew, 171

Meditation, 19, 29, 185, 186, 191

Memphite Theology, 27

Meskhenet, 93, 166

Metu Neter, 30, 141

Min, 34, 117, 136, 149, 159, 168

Mind, 143

Modern science, 130, 156

Moksha, 21

Moon, 143

Mortals, 29, 30

Moses, 163

Music, 53

Mysteries, 134, 135, 154, 169

Mysticism, 19, 164

Mythology, 22, 23, 24, 25, 28, 130

Nag Hammadi, 164

Nature, 91, 95, 134, 137, 150, 151

Nebertcher, 26, 27, 28, 29, 31, 53, 125, 131, 160, 177, 183

Nephthys, 32, 33, 51, 53, 57, 59, 65, 77, 81, 127, 132, 134, 135, 136, 137, 138, 147, 150, 151, 159, 160, 174, 178

Neter, 18, 26, 30, 31, 129, 174

Neters, 26

Neteru, 18, 26, 31

Netherworld, 125

Nubia, 119, 134, 140

Nun (primeval waters-unformed matter), 168

Nut, 32, 41, 43, 47, 51, 121, 123, 127, 132, 133, 147, 148, 150, 188

Om, 191

Osiris, 8, 14, 18, 24, 25, 26, 27, 28, 32, 33, 34, 35, 36, 37, 41, 51, 53, 55, 57, 59, 61, 63, 65, 73, 75, 79, 83, 85, 99, 101, 105, 107, 117, 119, 121, 123, 125, 127, 131, 132, 133, 134, 135, 136, 137, 138, 140, 144, 145, 146,

147, 149, 150, 151, 152, 155, 157, 159, 160, 161, 163, 164, 166, 167, 168, 169, 171, 172, 173, 174, 175, 176, 178, 179, 188, 189, 190, 191

Pa Neter, 25, 26, 28, 29, 162

Passion, 57

Peace (see also Hetep), 146, 147

Pert em Hru, 161

phallus, 33, 34, 65, 79

Philae, 27, 135

Philosophy, 7, 23, 25, 27, 169, 177

Phrygians, 134, 165

Plutarch, 35, 135, 174

Pontius Pilate, 163

Psycho-Mythology, 23

Ptah, 27, 79, 125, 131, 143, 173

Pyramid of Unas, 144

Pyramid Texts, 30, 35, 162, 163, 168, 169

Ra, 27, 28, 31, 34, 41, 43, 45, 47, 49, 51, 53, 57, 73, 77, 79, 81, 83, 85, 107, 109, 111, 115, 119, 121, 125, 128, 130, 131, 132, 137, 139, 140, 141, 145, 146, 149, 150, 161, 166, 168, 179

Rama, 130, 131, 142, 169

Ramakrishna, 21

Red Sea, 55

Reflection, 29

Reincarnation, 148

Religion, 7, 14, 18, 19, 25, 163, 168

Renenet, 166

Resurrection, 7, 21, 24, 27, 34, 57, 71, 127, 149, 174, 179, 186

Righteous action, 157

Rituals, 24, 175

Roman, 18, 163, 164, 171

Roman Catholic, 164, 171

Roman Empire, 18

Rome, 134, 164

Saa (spiritual understanding faculty), 63, 129, 154, 166, 168

Sages, 23, 28, 29, 35, 36, 133, 140, 156

Saints, 23, 156

Salvation, 21

Salvation . See also resurrection, 21

Samothracians, 165

Saraswati, 169

Sekhem, 81, 130, 159

Sekhmet, 168

Self (seeBasoulSpiritUniversal BaNeterHorus)., 14, 18, 19, 21, 35, 36, 128, 131, 132, 133, 137, 138, 139, 140, 141, 142, 146, 147, 149,

150, 151, 152, 155, 158, 159, 160, 161, 162, 167, 168, 169, 172, 173, 175, 179, 181, 187, 189, 191
Self-realization, 21, 142
Sema, 7
Serpent, 21, 65, 127, 136, 138, 145, 169
Serpent Power, 21, 127, 136, 138, 145, 169
Serpent Power (see also Kundalini and Buto), 21, 127, 136, 138, 145, 169
Set, 32, 33, 34, 51, 53, 57, 59, 65, 71, 73, 75, 79, 83, 105, 107, 109, 111, 113, 115, 117, 119, 121, 127, 132, 137, 139, 142, 143, 144, 146, 149, 150, 151, 152, 157, 159, 163, 169, 171, 173, 174, 175, 176, 178, 179
Sex, 103
Sexual energy, 158
Shabaka Inscription, 67
Shai, 166
Shakti (see also Kundalini), 151
Shetaut Neter See also Egyptian Religion, 19, 26, 30
Shiva, 33, 131, 151
Shu (air and space), 32, 41, 43, 47, 51, 79, 105, 107, 109, 119, 127, 129, 132, 135, 140, 168, 173
Sin, 153
Sirius, 176, 177, 178
Soul, 18, 97, 101, 128, 135, 136, 143, 151, 160, 161, 174
Spirit, 57, 91, 93, 97, 128, 129, 131, 134, 136, 137, 138, 145, 150, 151, 174, 178
Spiritual discipline, 154
Sufism, 164
Sun, 93, 107, 109, 157, 166
Supreme Being, 18, 19, 25, 26, 27, 28, 29, 31, 32, 125, 127, 128, 130, 131, 132, 138, 141, 143, 149, 150, 160, 162, 167, 169, 177, 188
Swami, 7
Swami Jyotirmayananda, 7
Syria, 32
Tantra, 154, 159
Tantra Yoga, 154, 159
Tantric Yoga, 19, 21
Tao, 21, 28, 36, 145
Tao Te Ching, 36
Taoism, 145
Tefnut, 32, 41, 43, 51, 79, 127, 132, 140
Tefnut (moisture), 32, 41, 43, 51, 79, 127, 132, 140
Tem, 51, 83, 136, 159
Ten Commandments, 163

The Absolute, 29, 131, 143
The All, 160
The God, 26, 28, 30, 89, 129, 162
The Pyramid Texts, 67, 162
The Self, 31, 161
Thebes, 27, 123
Third Eye, 169
Torah, 36
Transcendental Self, 160, 187
Triad, 135
Trinity, 26, 27, 30, 31, 34, 35, 131, 177
Truth, 146
Unas, 144, 169, 171
Understanding, 25
Uraeus, 21, 63, 139
Utchat, 143
Vedanta, 169
Vedantic. See also Vedanta, 142
Vishnu, 28, 131, 169
Water, 97, 186
Will, 93, 109, 157
Wisdom (also see Djehuti), 19, 133, 139
Witness, 89
Yahweh, 28
Yoga, 7, 14, 18, 19, 21, 23, 25, 29, 140, 142, 168
Yoga of Action, 21
Yoga of Devotion (see Yoga of Divine Love), 19, 21, 168
Yoga of Divine Love (see Yoga of Devotion), 21
Yoga of Meditation, 19
Yoga of Selfless Action. See also Yoga of Righteous, 19
Yoga of Wisdom (see also Jnana Yoga), 19, 21, 29
Yoga Vasistha, 142

The Ancient Egyptian Bible Part II

The Mystical Teachings of The Ausarian Resurrection

Initiation Into
The Third Level of Shetaut Asar

Take the next step in the study of The Ausarian Resurrection. *The Ausarian Resurrection: The Ancient Egyptian Bible* represents the first two levels of Shetaut Asar (Myth and Rituals of the Ausarian Religion).

In *The Mystical Teachings of The Ausarian Resurrection: Initiation Into The Third Level of Shetaut Asar* you can discover the mystical teachings contained in the verses of the myth and what they mean for the life of every spiritual aspirant.

Discover how to apply those teachings in your life so that you may attain the goal of Nehast (spiritual resurrection).

THE MYSTICAL TEACHINGS
OF
THE AUSARIAN RESURRECTION

This Volume will detail the myth of the Osirian Resurrection and The Story of Horus and Set and their mystical implications in the life of the aspirant/initiate. Then this volume will turn to a line by line mystical reading of the myth in order to uncover the mystical implications of the epic story. Mythology will come alive as a message from the Sages of ancient times to the initiates and not just as stories for entertainment. This Volume is special because it links the individual student to the myth and thereby gives her/him deep insight into his/her own true nature and how to practice the religion of Osiris, Isis and Horus. This volume may be used as a companion to the book *The Ausarian Resurrection: The Ancient Egyptian Bible* by Muata Ashby (see the description above). **232 pages 5.5"x 8.5" ISBN: 1-884564-22-4 $14.99**

The Sema Institute of Yoga Book Series
Books - Audio - Video
and
The Yoga Course Programs
P.O.Box 570459
Miami, Florida, 33257
(305) 378-6253 Fax: (305) 378-6253

This book is part of a series on the study and practice of ancient Egyptian Yoga and Mystical Spirituality. They are also part of the Egyptian Yoga Course provided by the Sema Institute of Yoga. You will find a listing of the other books in this series. For more information send for the Egyptian Yoga Book-Audio-Video Catalog or the Egyptian Yoga Course Catalog.

Now you can study the teachings of Egyptian and Indian Yoga wisdom and Spirituality with the Egyptian Yoga Mystical Spirituality Series. The Egyptian Yoga Series takes you through the Initiation process and lead you to understand the mysteries of the soul and the Divine.and attain the highest goal of life: EN-LIGHTENMENT. The *Egyptian Yoga Series*, takes you on an in depth study of ancient Egyptian mythology and their inner mystical meaning. Each Guide Book is prepared for the serious student of the mystical sciences and provides a study of the teachings along with exercises, assignments and projects to make the teachings understood and effective in real life. The Series is part of the Egyptian Yoga course but may be purchased even if you are not taking the course. The series is ideal for study groups.

$ Prices subject to change.

For a complete listing of titles send for the free *Senbet Yoga Catalog*

The Egyptian Yoga Catalog
Now on the Internet

Check out the latest books, audio and video presentations on Egyptian Yoga and seminars, classes and courses now on the World Wide Web!

INTERNET ADDRESS:
http://members.aol.com/Semayoga/index.htm

E-MAIL ADDRESS:
Semayoga@aol.com

Egyptian Yoga Vol. 1
Ancient Egyptian
Mystical Spirituality

A

A-1

Egyptian Yoga Vol. 2

The Paths of Mystical Religion

B

C

D

E

Ra-Osiris

Ptah

Amun

Initiation Into
Mystical Spirituality

F

G

The Paths of Yoga

Wisdom   **Devotion**   Action   **Meditation** **Tantrism**

H   I   J   K   L

More Books On The Paths of Yoga And Mystical Spirituality

M

N

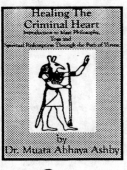

O

P

Q

R

S

T

U

V

W

198

THE YOGA AND MYSTICAL SPIRITUALITY BOOK SERIES

(A)
EGYPTIAN YOGA:
THE PHILOSOPHY OF ENLIGHTENMENT

An original, fully illustrated work, including hieroglyphs, detailing the meaning of the Egyptian mysteries, tantric yoga, psycho-spiritual and physical exercises. Egyptian Yoga is a guide to the practice of the highest spiritual philosophy which leads to absolute freedom from human misery and to immortality. It is well known by scholars that Egyptian philosophy is the basis of Western and Middle Eastern religious philosophies such as *Christianity, Islam, Judaism*, the *Kabbalah*, and Greek philosophy, but what about Indian philosophy, Yoga and Taoism? What were the original teachings? How can they be practiced today? What is the source of pain and suffering in the world and what is the solution? Discover the deepest mysteries of the mind and universe within and outside of your self.
216 Pages 8.5" X 11" ISBN: 1-884564-01-1 Soft $18.95 U.S.

(A-1)
EGYPTIAN YOGA II
The Supreme Wisdom of Enlightenment

In this long awaited sequel to *Egyptian Yoga: The Philosophy of Enlightenment* you will take a fascinating and enlightening journey back in time and discover the teachings which constituted the epitome of Ancient Egyptian spiritual wisdom. What is the supreme knowledge knowing which nothing is left unknown? What are the disciplines which lead to the fulfillment of all desires? Delve into the three states of consciousness (waking, dream and deep sleep) and the fourth state which transcends them all, Neberdjer, "The Absolute." These teachings of the city of Waset (Thebes) were the crowning achievement of the Sages of Ancient Egypt. They summarize and comprehensively explain the mysteries of the entire symbolism of the Ancient Egyptian pantheon of gods and goddesses that emanate from a Supreme Being who forms Creation while emerging as a Trinity. They establish the standard mystical keys for understanding the profound mystical symbolism of the Triad of human consciousness manifesting as the Trinity of gods, Amun-Ra-Ptah, symbolizing the mysticism of the soul, the mind, and creation, respectively. **ISBN 1-884564-39-9 8.5" X 11" $18.95 U.S.**

(B)
THE AUSARIAN RESURRECTION:
The Ancient Egyptian Bible

The Ancient Sages created stories based on human and superhuman beings whose struggles, aspirations, needs and desires ultimately lead them to discover their true Self. The myth of Isis, Osiris and Horus is no exception in this area. While there is no one source where the entire story may be found, pieces of it are inscribed in various ancient temples walls, tombs, steles and papyri. For the first time available, the complete myth of Osiris, Isis and Horus has been compiled from original Ancient Egyptian, Greek and Coptic Texts. This epic myth has been richly illustrated with reliefs from the temple of Horus at Edfu, the temple of Isis at Philae, the temple of Osiris at Abydos, the temple of Hathor at Denderah and various papyri, inscriptions and reliefs.

Discover the myth which inspired the teachings of the *Shetaut Neter* (Egyptian Mystery System - Egyptian Yoga) and the Egyptian Book of Coming Forth By Day. Also, discover the three levels of Ancient Egyptian Religion, how to understand the mysteries of the Tuat or Astral World and how to discover the abode of the Supreme in the Amenta, *The Other World*.

The ancient religion of Osiris, Isis and Horus, if properly understood, contains all of the elements necessary to lead the sincere aspirant to attain immortality through inner self-discovery. This volume presents the entire myth and explores the main mystical themes and rituals associated with the myth for understating human existence, creation and the way to achieve spiritual emancipation - *Resurrection*. The Osirian myth is so powerful that it influenced and is still having an effect on the major world religions. Discover the origins and mystical meaning of the Christian Trinity, the Eucharist ritual and the ancient origin of the birthday of Jesus Christ.
200 Pages 8.5" X 11" Hard Cover ISBN: 1-884564-12-7 $29.99 U. S. Soft Cover ISBN: 1-884564-27-5 $18.95

(C)
THE MYSTICAL TEACHINGS
OF
THE AUSARIAN RESURRECTION

This Volume will detail the myth of the Osirian Resurrection and The Story of Horus and Set and their mystical implications in the life of the aspirant/initiate. Then this volume will turn to a line by line mystical reading of the myth in order to uncover the mystical implications of the epic story. Mythology will come alive as a message from the Sages of ancient times to the initiates and not just as stories for entertainment. This Volume is special because it links the individual student to the myth and thereby gives her/him deep insight into his/her own true nature and how to practice the religion of Osiris, Isis and Horus. This volume may be used as a companion to the book *The Ausarian Resurrection: The Ancient Egyptian Bible* by Muata Ashby (see the description above). **232 pages 5.5"x 8.5" ISBN: 1-884564-22-4 $15.99**

(D)
THE PROPERTIES OF MATTER:
Egyptian Physics and
Yoga Metaphysics.

This Volume will go deeper into the philosophy of God as creation and will explore the concepts of modern science and how they correlate with ancient teachings. This Volume will lay the ground work for the understanding of the philosophy of universal consciousness and the initiatic/yogic insight into who or what is God? **200 pages. 5.5"x 8.5" ISBN 1-884564-07-0 $14.99**

(E)
THE HYMNS OF AMUN
The Mystical Wisdom of Ancient Egyptian Theban Theology

Take a fascinating journey back in time and discover the teachings which constituted the epitome of Ancient Egyptian spiritual wisdom. The teachings of the city of Thebes were the crowning achievement of the Sages and Saints of Ancient Egypt because they summarize and comprehensively explain the mysteries of the entire symbolism of the Ancient Egyptian pantheon of gods and goddesses that emanate from a Supreme Being who forms Creation while emerging as a Trinity. Theban Theology sheds light on the Trinity system of Christianity as well as that of Hinduism in India and establishes the standard mystical keys for understanding the profound mystical symbolism of the Triad of Human consciousness which leads to spiritual enlightenment. This volume introduces the teachings of Ancient Egypt through the religious hymns of Amun. **311 pages   5.5"x 8.5"   ISBN: 1-884564-08-9 $16.99**

(F)
INITIATION INTO EGYPTIAN YOGA:
The Secrets of Sheti

Sheti: Spiritual discipline or program, to go deeply into the mysteries, to study the mystery teachings and literature profoundly, to penetrate the mysteries.

♀ You will learn about the mysteries of initiation into the teachings and practice of Yoga and how to become an Initiate of the mystical sciences.

This insightful manual is the first in a series which introduces you to the goals of daily spiritual and yoga practices: Meditation, Diet, Words of Power and the ancient wisdom teachings. **150 pages 8.5" X 11" ISBN 1-884564-02-X   Soft Cover $16.99 U.S.**

(G)
THE GLORY OF INITIATION

A brief discussion of the theme of Initiation which was introduced in the book *Initiation Into Egyptian Yoga*. This volume explores the need for initiation and how a person is initiated into the teachings of mystical spirituality. Many new important topics are introduced such as: The Ancient Egyptian "Guru," The Mystical Sphinx, The Life of an Initiate of Yoga, The Importance of the Spiritual Name, Initiation With a Spiritual Preceptor and The Initiation Ritual. 40 pages $3.99 ISBN: 1-884564-37- 2

(H)

THE WISDOM OF ISIS
GOD IN THE UNIVERSE, GOD IN THE HEART
Who is God in the light of Yoga Philosophy?

Through the study of ancient myth and the illumination of initiatic understanding the idea of God is expanded from the mythological comprehension to the metaphysical. Then this metaphysical understanding is related to you, the student, so as to begin understanding your true divine nature. **243 pages 5.5"x 8.5" ISBN 1-884564-24-0 $15.99**

(I)
THE BLOOMING LOTUS OF DIVINE LOVE
The Process of Mystical Transformation and The Path of Divine Love

This Volume will focus on the ancient wisdom teachings and how to use them in a scientific process for self-transformation. Also, this volume will detail the process of transformation from ordinary consciousness to cosmic consciousness through the integrated practice of the teachings and the path of Devotional Love toward the Divine. **225 pages 5.5"x 8.5" ISBN 1-884564-11-9 $14.99**

(J)
THE WISDOM OF MAATI:
Spiritual Enlightenment Through the Path of Virtue

Known as Karma Yoga in India, the teachings of MAAT for living virtuously and with orderly wisdom are explained and the student is to begin practicing the precepts of Maat in daily life so as to promote the process of purification of the heart in preparation for the judgment of the soul. This judgment will be understood not as an event that will occur at the time of death but as an event that occurs continuously, at every moment in the life of the individual. The student will learn how to become allied with the forces of the Higher Self and to thereby begin cleansing the mind (heart) of impurities so as to attain a higher vision of reality. 210 **pages 5.5"x 8.5" ISBN 1-884564-20-8 $15.99**

(K)
MEDITATION
The Ancient Egyptian Path to Enlightenment

Many people do not know about the rich history of meditation practice in Ancient Egypt. This volume outlines the theory of meditation and presents the Ancient Egyptian Hieroglyphic text which give instruction as to the nature of the mind and its three modes of expression. It also presents the texts which give instruction on the practice of meditation for spiritual enlightenment and unity with the Divine. This volume allows the reader to begin practicing meditation by explaining, in easy to understand terms, the simplest form of meditation and working up to the most advanced form which was practiced in ancient times and which is still practiced by yogis around the world in modern times. **268 pages 5.5"x 8.5" ISBN 1-884564-27-7 $16.99**

(L)
EGYPTIAN TANTRA YOGA:
The Art of Sex Sublimation and Universal Consciousness

This Volume will expand on the male and female principles within the human body and in the universe and further detail the sublimation of sexual energy into spiritual energy. The student will study the deities Min and Hathor, Osiris and Isis, Geb and Nut and discover the mystical implications for a practical spiritual discipline. This Volume will also focus on the Tantric aspects of Ancient Egyptian and Indian mysticism, the purpose of sex and the mystical teachings of sexual sublimation which lead to self-knowledge and enlightenment. **203 pages 5.5"x 8.5" ISBN 1-884564-03-8 $15.99**

(M)
EGYPTIAN PROVERBS: TEMT TCHAAS

Temt Tchaas means: collection of Ancient Egyptian Proverbs
⚥ How to live according to MAAT Philosophy.
⚥ Beginning Meditation.
⚥ All proverbs are indexed for easy searches.
For the first time in one volume, Ancient Egyptian proverbs, wisdom teachings and meditations, fully illustrated with hieroglyphic text and symbols. EGYPTIAN PROVERBS is a unique collection of knowledge and wisdom which you can put into practice today and transform your life. **160 pages. 5.5"x 8.5" $9.95 U.S ISBN: 1-884564-00-3**

(N)
MYSTICISM OF USHET REKHAT:
Worship of the Divine Mother

The Supreme Being may be worshipped as father or as mother. *Ushet Rekhat* or *Mother Worship*, is the spiritual process of worshipping the Divine in the form of the Divine Goddess. It celebrates the most important forms of the Goddess including *Nathor, Maat, Aset, Arat, Amentet and Hathor* and explores their mystical meaning as well as the rising of *Sirius*, the star of Aset (Isis) and the new birth of Hor (Horus). The end of the year is a time of reckoning, reflection and engendering a new or renewed positive movement toward attaining spiritual enlightenment. The Mother Worship devotional meditation ritual, performed on five days during the month of December and on New Year's Eve, is based on the Ushet Rekhit. During the ceremony, the cosmic forces, symbolized by Sirius ✫ and the constellation of Orion ✫✫✫, are harnessed through the understanding and devotional attitude of the participant. This propitiation draws the light of wisdom and health to all those who share in the ritual, leading to prosperity and wisdom.
$9.99 - 146 pages. 5.5"x 8.5" ISBN 1-884564-18-6

(O)
HEALING THE CRIMINAL HEART
Introduction to Maat Philosophy, Yoga and Spiritual Redemption Through the Path of Virtue

Who is a criminal? Is there such a thing as a criminal heart? What is the source of evil and sinfulness and is there any way to rise above it? Is there redemption for those who have committed sins, even the worst crimes?

Ancient Egyptian mystical psychology holds important answers to these questions. Over ten thousand years ago mystical psychologists, the Sages of Ancient Egypt, studied and charted the human mind and spirit and laid out a path which will lead to spiritual redemption, prosperity and enlightenment.
This introductory volume brings forth the teachings of the Ausarian Resurrection, the most important myth of Ancient Egypt, with relation to the faults of human existence: anger, hatred, greed, lust, animosity, discontent, ignorance, egoism jealousy, bitterness, and a myriad of psycho-spiritual ailments which keep a human being in a state of negativity and adversity.
40 pages 5.5"x 8.5" ISBN: 1-884564-17-8 $3.99

(P)
EGYPTIAN YOGA EXERCISE
WORKOUT BOOK
Thef Neteru:
The Movement of The Gods and Goddesses

Discover the physical postures and exercises practiced thousands of years ago in Ancient Egypt which are today known as Yoga exercises. This work is based on the pictures and teachings from the Creation story of Ra, The Osirian Resurrection Myth and the carvings and reliefs from various Temples in Ancient Egypt. **130 Pages 8.5" X 11" ISBN 1-884564-10-0 Soft Cover $16.99 Exercise video $19.99**

(Q)
THE SERPENT POWER:
The Ancient Egyptian Mystical Wisdom
of the Inner Life Force.

This Volume specifically deals with the latent life Force energy of the universe and in the human body, its control and sublimation. How to develop the Life Force energy of the subtle body. This Volume will introduce the esoteric wisdom of the science of how virtuous living acts in a subtle and mysterious way to cleanse the latent psychic energy conduits and vortices of the spiritual body. **204 pages 5.5"x 8.5" ISBN 1-884564-19-4 $15.99**

(R)
THE CYCLES OF TIME:
The Ancient Origins of Yoga in Egypt and India

This Volume will cover the ancient origins of Yoga and establish a link between the cultures of Ancient Egypt and ancient and modern India. This Volume is of paramount importance because it shows that Egyptian Philosophy began over 30,000 years ago and did not die out along with Egyptian society but that it was carried on by the Sages and Saints who left Egypt at the time of its social collapse. **200 pages. 5.5"x 8.5" ISBN 1-884564-13-5 $14.99**

(S)
THE MYSTERIES OF SHETAUT PAUTI
The Mystical Teachings of The Ancient Egyptian Creation Myth

Discover the mystical teachings contained in the Creation Myth and the gods and goddesses who brought creation

and human beings into existence. The Creation Myth holds the key to understanding the universe and for attaining spiritual enlightenment.
ISBN: 1-884564-38-0 40 pages $5.99

(T)
GROWING BEYOND HATE
The Mystic Art
of Transcending Hate and Discovering
Spiritual Enlightenment Through Yoga

What is the source of animosity between human beings? What is the basis for negativity in the human heart and is there a way to deal with it? How can the teachings of Yoga Philosophy be used to resolve animosity and to transcend hatred in order to attain spiritual enlightenment and promote harmony in society.

Human Relations is an important issue in modern times. This volume is an introductory guide to understanding why people engage in various forms of animosity including hatred, hostility, racism, sexism, etc. towards others. It provides insights into the nature of the mind and the process of spiritual development which leads to purity of heart and spiritual emancipation. 64 Pages ISBN: 1-884564-34-8 $5.99

(U)
THE SLOWNESS MEDITATION
How to Discover
The Inner Witnessing Self

The Slowness meditation is the art of concentrating on movement and discovering the inner light of the Self

What is the *Inner Witnessing Self* and how can slowness lead a person to discover it? What is *automatic consciousness* and what does it operate in the mind of most human beings?

Discover the discipline of meditation which will allow you to go beyond the mundane realities of life so that you may discover inner peace, expansion of consciousness, inner fulfillment and contentment.

This is the Slowness Meditation Program 40 Pages ISBN: 1-884564-36-4 $4.99

(V)
THE STORY OF ASAR, ASET AND HERU:
An Ancient Egyptian Legend

Now for the first time, the most ancient myth of Ancient Egypt comes alive for children. Inspired by the books *The Ausarian Resurrection: The Ancient Egyptian Bible* and *The Mystical Teachings of The Ausarian Resurrection*, **The Story of Asar, Aset and Heru** is an easy to understand and thrilling tale which inspired the children of Ancient Egypt to aspire to greatness and righteousness.

If you and your child have enjoyed stories like *The Lion King* and *Star Wars you will love* **The Story of Asar, Aset and Heru.** Also, if you know the story of Jesus and Krishna you will

discover than Ancient Egypt had a similar myth and that this myth carries important spiritual teachings for living a fruitful and fulfilling life.

This book may be used along with *The Parents Guide To The Ausarian Resurrection Myth: How to Teach Yourself and Your Child the Principles of Universal Mystical Religion.* The guide provides some background to the Ausarian Resurrection myth and it also gives insight into the mystical teachings contained in it which you may introduce to your child. It is designed for parents who wish to grow spiritually with their children and it serves as an introduction for those who would like to study the Ausarian Resurrection Myth in depth and to practice its teachings. **41 pages 8.5" X 11" ISBN: 1-884564-31-3 $8.99**

(W)
THE PARENTS GUIDE TO THE AUSARIAN RESURRECTION MYTH:
How to Teach Yourself and Your Child
the Principles of Universal Mystical Religion.

This insightful manual brings for the timeless wisdom of the ancient through the Ancient Egyptian myth of Asar, Aset and Heru and the mystical teachings contained in it for parents who want to guide their children to understand and practice the teachings of mystical spirituality. This manual may be used with the children's storybook *The Story of Asar, Aset and Heru* by Dr. Muata Abhaya Ashby. **64 pages 5.5"x 8.5" ISBN: 1-884564-30-5 $5.99**

The Egyptian Yoga Audio Lecture Series

All cassettes on Sale for only $ 9.99

Tapes with WC refer to the ongoing Weekly Class Series
Use the number when ordering.

Tape 100   Tape 102   Tape 204-205

Tape 300-301   Tape 203   Tape 601

Tape 700-701-702   Tape 703   Tape 113

Tape 303   Tape 305   Tape 800

100 Introduction to Egyptian Yoga, the paths of Yoga and Mystical Religion $9.99
102 What is Yoga and how can it transform your life? Radio Interview in LA - $4.99
103 Wisdom of Egyptian Yoga Part 1 $9.99 - 90min (103 & 104 - 2 tape set)
104 Wisdom of Egyptian Yoga Part 2 $9.99 - 90min (103 & 104 - 2 tape set)
105 Maat Workshop Part 1: How to Practice the Teachings - $9.99- 90min (105 & 106-2 tape set)
106 Maat Workshop Part 2: How to Practice the Teachings -$9.99- 90min (105 & 106 -2 tape set)
107 Pert Em Heru: Introduction to the Book of Coming Forth By Day Part 1-$9.99 (107 &108 set)
108 Pert Em Heru: Introduction to the Book of Coming Forth By Day Part 2-$9.99 (107 &108 set)
109 Initiation Into Shetaut Aset Part 1: The Teachings of The Temple of Isis- $9.99(109 & 110 set)
110 Initiation Into Shetaut Aset Part 2: The Teachings of The Temple of Isis - $9.99 -(109 & 110 set)
111 The Cycles of Time - $14.99 - 2 hours
112 Race Relations in the light of Yoga Philosophy $9.99 - 90 min
113 The Story of Asar, Aset and Heru $9.99
200 Initiation Into Egyptian Yoga Part I- $9.99 (200 & 201 - 2 tape set) 90min
201 Initiation Into Egyptian Yoga Part II- $9.99 (200 & 201 - 2 tape set) 90 min.
203 WC1 Initiation: How to be a Disciple of Yoga: - $9.99 - 90 min
204 WC2 Initiation: The Ten Virtues of a Spiritual Aspirant Part 1 -$9.99- 60 min (204 & 205 set)
205 WC3 Initiation: The Ten Virtues of a Spiritual Aspirant Part 2 -$9.99 - 60 min (204 & 205 set)
206 WC4 Introduction to Meditation: The Art of Concentration $9.99 - 60 min
207 WC5 Introduction to Meditation: The Art of Concentration $9.99 - 60 min
208 WC6 Initiation: Health, Vegetarianism and Yoga $9.99 - 90 min
209 Sheti Workshop Part 1
210 Sheti Workshop Part 2
211 The Initiatic Way of Education - $14.99 -Two hours
300 Ausarian Resurrection, Part 1- $9.99
301 Ausarian Resurrection, Part 2- $9.99
302 WC7 The Three Levels of Religion - $9.99 - 90 min.
303 WC8 The Story of Hethor and Tehuti: The Three States of Consciousness - $9.99 - 90 min.
304 WC9 The Story of Ra and Aset $9.99 - 90 min.
305 WC10 Understanding the mind and how to transcend the Ego $9.99
306 WC11 The Glory of Devotional Love, Part 1 - $9.99 - 90 min
307 WC12 The Glory of Devotional Love, Part 2 - $9.99 - 90 min
308 WC13 The Birth of Heru & the Meaning of Happiness - $9.99 - 90 min
309 WC14 The Death of Heru: How Egoism Poisons Spiritual Aspiration $9.99 - 90 min
310 WC15 The Glory of Listening to the Teachings - $9.99 - 90 min
311 WC16 The Initiation of Heru $9.99 - 90 min
312 WC17 How the soul becomes incarnated and trapped in the body $9.99 - 60 min
313 WC18 How the soul operated through mind and senses and ego $9.99 - 90 min
501 Ushet Morning Worship: Adorations to Ra-Kheperi and Hethor $9.99 - approx. 30 min.
502 Ushet Morning Worship: Adorations to Amun - $9.99 - 60 min.
600 WC The Egyptian Yoga Exercise Workout with Vijaya Level I- short session $9.99 45 min.
601 WC The Egyptian Yoga Exercise Workout with Vijaya Level II- long session $9.99 - 90min
603 WC The Egyptian Yoga Exercise Workout with Muata Level III - long session $9.99 - 90min
700 Meditation Lecture Series Part 1 (St. Louis)- $9.99 -60 min. (700, 701 & 702 - 3 tape set)
701 Meditation Lecture Series, Part 2 (St. Louis) - $9.99 - 60 min.(700, 701 & 702 - 3 tape set)
702 Meditation Lecture Series, Part 3 (St. Louis) - $9.99 - 60 min.(700, 701 & 702 - 3 tape set)
703 Guided Meditation Session $9.99
800 Serpent Power Level I: Lecture, Music and Meditation -$9.99 - 90min
801 Serpent Power Level II: Lecture, Music and Meditation - $9.99 - 90min
900 Ushet Devotional Chanting of Hekau *Amma Su En Pa Neter* - $9.99 - 60 min.
901 Ushet Devotional Chanting of Divine Name Hekau: *Om Amun Ra Ptah* - $9.99 - 60 min.
902 Ushet Devotional Chanting of Divine Name Hekau: *Om Asar, Aset, Heru* - $9.99 - 60 min.
1000 Introduction to Christian Yoga-Lecture at Unity Church in Los Angeles $9.99

Egyptian Yoga® Video Lectures

Introduction to EGYPTIAN YOGA Video Lecture by Muata Ashby

INTRODUCTION TO EGYPTIAN YOGA
A VIDEO LECTURE
(NEW VIDEO)

—Discover the Origins of Yoga and World Religions, Indian Philosophy and Mythology
—Learn the ancient art of the Egyptian Yoga, the Mysteries of Osiris and Isis, the correlations between ancient Egyptian Mysticism and Modern Physics, The Pyramid Texts, The Papyrus of Ani, The Origins of Christianity and more. 1 hr. 30 min. **$19.99**

Indus-Kamit-Kush

is a journey of discovery from the ancient origins of Ethiopia and Egypt in north-east Africa to the Indus valley in India. How were Ethiopia, Egypt and India related in ancient times and is the ancient philosophy of Egypt still being practiced in modern day Indian Yoga philosophy? The study of Indian Yoga and Vedanta philosophy and Shetaut Neter (Egyptian Mysteries) gives insights into the ancient texts which prove the cultural, religious and mythological synchronicity between these lands. The new insights into the ancient mystical philosophy of India, Ethiopia and Egypt will allow you to effectively understand and practice Indian Yoga (Vedanta) and Egyptian Yoga and mystical philosophy (Shetaut Neter) Video $19.99 - Audio Cassette $14.99

The Ancient History, Unity and Mystical philosophy of India, Egypt and Ethiopia
A Video Journey by Dr. Muata Ashby

The Trinity by Dr. Muata Ashby 2 Hour Lecture

Thef Neteru: The Movement of The Gods and Goddesses
The Egyptian Yoga Exercise Workout Video

Discover the physical postures and exercises practiced thousands of years ago in ancient Egypt which are today known as Yoga exercises. This work is based on the pictures and teachings from the Creation story of Ra, The Osirian Resurrection Myth and the carvings and reliefs from various Temples in ancient Egypt. **Video $19.99 - Audio $9.99**

THE INNER MEANING OF THE TRINITY AND THE THREE LEVELS OF RELIGION

☥ This lecture takes you on a journey through the development of religion in its three stages: Ritual, Mythological and Metaphysical/Philosophical.
☥ Discover the inner meaning and the correct practice of religion in all of its important stages through this insightful video slide presentation (Also available on audio cassette $14.99).
2 Hours - Video $19.99

Other Videos:
Meditation Workshop 6/21/97 $29.99
Initiation Into Egyptian Yoga two tape set with manual $29.99

204

Video Lecture -Slide Presentation

The Mystical Teachings of
The Ausarian Resurrection
by
Dr. Muata Abhaya Ashby

$24.99

Also Available on Audio Cassette

$14.99

THE EGYPTIAN YOGA GUIDE
Introduction to Egyptian Yoga and the Egyptian Yoga Book Series

The Egyptian Yoga Guide is a comprehensive pamphlet which helps you to navigate through the Egyptian Yoga Book Series as well as the program of yoga and or religious studies based on the book series. The Egyptian Yoga Guide assists you in understanding the meaning and purpose of Egyptian Yoga by introducing the main concepts and goals. Then the guide helps you to determining what kind of personality you have and what form of spiritual study and practice is best suited for you. Then the guide helps you to understand the process of spiritual evolution and the way to promote spiritual knowledge through the integral Egyptian Yoga Studies program. $2.95 . ISBN 1-884564-29-1

What is Religion? What is Yoga? What is Spirituality?
How can I end pain and sorrow in my life?
What is my purpose in life?
Is it really possible to discover peace and immortality?
How can I discover my Higher Self and benefit humanity?
How do I become a practitioner of Yoga?
and
How can the Egyptian Yoga Book Series help me to discover my spiritual path?

Many people have written and called us asking these questions. In response we have created a small and easy to read volume called the *Egyptian Yoga Guide*.

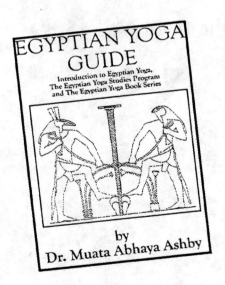

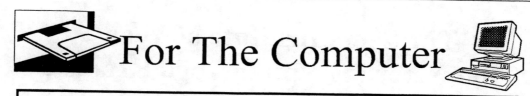

For The Computer

ScribeSoft™ Font Library
Egyptian Hieroglyphic Clip Art for the Computer

Hieroglyphics for IBM and MAC compatible PC's. *Scribesoft Clip Art Library* is a collection of over 750 ancient Egyptian Hieroglyphics similar to those used to produce the Scribesoft Fonts. Available on 3.5" diskettes.

Scribesoft Clip Art Library:

Scribesoft Font Library $39.99 + 4.50 S/H Diskettes

ScribeSoft™ Font Alphabet:

Hieroglyphics for IBM and MAC compatible PC's. Now adding hieroglyphics to your documents or computer projects is as easy as adding a new Font style. *Scribesoft Alphabet* comes in one font file which may be easily added to your computer. *Scribesoft Alphabet* is a font collection which matches the English keyboard to the Ancient Egyptian alphabet so when you type an English letter its corresponding hieroglyph is printed on the screen..

A B C D E F G H I J K L M N O P Q

R S T U V W X Y Z

ScribeSoft™ Clip Art Library I
Egyptian Hieroglyphic Clip Art for the Computer

Hieroglyphics for IBM compatible PC's. *Scribesoft Clip Art Library* is a collection of over 750 ancient Egyptian Hieroglyphics similar to those used to produce the Scribesoft Fonts. Each picture is in .PCX Format. Available on 3.5" diskettes.

Scribesoft Clip Art Library:

Scribesoft Clip Art Library $39.99 + 4.50 S/H

ScribeSoft™ Grayscale Images Library I
Ancient Egyptian Images for the IBM Computer

**Gods and Goddesses - Symbols
and more...
Scribesoft Grayscale Images
Library I CD ROM $39.99 + 4.50 S/H**

The Sema Institute of Yoga
Thef Neteru Egyptian Yoga Exercise
Teachers Training Course

Coming in 1998

In response to many requests a new program specifically designed for those interested in teaching Egyptian Yoga has been prepared.

Yoga is a spiritual discipline for promoting spiritual enlightenment. However, the first step towards spiritual health is physical health because the body is the vessel of the spirit. It is the vehicle by which the spirit can be discovered. Therefore, the correct practice of Yoga requires purification of the mind and body first in preparation for study of the higher wisdom teachings and meditation which leads a human being to the higher goals of life.

You will learn how to practice and lead others in practicing the Ancient Egyptian Exercise forms for health and spiritual enlightenment. The program consists of Assignments which introduce the student to the practice of the Ancient Egyptian Yoga Postures of *Thef Neteru Egyptian Yoga*. It also initiates the student into the Mystical Wisdom of the Postures. The assignments will be reviewed as you work with an instructor. The Program concludes with an Egyptian Yoga Exercise Workout Seminar where the student will work with Dr. Ashby directly and also conduct an exercise class. Each assignment has certain book and or audio/video tapes from the Egyptian Yoga Catalog as requirements to assist your studies. A certificate will be awarded to all who successfully complete the program. They will be able to practice the teachings of Yoga correctly and to instruct others on the teachings of universal Yoga Spiritual Living. The course is designed to be completed over a period of 3-6 months. Send for the Thef Neteru Egyptian Yoga Exercise Teachers Training Course Catalog ($5.00 + $2 Postage) for more information or call Sema Institute (305) 378-6253

208

ABOUT DR. ASHBY

Reginald Muata Ashby holds a Doctor of Philosophy Degree in Religion, and a Doctor of Divinity Degree in Holistic Healing. He is also a Pastoral Counselor and Teacher of Yoga Philosophy and Discipline. Dr. Ashby is an adjunct faculty member of the American Institute of Holistic Theology. Dr. Ashby has been an independent researcher and practitioner of Egyptian, Indian and Chinese Yoga and psychology as well as Christian Mysticism. Dr. Ashby has studied advanced *Jnana, Bhakti and Kundalini Yogas* under the guidance of Spiritual Masters and is a disciple of Swami Jyotirmayananda, a world renowned Yoga Master. He has extensively studied mystical religious traditions from around the world and is an accomplished lecturer, author and artist. He is an Ordained Minister and Spiritual Counselor and also the founder the *Sheti Association*, a membership group for the study and practice of Egyptian Yoga as well as the *Sema Institute*, a non-profit organization dedicated to spreading the wisdom of Yoga and ancient Egyptian mystical wisdom..

Order Form

Telephone orders: Call Toll Free: 1(305) 378-6253. Have your AMEX, Optima, Visa or MasterCard ready.
Fax orders: 1-(305) 378-6253

Postal Orders: Sema Institute of Yoga, P.O. Box 570459, Miami, Fl. 33257. USA.

Please send the following books and / or tapes.

ITEM

_____ Cost $_____
_____ Cost $_____
_____ Cost $_____
_____ Cost $_____
_____ Cost $_____

Total $_____

_____Please send the latest *Egyptian Yoga Catalog* to me FREE.
_____Please add my name to the *Sheti Association* so that I may receive more
information on upcoming Yoga Seminars and other events.

Name:_____ Address:
_____City:_____ State:_____ Zip:
_____

Sales tax: Please add 6.5% for books shipped to Florida addresses

Shipping:

_____Book Rate: $2.00 for the first book and 75 cents for each additional
book (Surface shipping may take three to four weeks)
_____Air Mail or UPS: $4.00 for first book and $.50 for each additional

_____Payment:_____
_____Check_____

_____Credit card: _____ Visa, _____ MasterCard, _____ Optima,
_____ AMEX.

Card number:_____

Name on card:_____ Exp. date:_____/_____

*Donations: I would like to Donate $_____ to the Inmate Education Program.
*Donations: I would like to Donate $_____ to the Yoga Center Book program.
Tax Deductible.

TO PLACE AN ORDER, contact your local bookstore or send CK or MO for the cost of each item plus shipping and handling to the address below. Shipping cost $4.00 first item, .50¢ each additional item. (Prices subject to change) *Ordering from outside U.S.* send equivalent to U.S. currency plus $5 in U.S. currency for the first item and $3 for each additional for shipping. Send to C.M. Books, P.O. Box 570459, Miami, Fl. 33257 or Visa-Master Card <u>INCLUDE Physical address and Driver's license # if you are sending a check as payment.</u> Bookstores: You may purchase directly from C.M. Books AT 40% DISCOUNT- CALL 305-378-6253 C.M. BOOKS, P.O. BOX 570459, MIAMI, FL. 33257 -